THE LITERATURE MATRIX
OF CHEMISTRY

THE LITERATURE MATRIX OF CHEMISTRY

HERMAN SKOLNIK
Hercules Inc., Hercules Research Center
Wilmington, Delaware

A Wiley-Interscience Publication

JOHN WILEY & SONS
New York   Chichester   Brisbane   Toronto   Singapore

Copyright © 1982 by John Wiley & Sons, Inc.

All rights reserved. Published simultaneously in Canada.

Reproduction or translation of any part of this work
beyond that permitted by Section 107 or 108 of the
1976 United States Copyright Act without the permission
of the copyright owner is unlawful. Requests for
permission or further information should be addressed to
the Permissions Department, John Wiley & Sons, Inc.

Library of Congress Cataloging in Publication Data

Skolnik, Herman.
  The literature matrix of chemistry.

  "A Wiley-Interscience publication."
  Includes index.
  1. Chemical literature. I. Title.
QD8.5.S58   540'.72   81-22002
ISBN 0-471-79545-3   AACR2

Printed in the United States of America

10 9 8 7 6 5 4 3 2 1

PREFACE

The literature of chemistry and chemical technology is a rich and vast knowledge resource through which we can interact with those who have shaped our past and who are shaping our present.

On accepting the invitation to write this book, I hoped to achieve the following objectives:

To give the reader an appreciation of the value of the literature matrix and the vital role it has played in the progress of chemistry and technology.

To delineate the scope and content of the literature matrix so that the reader can interact with and gain access to it effectively.

To orient the book to students majoring in chemistry and chemical engineering and to scientists and engineers employed by the chemical industry in research and development and in plant operations.

Whereas a minority of chemists and chemical engineers affect the literature as authors, all are affected by the literature as readers and users. Reading and using the literature are not only a tradition; they are a necessity if we are to maintain scientific growth (self-education), relate facts (idea seeking), and establish background information for new research programs (insurance against repeating what has already been done).

Too many graduates leave the educational environment with the belief that learning goes on in academic buildings and nowhere else. To limit thinking within the bounds of formal education and training makes us artisans and our science an art, and courts technical obsolescence within a decade.

The chemical literature offers professional chemists and chemical engineers an opportunity for continuous, lifelong self-education. Ideally, every course in science and engineering curriculums should train students to utilize the literature for self-education. The student should be taught not only segmented disciplines, but also how to learn science and technology that is changing rapidly in directions that cannot be anticipated easily.

The amount of information to be taught has increased so much that most professors find little time to teach the literature. Furthermore, chemistry and chemical technology are increasingly segmented into new disciplines and subdisciplines, such as polymer chemistry, material science, and environmental science. The need to teach electronics and computer science in addition to the new disciplines have forced the elimination of courses in literature, history, and philosophy of chemistry from the majority of curriculums. Of the approximately 2000 colleges and universities that grant degrees in chemistry, only a few offer courses in the literature of chemistry and still fewer in the history and philosophy of chemistry. Paradoxically, when the chemical literature was relatively small, the literature and history of chemistry were considered to be important components of the curriculum, and a high percentage of colleges and universities had courses in those subjects. Many textbooks written for students of the late nineteenth and the first three decades of the twentieth century emphasized the literature and history of chemistry. Unfortunately, this is no longer the case.

The twentieth century has been a period of rapid growth in the chemical industry and in governmental laboratories, in research and development funding by both the chemical industry and the federal government, and in the numbers of chemists and chemical engineers. The result has been a correspondingly rapid growth of the literature in a multitude of fragmented disciplines and subdisciplines. The size, growth, and complexity of the literature became such in the twentieth century, and particularly since 1940, that a multitude of information services were created and a number of guide books were written to aid the user of the literature. One of the best-known of these was *A Guide to the Literature of Chemistry* by E.J. Crane and A. M. Patterson, published in 1927 by John Wiley & Sons. This book enjoyed wide use as a text for courses in the literature of chemistry, as did the second edition (1957) by Crane, Patterson, and E.B. Marr. Two other highly regarded and much used texts were *Chemical Publications—Their Nature and Use* by M.G. Mellon (1928, 1940, and 1948; McGraw-Hill) and *Library Guide for the Chemist* by B.A. Soule (1938, McGraw-Hill).

Another response to the size, growth and complexity of the literature was the appearance of a new specialist, the chemical information scientist, and a new subdiscipline of chemistry, chemical information science—now a well-established career for thousands of chemists. Although the activities engaged in by these chemists are taught in colleges and universities, the courses are not a part of the chemistry curriculum, nor do they constitute a curriculum for chemical information science. Chemical information scientists edit and write technical material, translate, index, abstract, search the literature, design information systems, and relate the literature to the needs of an environment. As computers became increasingly important in processing information, chemical information scientists played an important role in employing this new tool for computerized information systems and services.

In the nineteenth century the literature of chemistry consisted of personal contacts, lectures, correspondence, books, and a few journals. As late as World War I it was not very difficult for a chemist to read practically everything of importance published in chemistry. Thereafter it became increasingly difficult, and by the 1930s it was impossible to read everything of importance.

Today, the chemical literature consists of books, encyclopedias, treatises, data compilations, handbooks, patents, journals, abstract journals, trade literature, government publications, market research reports, and a variety of computer-based information services. Although a part of this literature matrix is discussed in books by Crane, Patterson, and Marr; Mellon; Soule; and others, the character of the literature has changed radically since these books were written. The present book includes the earlier literature, which is still of importance for retrospective searching, and the significant traditional literature and information services, which are essential for maintaining current awareness and for retrospective searching.

Books, encyclopedias, treatises, data compilations, etc., are the vade mecum of students in all subject areas, especially in science and engineering. These are the subjects covered in Chapters 1, 2, and 3.

Books are the major resource utilized in the educational process, and one who has not learned how to use school and public libraries can hardly claim to be educated. The books one acquires during the academic years are but a drop in the ocean of literature, and this drop evaporates rather quickly into obsolescence. Throughout one's professional career it is important to gain familiarity with a large number of books, encyclopedias, treatises, etc., and with sources that give information about new books. The survey of books in Chapter 1 is neither definitive nor all-inclusive; it is, however, highly selective, based on my own use of many of the books listed or on the evaluations of others. Year of publication is not given for every book because many undergo periodic revision; the reader should seek the latest edition.

Familiarity with treatises and encyclopedias, such as those listed and discussed in Chapter 2, is a sine qua non for all practicing chemists and engineers. Organic chemists cut their teeth on Beilstein and Houben-Weyl, and inorganic chemists on Gmelin. The most important general reference book today is the *Kirk–Othmer Encyclopedia of Chemical Technology*. Considerable searching and learning time is saved by knowing and consulting these encyclopedias and treatises. Like most other tools of chemistry, expertise comes with frequent use.

Every chemist and chemical engineer should have a personal copy of a single-volume handbook, such as Lange's, Perry's, or CRC's, and should be aware of and frequently consult comprehensive works, such as Landolt-Börnstein, *International Critical Tables*, and the special data compilers of critical data discussed in Chapter 3.

Patents constitute an integral resource of the chemical literature. They have a unique literary form, written to satisfy legal requirements, and very unlike that used for reports or journal literature. Most important, they are an essential and useful source of chemical technology, and they play a critical role in the conduct of research and development in the chemical industry. The number of abstracts of basic patents published in *Chemical Abstracts*, which very recently has been in excess of 60,000 per year, gives an indication of the size of this literature. Chapter 4 discusses patents as a resource and how to use them.

Journal literature has been the fastest growing segment of the chemical literature. Whereas books, encyclopedias, and treatises discuss the past events of chemistry, journals record the current happenings. Journals came into existence in the seventeenth century as a better and faster communication medium than letter, pamphlet, or book, and slowly evolved into the dominant medium for reporting and communicating activities in the laboratory. As chemistry was increasingly subdivided into specialties and the products of chemical industries increasingly used by other industries, the journal literature grew to cover these areas of interest. In addition to reporting current research, journals were introduced to review the literature and to serve the needs of trade groups. As the number of journals in chemistry, chemical technology, and allied fields increased to the present 20,000–40,000, the journal literature also became the dominant resource for retrospective searching. Chapter 5 puts this vast resource into perspective, identifying the important journals by period of publication, country of publication, and—for journals currently published—subject area covered. Because there are so many journals being published today, only the major journals in various subdisciplines are listed.

In the nineteenth century, the size and complexity of the journal literature already prompted the introduction of *Pharmaceutisches Centralblatt* (1830) [name changed to *Chemisches Zentralblatt* (1856)], the first journal in chemistry consisting wholly of abstracts. It was followed by *Science Abstracts* in 1898 and *Chemical Abstracts* in 1907. There are now over 1500 indexing/abstracting publications, covering the journal, report, patent, and book literature. Chapter 6 discusses these services as they evolved over the centuries. Chapter 7 is a fairly detailed discussion of *Chemical Abstracts* and Chapter 8 of other indexing/abstracting services.

The introduction of computer-based information services, the subject of Chapter 9, added a new dimension to the chemical literature matrix. Since the mid-1960s, online data bases have become a major tool for searching the chemical literature. They are a tool, however, that requires knowledge of the contents and limitations of data bases and how to access the data bases through the systems imposed by data base brokers. Despite the increasing number of data bases available online from various data base brokers, most chemists use the new tool mostly through intermediaries. Terminals, a maze of operating systems, programming languages, and intermediaries are still barriers between the scientist and the computer. But there is hope that through proper management computers and telecommunications can bring the literature of chemistry to us according to our specific needs and in our terms.

Of the various components of the literature matrix, computer-based information services are undergoing the most rapid changes. For about two months in 1981, I was given an opportunity to update the present book before it went to the publisher. I added new information to every chapter, but the greatest number of changes and additions were in the chapter on computer-based information services. Data base producers especially are undergoing changes toward improving their products. A salient example of the changing nature of computer-searchable information systems is Chemical Abstracts Service, whose products CASIA, CA Condensates, and Patent Concordance, no longer produced, have been replaced by far superior products, CA BIBLIOFILE and CA SEARCH.

Most scientists and engineers prefer the dreams of the future above the history of the past. But our constantly evolving present is a consequence of our expanding past, and the best of today's chemistry will be a part of the past. The study of history is more than a luxury. The past has played a tremendous role in shaping our literature and continues to be a part of our total knowledge. The chemical literature, although young and vigorous, is steeped in history. Those who have made this history and literature are discussed in Chapter 10. Chapter 11 traces the development of American chemistry and its literature from colonial times to the twentieth century. Only deceased chemists are considered in this chapter; otherwise chapter 11 would have been the longest in the book.

Communications has been the most pervasive force in the creation and maintenance of chemistry and chemical technology. The printing press was the magic wand that made this possible. But like the "sorcerer's apprentice," we do not know how to control the outpouring; we seem to have more documents than we want or need; or else, the ones we want and need are diluted with too many which are not relevant. Information storage and retrieval are still based on the printing press and paper, the filing cabinet, and library shelves. For the reader, microfiche and microfilm, introduced to save space and costs, are inferior to paper. Despite the progress that has been and is being made in computerized information systems and in telecommunications, most of us will continue to read and file printed documents for some time to come. But the paperless society is on the horizon and will be part of our future.

HERMAN SKOLNIK

Wilmington, Delaware
January 1982

CONTENTS

THE LITERATURE MATRIX
OF CHEMISTRY

BOOKS

Books, personal libraries, and library networks are the essential components in the continuance of scientific and technological progress which serve to allow each generation to broaden its view and deepen its knowledge by standing on the shoulders of the generations preceding it.

The beginning of preserved records has been traced as far back as the Sumerian civilization of about 3600 B.C. These first records were made with a pointed stylus on wet clay, which was then baked into a durable record. According to a *Wall Street Journal* front page story on June 18, 1979, a 4500-year-old library in the ancient city of Ebla, which flourished between 2400 and 2250 B.C., was discovered in Syria. At least 20,000 tablets have been unearthed, some the size of chocolate bars, others more than a foot square with as many as 30 columns and 3000 lines on each face. The tablets are records of everyday life in the city: diplomatic records, trade agreements, and school exercises. In Egypt as early as 2000 B.C. libraries were established in which papyri rolled and packed in labeled jars were arranged chronologically on shelves. During the Greek civilization, many books were written on papyrus or parchment, and personal libraries became common among the elite. *Timaeus*, one of Plato's *Dialogues*, written about 350 B.C., had a great influence on the posterity of science as did Aristotle's *Physics* (335–323 B.C.).

The famous Alexandrian library, founded in the third century B.C., contained over 500,000 scrolls (equivalent to about 100,000 books of today). Scrolls brought to Alexandria by their owners had to be deposited in the library and exchanged for a copy. The Pergamum library, which existed in the same period, had a collection of about 200,000 scrolls.

Through the decline of Greece and the ascendency of the Roman empire, these great libraries were the means by which the heritage of the Greek civilization was transmitted throughout the Roman world and into the stream of history. In 77, Pliny the Elder (23–79) wrote *Historia Naturalis*, an encyclopedic summary of the science of his age. Pliny covered 20,000 topics and referred to 2000 volumes by nearly 500 authors. About 200 copies of Pliny's work made during the medieval and Renaissance periods are still in existence.

After the collapse of the Roman empire, and through the long years of the Dark Ages, the Church maintained a degree of literacy through monks, who, in the many monasteries throughout Europe, patiently copied page after page of manuscripts into liturgical Latin. Parchment made from sheepskin was the usual writing medium until the twelfth century, when paper became common in Europe.

During the so-called Dark Ages of Europe, the continuity of science from Egypt, India, Greece, and Byzantium to Spain was maintained and enhanced in Eastern Islam. By the ninth century, most of the classic Greek writings in science, mathematics, astronomy, and medicine had been translated into Arabic. Indeed, the experimental beginnings of chemistry were initiated by the Moslems, who learned to analyze chemical substances, studied and isolated many drugs, and made alchemy, which they inherited from Egypt, into a popular pursuit [the most famous of these alchemists was Jabit ibn Hayyan (702–765), who became known in Europe under the name Gebir]. The many books published on alchemy stimulated the practice of chemistry throughout Europe after the tenth century.

During the Middle Ages, beginning about the tenth century, universities were founded, first to train clerics in holy orders, then to teach law and, eventually, medicine. The Renaissance, a transitional period in Europe between medieval and modern times (from the fourteenth to the seventeenth century), saw the introduction of learned societies and academies of learning. Even books of few pages in medieval Europe were a luxury, and libraries of the wealthy were relatively small, usually less than 100 volumes. With the coming of universities, corps of copyists were organized to transcribe books for teachers and students— but original authors were not paid; indeed, they had to pay to have copies made. Literacy was confined for the most part to the clerics and professionals (such as doctors and governmental officials) until the twelfth and thirteenth centuries; yet libraries multiplied rapidly, especially in the monasteries, cathedrals, and universities.

Many classical Greek works and Arabic manuscripts were translated into Latin during the twelfth and thirteenth centuries. This transfusion of ancient knowledge, which occurred principally in Spain and Italy, was the beginning of the reawakening of scholarship throughout Europe and the secularization of education. From the tenth century onward, the translation of Arabic alchemical texts into Latin was the impetus for alchemical activity throughout Europe—including in monasteries, even after the Church condemned the practice in 1307. One of the more famous of the medieval scientists was Roger Bacon (1214–1292), who studied medicine at Oxford. His major work was *Opus Majus* (1266–

1267), a six-volume encyclopedia emphasizing the importance of mathematics and experimentation in scientific work. An alchemical book by Bacon was also published, but was not generally available until 1541. The printed version of *Opus Majus* became available in 1733.

Several factors combined to create a book publishing industry in Europe during the fifteenth century. Moslems introduced paper manufacture into Spain. Clothing was made of linen, and cast-off clothes provided cheap rags for paper. An oil-based ink had been developed. Literacy was increasing rapidly beyond the clergy, especially among the mercantile and industrial sectors. Finally, Johann Gutenberg introduced movable type at Mainz in the 1450s. Before the century was over, books were being printed in Germany, the Netherlands, France, Spain, England, and Italy. In terms of printing, paper, and binding qualities, most of these books were of very high quality, not matched again until the eighteenth century.

After Gutenberg, the malady *insanabile scribendi cacoethes*, or the itch to publish, reached almost epidemic proportion. This urge was not at all profitable for the writers because there was no copyright protection and pirating among the publishers was extremely common. Printing and publishing were done by the same printing house, and this was where the profits and glory were. The Frankfurt Book Fair was established so that publishers and booksellers could meet twice a year. At the 1548 fair, the first newspaper—one sheet—was printed and distributed. Among the flood of books made available at relatively low cost were Biringuccio's *De la Pirotechnia*, a 10-volume treatise printed in 1540, and Agricola's 12-volume *De Re Metallica*, printed in 1556. These two important, widely read works initated the rise in technology. Other important books in the advancement of the science and technology of chemistry are discussed in Chapter 10.

USING THE LIBRARY

Books are one of the most important forms of the literature of chemistry, chemical technology, and related sciences. It is the form that guides and dominates the educational process from kindergarden through college, and, to some degree, even through graduate school. A good educational background is based not on only text and reference books but also on how to use the school, college, university, and public libraries and how to accumulate our own personal libraries.

Books are considered so essential to the educational process that beginning in the nineteenth century, many were produced by the world's university presses. Whereas the commercial press is dominated by economic considerations, the university press has been motivated to publish works that could be helpful to students and that might be necessary for scholarship. Over the past century, several scientific and technological societies and trade associations also were motivated to publish books that commercial publishers considered economic risks. Since World War II, however, the commercial press has discovered that the "making of many books" is a highly profitable business, so much so that independent book publishers have been prime candidates for takeovers by conglomerates, such as Xerox, RCA, and CBS, or by the larger book publishers.

According to *Scientific and Technical Books and Serials in Print 1979* (Bowker, New York), there are 67,500 scientific and technical books currently in print, produced by about 2100 publishers. As measured by the shelf space required for books in the National Library of Medicine, the space requirement doubles every 25 years. Based on the 1958 and 1963 *Census of Manufacturers*, the number of scientific and technical books sold went from 15.6 million in 1958 to 29.6 million copies in 1963. There are over two million books in the Library of Congress, and there are about 530 miles of bookshelves in the New York Public Library (for books, bound journals, and other documents).

Important sources for finding out what books exist are the following:

Scientific and Technical Books and Serials in Print, Bowker, New York. Issued annually, it lists books by author and title.

Cumulative Book Index, Wilson, New York. Issued monthly and accumulated periodically, the index lists books published in the United States and England by author and title.

Library of Congress Catalog of Printed Cards, Library of Congress, Washington, D.C. The catalog is issued by Library of Congress (LC) class periodically. The one on "Technology T" was issued in two parts: Part I—pre-1976 cumulation, 15 volumes with about 480,000 titles; and Part II—quarterly supplements. These are issued with the following indexes: author, title, LC number, Dewey number, and LC subject heading.

Technical Book Review Index, Special Libraries Association, New York. Issued ten months each year since 1935, books are indexed annually for locating reviews.

Other sources are the following:

Chemical Abstracts. Current issues contain 80 sections of published books. *Chemical Abstracts* indexes denote each entry for a book with a "B" following the abstract number.

Science Books—A Quarterly Review. Issued by the AAAS since 1965, about 1000 books each year are critically reviewed and evaluated by experts.

In addition, the following journals carry high quality reviews of current books:

Journal of Chemical Education
Journal of the American Chemical Society
Science
Nature
Education in Chemistry
Chemistry and Industry
Science Progress
Angewandte Chemie
Chemistry in Britain

Other valuable and convenient sources are the advertisements and publications of book publishers.

Because libraries—in particular, their reference sections—are essential to our continuing education, we should know how they are arranged and how to use them effectively.

Classification is a process of differentiation in which objects or ideas are brought together by similarities and separated by differences. Classification schemes have played primary roles in the history of knowledge and education. The family–genus–species concept that Linnaeus introduced in 1738 is an outstanding classification system that marks the beginning of the systematization of botany. Mendeleev's periodic table, first published in 1869, is an example of a classification system in chemistry that pointed out potential errors of existing information and predicted the discovery of new elements and their properties; it motivated and advanced research, and it is still a powerful teaching aid.

The classification of knowledge has played an important role in how documents are arranged in libraries. Well into the nineteenth century, the majority of libraries arranged books alphabetically by author or title or by size, color, or accession. Library science took a giant step forward in 1876 with Melvil Dewey's introduction of his decimal classification system for the arrangement of books in libraries. This system was adopted quickly as is or in modified form by many libraries.

There are three major library book classification systems used today: Dewey, Library of Congress (LC), and universal decimal classification (UDC), a modified Dewey widely used in European libraries. These three classification systems are based on traditional disciplines; they largely reflect the spectrum of academic curricula. Thus, the Dewey decimal classification divided knowledge into the following nine classes plus one for general works:

000	General Works	500	Pure Science
100	Philosophy	600	Technology or Useful Arts
200	Religion	700	Fine Arts
300	Social Sciences	800	Literature
400	Language	900	History, Geography, Biography

Each of these ten major divisions is further subdivided into a maximum of 99 subdivisions, and further divided, as shown in the following abridgment of two major classes, science and technology:

500	Pure Science		Starch
510	Mathematics		Cellulose
520	Astronomy		High Polymers
530	Physics		Rubber
			Synthetic Resins
540	Chemistry, Crystallography, Mineralogy	548	Crystallography
541	Physical and Theoretical Chemistry	549	Mineralogy
		550	Earth Sciences
542	Apparatus and Equipment	560	Paleontology
		570	Biological Sciences
543	Analytical Chemistry— General	580	Botanical Sciences
		590	Zoological Sciences
544	Qualitative Analysis	600	Technology
545	Quantitative Analysis	610	Medical Sciences
546	Inorganic Chemistry	630	Agriculture
547	Organic Chemistry	660	Chemical Technology

547.013	Polymerization		660.28	Chemical Engineering
547.920	Special Fields of Organic Chemistry		661	Industrial Chemicals
663	Beverages, Stimulants		662.	Explosives, Fuels
664	Food Technology		668.44	Plastics from Cellulose
665	Oils, Fats, Waxes, Gases		669	Metallurgy
666	Ceramics		670	Other Manufacturers
667	Cleaning and Color Industries		767	Pulp and Paper Industries
668	Other Organic Chemical Materials and Products		677	Textile and Fiber Manufacturers
668.4	Plastics Industries, Resins, Gums		677.46	Rayon
668.422	Condensation Plastics, e.g., Phenolics		678	Rubber
668.423	Linear Polymer Plastics, e.g., Polyethylene		678.3	Natural Rubber
			678.7	Elastomers
			678.72	Synthetic Rubber
			678.722	Polymerization to Synthetic Rubber

Conceived in 1895 and introduced in 1905, universal decimal classification, an international adaptation of the Dewey decimal classification system, has been adopted by many European libraries. Considerably more detailed than the Dewey system, UDC has been used as an indexing scheme as well as a document classification. As shown in the following abbreviated divisions for the two classes science and technology, there is a close relationship between the subclasses in Dewey and UDC.

5	Natural Sciences		547.284.3	Acetone
54	Chemistry		547.3	Acyclic, Unsaturated
543	Analytical Chemistry		547.313.2	Ethylene
547	Organic Chemistry		6	Applied Sciences
547.2	Acyclic, Aliphatic Compounds		66	Chemical Technology
547.28	Carbonyl Compounds		67	Manufacturers
547.284	Ketones		677	Textiles
			677.4	Synthetic Fibers

678	Macromolecular Materials	678.544	Cellulose Esters
678.01:53	Physical Properties	678.546	Cellulose Ethers
678.01:536	Thermal Properties	678.6	Polycondensates
678.06	Applications	678.632	Phenol-Aldehyde
678.06:621	Engineering	678.7	Synthetic Rubber, Resins
678.06:621.3	Electrical	678.742.2	Polyethylene
678.4	Rubber and Natural Macro-molecules	678.742.3	Polypropylene
		678.743.22	Poly(vinyl Chloride)
678.5	Plastics Based on Cellulose	678.744.322	Poly(acrylic Acid)
		678.746.22	Polystyrene
678.542	Cellulose	678.762.2	Polybutadiene

The other standard book classification, and the one which most Americans will encounter, is the Library of Congress classification system (LC), which was also conceived and introduced in the last part of the nineteenth century (its printed catalog cards have been available since 1902). Originally designed for the Library of Congress only, LC was based on the over three million books in its collection at that time. Unlike Dewey and UDC, LC is not a decimal system; it has 21 major classes of knowledge, and is based on an alphabetical and numerical representation for the classes, as follows:

A	General Works	M	Music
B	Philosophy and Religion	N	Fine Arts
C	Auxiliary Sciences of History	P	Language and Literature
		Q	Science
D	Universal History	R	Medicine
E and F	American History	S	Agriculture
G	Geography	T	Technology
H	Social Science	U	Military Science
J	Political Science	V	Naval Science
K	Law	Z	Bibliography, Library Science
L	Education		

The first subdivisions of the 21 major classes are also indicated with capital letters, as in the following breakdown of science:

Q	Science	QH	Natural History
QA	Mathematics	QK	Botany
QB	Astronomy	QL	Zoology
QC	Physics	QM	Human Anatomy
QD	Chemistry	QP	Physiology
QE	Geology	QR	Bacteriology

Each subdivision is divided by a numerical system, as illustrated below for chemistry and chemical technology:

QD	Chemistry	QD281.86	Polymerization
QD1	Chemical Societies	QD301–319	Aliphatic Compounds
QD7	Nomenclature	QD410	Organometal Compounds
QD11–18	History		
QD45	Laboratory Manuals	QD419	Gums and Resins
		TP	Chemical Technology
QD71–145	Analytical Chemistry		
		TP155	Chemical Engineering
QD81–95	Qualitative		
QD101–142	Quantitative	TP977–982	Gums and Resins
QD151–199	Inorganic Chemistry	TP986	Plastic Materials
		TP986.A5	Special Plastics
QD241–449	Organic Chemistry	TP986.A5.B3	Bakelite

In many libraries, books are arranged on shelves by call number, a combination of the book classification code and the Cutter author code. The Cutter code consists of the first letter of the author's surname followed by a two- or three-digit number. The numbers, arranged in a tabular form, represent Charles A. Cutter's statistical distribution of letters in authors' names. For example, the Cutter two-digit designation for Huntress is H92. Moderate size libraries, such as those of industrial research and development laboratories or of chemistry departments, prefer an alphabetical Cutter code, in which, Huntress, for example, is designated HUN.

None of the three primary book classification systems allows easy browsing in the library, especially in the rapidly changing science and technology sections. Library clients, even those knowledgeable in the classification systems, are advised to consult the book catalog under subjects of interest, authors, and titles. Many libraries have subject heading books or authority lists that relate subjects with classifications. One such publication, issued regularly by the Library of Congress, is a working tool for most catalog librarians.

In attempting to be all things to all areas of knowledge, the three primary book classification systems fail to bring like things together for the community of scientists and engineers concentrated in a specific discipline, such as in the sciences and technologies related to chemistry. The three major library classification systems are based primarily on and reflect for the most part the spectrum of academic curricula of major universities, which is not always congruent with the real world of knowledge and practice. Moreover, none of the three has been able to keep pace with the advances of science and the changes of technology. The dichotomization of science into "pure" and "applied" is anachronistic to newer disciplines, such as polymer science, space technology, computer science, information science, or chemical propulsion, to cite a few examples.

The following four examples illustrate the dispersion of polymer books by the LC and Dewey call numbers [see H. Skolnik, "A Classification System for Polymer Literature in an Industrial Environment," *J. Chem. Info. Comput. Sci. 19*, 76–79 (1979)]:

1. F.E. Bailey, Jr., and J. V. Koleski, *Poly(ethylene Oxide)*
    Academic Press, New York, 1976
    LC: TP1180.P653B34
    Dewey: 668.4'234

2. E.J. Vandenberg (ed.), *Polyethers*, ACS Symposium Series 6, American Chemical Society, Washington, D.C., 1975
    LC: QD380.P63
    Dewey: 547'.84

3. J.P. Kennedy, *Cationic Polymerization of Olefins: A Critical Inventory*, Wiley–Interscience, New York, 1975
    LC: QD305.H7K38
    Dewey: 547'.8432'234

4. J. Schultz, *Polymer Materials Science*, Prentice–Hall, New York, 1974
LC: TA455.P58S36
Dewey: 620.1'92

Books 1 and 2 above are concerned with linear polymers of ethylene oxide, yet 1 is classified in "Applied Science" and 2 in "Pure Science," 1 in "Plastic Materials" under "Chemical Technology" and 2 under "Organic Chemistry" in the LC system, which places them very far apart in even a special library. These two books are separated similarly by the Dewey classification, with 1 classified in the "Plastics Industries, Resins, Gums" under "Applied Science" and 2 in "Polymerization" under "Organic Chemistry." Book 3, on the other hand, is shelved by LC and Dewey reasonably close to book 2, yet not so close that both could be spotted easily by browsing in the stacks. Book 4 is completely isolated from the totality of polymer science and technology books.

Inasmuch as a very large number of chemists and chemical engineers are engaged in research and development in polymer science and technology, and polymer science and technology is second to only the pharmaceutical/medical sciences in industrial research and development expenditures, polymer science and technology deserves the status of a major discipline of chemistry, not as a subclass or sub-subclass of organic chemistry, physics, physical chemistry, or applied science.

REFERENCE WORKS AND BOOKS

The remainder of this chapter is devoted to a list of the major, recently published reference works and books. (The classics are discussed in Chapters 10 and 11.) Because many of these books undergo frequent revisions, the year of publication is not cited; it is understood that one would request the most recent edition from the library or the publisher. The reference works and books are categorized under the following outline, which is more relevant than any of the three primary classification systems to the interests of the chemical community:

I.   General reference
    A.   Directories
        Publications
        People

      B. Polymerization

      C. Specific polymers

XII. Industrial chemistry

      A. General

      B. Adhesives

      C. Ceramics

      D. Cosmetics

      E. Dyes and pigments

      F. Explosives, propellants, space science

      G. Fertilizers

      H. Food science and technology

      I. Paper

      J. Petroleum

      K. Pesticides

      L. Solvents and coatings

      M. Surfactants

      N. Textiles

I. General reference

      A. *Directories*

         Publications

         1. *Ayer's Directory of Publications*, Ayer Press, Philadelphia

         2. *Ulrich's International Periodicals Directory*, Bowker, New York

         3. *Union List of Serials in Libraries of the U.S. and Canada*, supplemented by *New Serial Titles*, Library of Congress, Washington, DC

         4. *World List of Scientific Periodicals* and *British Catalogue of Periodicals*, both updated quarterly and annually, Butterworth, London

         5. *Subject Guide to Books in Print*, Bowker, New York

         6. *Bibliography of Textile Books*, American Association of Textile Technologists, New York

         7. *CASSI—The Chemical Abstracts Service Source Index* (see Chapter 5), Chemical Abstracts Service, Columbus, OH

         8. *Standard Periodical Directory*, Oxbridge, New York

9. *Abstracting Services—Science and Technology*, Federation Internationale de Documentation, The Hague, Netherlands

10. *Directory of Information Resources in the United States*, U.S. Government Printing Office, Washington, D.C.

11. A.T. Kruzas (ed.), *Directory of Special Libraries and Information Centers*, Gale Research, Detroit

12. *Bacon's Publicity Checker*, Vol. 1, "Magazines," Bacon's, Chicago

People

1. *Who's Who in America*, Marquis, Chicago

2. *American Men and Women of Science*, Cattell Press, Tempe, Ariz.

3. Society Memberships
   a. American Institute of Chemical Engineers
   b. American Oil Chemists' Society
   c. ASTM
   d. ACS Divisions, e.g., Analytical Chemistry, Chemical Marketing and Economics, Fuel Chemistry, Petroleum Chemistry, Rubber, etc.
   e. American Physical Society
   f. Society of the Plastics Industry
   g. Technical Association of the Pulp and Paper Industry

4. *Directory of British Scientists*, Ernest Benn, London

5. *Address Book of German Chemists*, German Chemical Society and Verlag Chemie, Weinheim, West Germany

6. *World of Learning*, Europa, London

7. *College Chemistry Faculties*, American Chemical Society, Washington, D.C.

Companies

1. *Jane's Major Companies of Europe*, McGraw–Hill, New York

2. *Industrial Research Laboratories*, Bowker, New York

3. *Federation of British Industries*, The Federation, London

4. *Directory of Chemical Producers,* SRI, Menlo Park, Calif.
5. *Thomas Register of American Manufacturers,* New York
6. *Consulting and Laboratory Services: A Directory,* Lundy Enterprises, State College, Pa.
7. *Information Industry Market Place 1981,* Bowker, New York

Societies and associations
1. *Scientific, Technical, and Related Societies of the United States,* National Academy of Sciences, Washington, D.C.
2. *United States Trade Associations,* Johnson, Loveland, Col.
3. *Encyclopedia of Associations,* Gale Research, Detroit
4. *Directory of International Scientific Organizations,* UNESCO, New York
5. *Education Directory, Colleges and Universities,* U.S. Government Printing Office, Washington, D.C.
6. C.E. Lovejoy, *College Guide,* Simon & Schuster, New York
7. J. Gourman, *Gourman Report,* National Education Standards, Los Angeles

B. *General encyclopedias*
1. The *Encyclopedia Americana,* Americana, New York
2. *Encyclopedia Britanica,* Encyclopedia Britannica, Chicago
3. The *Columbia Encyclopedia,* Columbia Univ. Press, New York
4. The *World Book,* Field Enterprises, Chicago

C. *General dictionaries*
1. The *American College Dictionary,* Random House, New York
2. *Funk and Wagnall's New Standard Dictionary,* Funk & Wagnalls, New York
3. *Webster's New Collegiate Dictionary,* Merriam, Springfield, Mass.

4. E. Ehrlich et al. (eds.), *Oxford American Dictionary*, Oxford Univ. Press, New York

5. W. Morris (ed.), *American Heritage Dictionary of the English Language*, Houghton Mifflin, Boston

6. *Webster's Unabridged Dictionary*, Merriam, Springfield, Mass.

7. *Roget's International Thesaurus*, Crowell, New York

8. *Fowler's Dictionary of Modern English Usage*, Oxford Univ. Press, Fair Lawn, N.J.

D. *Technical dictionaries*

1. G. G. and A. W. Hawley, *Hawley's Technical Speller*, Reinhold, New York

2. A. and E. Rose, *Condensed Chemical Dictionary*, Reinhold, New Yrok

3. H. Bennett (ed.), *Concise Chemical and Technical Dictionary*, Chemical Pub., New York

4. *Hackh's Chemical Dictionary*, McGraw–Hill, New York

5. *SOCMA Handbook*, ACS, Washington, D.C.

6. *Chemist's Dictionary*, Van Nostrand, New York

7. G. L. Clark and G. G. Hawley, *The Encyclopedia of Chemistry*, Reinhold, New York

8. *Chamber's Technical Dictionary*, Macmillan, New York

9. *International Encyclopedia of the Chemical Sciences*, Van Nostrand, New York

10. M. Orchin and F. Kaplan, *Vocabulary of Organic Chemistry*, Wiley, New York

11. *Merck Index of Chemicals and Drugs*, Merck, Rahway, N.J.

12. *Stedman's Medical Dictionary*, Williams & Wilkins, Baltimore

13. *Dorland's Illustrated Medical Dictionary*, Saunders, Philadelphia

14. *New and Nonofficial Drugs*, American Medical Association, Chicago

15. *Parr's Concise Medical Encyclopedia*, American Elsevier, New York

16. *Pharmacopedia of the United States*, Mack, Easton, Pa.

17. *Proprietary Names of Official Drugs*, American Pharmaceutical Association, Washington, D.C.

E. Handbooks

1. R. C. Weast (ed.), *The Handbook of Chemistry and Physics*, Chemical Rubber, Cleveland

2. M. A. Lange, *Handbook of Chemistry*, McGraw–Hill, New York

3. J. H. and R. H. Perry, *Engineering Manual*, McGraw–Hill, New York

4. R. H. Chilton, S. D. Kirkpatrick, and J. H. Perry, *Chemical Engineers' Handbook*, McGraw–Hill, New York

5. D. E. Gray (ed.), *Handbook of Physics*, McGraw–Hill, New York

F. Trade information

1. *Index of Trademarks*, U.S. Patent Office, Washington, D.C.

2. Haynes, W., *Chemical Trade Names and Commercial Synonyms*, Van Nostrand, New York

3. Zimmerman, O. T., and I. Lavine, *Handbook of Material Trade Names*, Industrial Research Service, Dover, N.H.

4. E. T. Crowley (ed.), *Trade Names Dictionary*, Gale Research, Detroit

5. Gardner, W., and E. I. Cook, *Chemical synonyms and Trade Names*, Chemical Rubber, Boca Raton, Fl.

6. *Chemicals of Commerce*, Van Nostrand, New York

7. Bennett, H., *The Chemical Formulary*, Chemical Publishing, New York

8. *Chemical Business Handbook*, McGraw-Hill, New York

9. *C.E.C. Chemical Engineering Catalog*, Reinhold, New York

10. *Buyers Guide*, Chemical Week, McGraw-Hill, New York

11. *Thomas Register of American Manufacturers* Thomas, New York

12. *Chemical Economics Handbook*, Standford Research Inst. Stanford, Calif.

13. *Commodity Yearbook*, Commodity Research Bureau, New York

14. *Chem. Sources–U.S.A.*, Directories Pub., Flemington, N.J.

15. *Chem Sources–Europe*, Directories Pub., Flemington, N.J.

16. *Chemical Industry Facts Book*, Chemical Manufacturers Association, New York

17. *Chemical Statistics Handbook*, Chemical Manufacturers Association, New York

18. *Statistical Abstract of the United States*, U.S. Bureau of the Census, Washington, D.C.

19. Anon., *Chemistry in the Economy*, ACS, Washington, D.C.

20. *Preprints*, ACS Division of Chemical Marketing and Economics

21. R. Ferber, *Handbook of Marketing Research*, McGraw–Hill, New York

22. E. A. Gee and C. Tyler, *Managing Innovation*, Wiley, New York

23. D. D. Lee, *Industrial Marketing Research*, Technomic, Westport, Conn.

24. W. J. Stanton, *Fundamentals of Marketing*, McGraw–Hill, New York

25. N. H. Giragosian (ed.), *Chemical Marketing Research*, Reinhold, New York

G. *Foreign language dictionaries*

1. *Cassell's New French–English, English–French Dictionary*, Funk and Wagnalls, New York

2. L. DeVries, *French–English Science Dictionary*, McGraw–Hill, New York

3. A. M. Patterson, *A French–English Dictionary for Chemists*, Wiley, New York

4. H. Fromberg and A. King, *French–English Chemical Terminology*, trans. by J. Jousset, Verlag Chemie, Weinheim, West Germany

5. L. DeVries, *German–English Science Dictionary*, McGraw–Hill, New York

6. A. M. Patterson, *A German–English Dictionary for Chemists*, Wiley, New York

7. D. W. Unseld, *Medical Dictionary of the German and English Languages* Wissenshaftliche Verlag, Stuttgart, West Germany

8. A. Webel, *German–English Dictionary of Technical, Scientific and General Terms*, Dutton, New York

9. A. F. Dorian *"Dictionary of Science and Technology,"* English–German and also German–English, Elsevier, New York

10. H. Fromberg and A. King, *English–German Chemical Terminology*, Verlag Chemie, Weinheim, West German

11. M. S. Welling, *German–English Glossary of Plastics Machinery Terms*, Carl Haneer, Munich

12. G. Marolli, *Technical Dictionary: English–Italian, Italian–English*, Heineman, New York

13. L. I. Callahan, *Russian–English Chemical and Medical Dictionary*, Wiley, New York

14. M. Goldberg, *Spanish–English Chemical and Medical Dictionary* McGraw–Hill, New York

H. *Technical encyclopedias and compendia*

1. *Kirk–Othmer Encyclopedia of Chemical Technology*, Wiley–Interscience, New York

2. F. Ullmann, *Encyclopedia der technischen Chemie*, Verlag Chemie, Weinheim, West Germany

3. W. H. Crouse (ed.), *Encyclopedia of Science and Technology*, McGraw–Hill, New York

4. J. F. Thorp and M. A. Whitley, *Thorpe's Dictionary of Applied Chemistry*, Longman, New York

5. *Encyclopedia of Chemical Process Equipment*, Reinhold, New York

6. J. J. McKette and W. A. Cunningham, *Encyclopedia of Chemical Processing and Design*, Dekker, New York

7. H. F. Mark (ed.), *Encyclopedia of Polymer Science and Technology*, Wiley, New York

8. *Dictionary of Named Effects and Laws*, Chapman–Hall, New York

9. Anon., *Colour Index*, Society of Dyers and Colourists, Bradford, England

10. R. Stelzner, *Literatur-Register der organischen Chemie*, Verlag Chemie, Weinheim, West Germany

11. F. Richter *Lexikon der Kohlenstoffverbindungen*, Verlag von Leopold Voss, Hamburg, W. Germany

12. H. G. Bait et al., *Beilstein's Handbuch der organischen Chemie*, Springer, Berlin, Germany

13. F. Radt (ed.), *Elsevier's Encyclopedia of Organic Chemistry*, Elsevier, New York

14. I. M. Heilbron and H. M. Brunbury, (ed.), *Dictionary of Organic Compounds*, Oxford Univ. Press, London

15. E. Muller (ed.), *Houben–Weyl's Methoden der organischen Chemie*, George Thieme Verlag, Stuttgart, Germany

16. R. Adams et al., *Organic Syntheses*, Wiley, New York

17. R. Adams et al., *Organic Reactions*, Wiley, New York

16. E. H. Rodd (ed.), *Chemistry of Carbon Compounds*, Elsevier, New York

19. W. Theilheimer, *Synthetic Methods of Organic Chemistry*, Wiley, New York

20. A. Weissberger (ed.), *Techniques of Organic Chemistry*, Wiley, New York

21. Gmelin Institute, *Gmelin's Handbuch der anorganischen Chemie,*, Verlag Chemie, Weinheim, West Germany

22. *Inorganic Syntheses*, McGraw–Hill, New York

23. C. A. Jacobson, *Encyclopedia of Chemical Reactions*, Reinhold, New York

24. J. W. Mellor, *Comprehensive Treatise on Inorganic and Theoretical Chemistry*, Longman, New York

25. M. C. Snead, J. L. Maynard, and R. C. Brasted, *Comprehensive Inorganic Chemistry*, Van Nostrand, New York

26. N. J. Friend, *Textbook of Inorganic Chemistry*, Griffin, London

27. A. Eucken (ed.), *Landolt-Börnstein: Zahlenwerte und*

Funktionen aus Physik, Chemie, Astronomie, Geophysik and Technik, Springer, Berlin

28. Rompps Chemie-Lexikon, Frank'sche Verlagshandlung, Stuttgart, Germany

29. E. W. Washburn (ed.), International Critical Tables, McGraw–Hill, New York

30. D. R. Stull and H. Prophet, JANAF Thermochemical Data, National Standard Reference Data series, National Bureau of Standards, report no. 37, Washington, DC

31. D. R. Stull, E. F. Westrum, and G. C. Sinke, The Chemical Thermodynamics of Organic Compounds, Wiley, New York

32. Selected Values of Chemical Thermodynamic Properties, National Bureau of Standards technical note 270 (issued in parts), Washington, DC

33. Van Nostrand's Scientific Encyclopedia, Van Nostrand, New York

34. H. J. Gray (ed.), Dictionary of Physics, Longman, New York

35. J. Thewlis, D. J. Hughes, and A. R. Meetham (eds.), Encyclopaedic Dictionary of Physics, Pergamon, New York

36. S. Fluegge (ed.), Handbuch der Physik/Encyclopedia of Physics, Springer, Berlin

37. C. A. Hampel (ed.), Encyclopedia of Electrochemistry, Reinhold, New York

38. Tables annuelles de constantes et donnees numeriques, McGraw–Hill, New York

39. H. and T. Stephen (ed.), Solubilities of Inorganic and Organic Compounds, Pergamon, New York

40. A. Seidell, Solubilities of Inorganic, Organic, and Metal Organic Compounds, Van Nostrand, New York

41. A. S. Kertes (ed.), Solubility Data Series (an IUPAC sponsored comprehensive series of critically evaluated solubility data), Pergamon, New York

II. Industrial functions

    A. Management

        1. American Management Association publications

2. Conference Board publications
3. P. F. Drucker, *The Effective Executive*, Harper, New York
4. P. F. Drucker, *Managing for Results*, Harper, New York
5. P. F. Drucker, *Management: Tasks, Responsibilities, Practices*, Harper, New York
6. P. F. Drucker, *Technology, Management, and Society*, Harper, New York
7. J. K. Galbraith, *The New Industrial State*, Houghten–Mifflin, Boston
8. C. Heyel (ed.), *Encyclopedia of Management*, Van Nostrand, New York
9. J. R. Bright, *Technology Forecasting*, Permaquid Press, Austin, Tex.
10. V. Bush, *Science—The Endless Frontier*, NSF, Washington, DC
11. C. E. K. Mees and J. A. Leermakers, *The Organization of Industrial Scientific Research*, McGraw–Hill, New York
12. E. B. Wilson, *An Introduction to Scientific Research*, McGraw–Hill, New York
13. *Professionals in Chemistry: 1977*, ACS, Washington, DC
14. P. F. Drucker, *Managing in Turbulent Times*, Harper, New York
15. T. Gordon, *Leader Effectiveness Training, LET*, Wyden, New York
16. G. Gale, *Theory of Science*, McGraw–Hill, New York
17. J. L. Meyer and M. W. Donaho, *Get the Right Person for the Job. Managing Interviews and Selecting Employees*, Prentice–Hall, New York
18. T. H. Patten, Jr., *Classics of Personnel Management*, Moor, Oak Park, Ill.
19. K. Knight (ed.), *Matrix Management*, Petrocelli, New York

B. Writing
  1. M. Brogan, *Handbook for Authors*, ACS, Washington, DC

2. *Style Manual*, U.S. GPO, Washington, DC
3. *A Manual of Style*, Chicago Univ. Press, Chicago
4. W. Strunk and E. B. White, *The Elements of Style*, Macmillan, New York
5. L. F. and M. Fieser, *Style Guide for Chemists*, Reinhold, New York
6. R. Gunning, *The Technique of Clear Writing*, McGraw–Hill, New York
7. H. J. Tichy, *Effective Writing for Engineers, Managers, Scientists*, Wiley, New York
8. F. H. Rhodes, *Technical Report Writing*, McGraw–Hill New York
9. J. N. Ulman, *Technical Reporting*, Holt, New York
10. B. H. Weil, *Technical Editing*, Reinhold, New York
11. M. O'Connor, *The Scientist as Editor: Guidelines for Editors of Books and Journals*, Wiley, New York
12. R. A. Day, *How to Write and Publish a Scientific Paper*, Institute for Scientific Information Press, Philadelphia
13. J. Monroe and C. Meredith, *The Science of Scientific Writing*, Kendall/Hunt, Dubuque, Iowa

C. *Information and library science*

1. J. Becker and R. M. Hayes, *Information Storage and Retrieval*, Wiley, New York
2. R. T. Bottle (ed.), *The Use of the Chemical Literature*, Archon, London
3. C. P. Bourne, *Methods of Information Handling*, Wiley, New York
4. C. R. Burman, *How to Find Out in Chemistry*, Pergamon, New York
5. C. H. Davis and J. E. Rush, *Information Retrieval and Documentation in Chemistry*, Greenwood, Westport, Conn.
6. M. P. Crosland, *Historical Studies in the Language of Chemistry*, Harvard University Press, Cambridge, Mass.
7. F. M. Lancaster, *Toward Paperless Information Systems*, Academic Press, New York
8. F. M. Lancaster, *The Measurement and Evaluation of*

Library Services, Information Resources Press, Washington, DC

9. S. Herner, *A Brief Guide to Sources of Scientific and Technical Information*, Information Resources Press, Washington, DC

10. A. Kent and H. Lancour (eds.), *Encyclopedia of Library and Information Science*, Dekker, New York

11. D. W. King and E. C. Bryant, *The Evaluation of Information Services and Products*, Information Resources Press, Washington, DC

12. A. T. Kruzas (ed.), *Encyclopedia of Information Systems and Services*, Gale Research, Detroit

13. A. N. Grosch, *Minicomputers in Libraries*, American Society for Information Science, Washington, DC

14. *The Annual Review of Information Science and Technology*, American Society for Information Science, Washington, DC

15. T. E. R. Singer (ed.), *Literature Resources for Chemical Process Industries*, American Chemical Society, Washington, DC

16. M. G. Mellon (ed.), *Training of Literature Chemists*, American Chemical Society, Washington, DC

17. T. E. R. Singer (ed.), *Searching the Chemical Literature*, American Chemical Society, Washington, DC

18. J. F. Smith (ed.), *Literature of Chemical Technology*, American Chemical Society, Washington, DC

19. L. J. Strauss, I. M. Strieby, and A. L. Brown, *Scientific and Technical Libraries*, Wiley, New York

20. E. J. Crane, A. M. Patterson, and E. B. Marr, *A Guide to the Literature of Chemistry*, Wiley, New York

21. G. M. Dyson, *A Short Guide to Chemical Literature*, Longman, New York

22. *M. G. Mellon, Chemical Publications*, McGraw–Hill, New York

23. *Library Guide for the Chemist*, B. A. Soule, McGraw–Hill, New York

24. H. M. Woodburn, *Using the Chemical Literature*, Dekker, New York

25. R. E. Maizell, *How to Find Chemical Information*, Wiley, New York

26. B. Katz and A. Tarr (eds.), *Reference and Information Services*, Scarecrow Press, Metuchen, N. J.

27. L. Maranjian and R. W. Boss, *Fee-Based Information Services, A Study of a Growing Industry*, Bowker, New York

28. F. W. Lancaster, *Vocabulary Control for Information Retrieval*, Information Resources Press, Washington, D.C.

29. F. W. Lancaster, *Information Retrieval Systems: Characteristics, Testing, and Evaluation*, Wiley, New York

30. *Records Retention and Files Management*, Wilds, New York

D. *Industrial toxicology*

1. L. J. Casarett and J. Doull (eds.), *Toxicology, the Basic Science of Poisons*, Macmillan, New York

2. G. D. and F. E. Clayton, *Patty's Industrial Hygiene and Toxicology*, Wiley, New York

3. W. B. Deichmann and H. W. Gerarde, *Toxicology of Drugs and Chemicals*, Academic Press, New York

4. H. B. Elkins, *The Chemistry of Industrial Toxicology*, Wiley, New York

5. E. J. Fairchild (ed.), *Registry of Toxic Effects of Chemical Substances*, NIOSH, U.S. Government Printing Office

6. A. Hamilton and H. L. Hardy, *Industrial Toxicology*, PSG Pub., Littleton, MA

7. *Encyclopedia of Occupational Health and Safety*, International Labour Office, Geneva

8. F. A. Patty, (ed.), *Industrial Hygiene and Toxicology*, Wiley, New York

9. E. R. Plunkett, *Handbook of Industrial Toxicology*, Chemical Publishing, New York

10. *Environmental Toxicology—A Guide to Information Sources*, Gale Research, Detroit

11. L. S. Schieler and D. Panze, *Hazardous Materials,* Van Nostrand, New York

12. H. E. Sax, *Dangerous Properties of Industrial Materials,* Van Nostrand, New York

13. Anon., *Threshold Limit Values for Chemical Substances in Workroom Air Adopted by ACGIH for 1980,* American Conference of Governmental Industrial Hygienists, Cincinnati

14. Anon., *Prudent Practices for Handling Hazardous Chemicals in Laboratories,* National Research Council, Washington, D.C.

E. *Pollution control*

1. *Preprint* Series of ACS Divisions of Environmental Chemistry and Water, Air, and Waste, *ACS Advances in Chemistry* series, and *ACS Symposium* series American Chemical Society, Washington, DC

2. AIChE Symposium series on *Waste Water Treatment* and on *Air Pollution,* American Institute of Chemical Engineers, New York

3. Bibliographic series on *Institute of Paper Chemistry, Air* and on *Water Pollution in the Pulp and Paper Industry,* Appleton, Wis.

4. *Industrial Waste Conference Proceedings,* Purdue University, Lafayette, Ind.

III. *Mathematics*

1. G. and R. C. James, *Mathematics Dictionary,* Van Nostrand, New York

2. C. E. Pearson (ed.), *Handbook of Applied Mathematics,* Van Nostrand, New York

3. R. C. Weast (ed.), *Handbook of Tables for Mathematics,* CRC, Boca Raton, Fla.

4. C. L. Perrin, *Mathematics for Chemists,* Wiley, New York

5. R. L. Ackoff, *Scientific Method: Optimizing Applied Research Decision,* Wiley, New York

6. E. L. Bauer, *Statistical Manual for Chemists,* Academic Press, New York

7. G. E. P. Box and W. G. Hunter, *Statistics for Experimenters,* Wiley, New York

8. A. Naiman, R. Rosenfeld, and G. Zirkel, *Understanding Statistics*, McGraw–Hill, New York

9. B. E. Gillett, *Introduction to Operations Research*, McGraw–Hill, New York

IV. *Physics*

1. E. U. Condon and H. Odishaw, *Handbook of Physics*, McGraw–Hill, New York

2. *Handbuch der Physik: Encyclopedia of Physics*, Springer–Verlag, Secaucus, N.J.

3. J. T. Glazebrook, *Dictionary of Applied Physics*, Macmillan, New York

4. J. Thewlis (ed.), *Encyclopedic Dictionary of Physics*, Pergamon, New York

5. D. Halliday and R. Resnick, *Fundamentals of Physics*, Wiley, New York

6. D. Williams (ed.), *Methods of Experimental Physics*, Academic Press, New York

7. F. H. Field et al., *Pure and Applied Physics*, Academic Press, New York

V. *Chemical Engineering*

1. American Chemical Society, Advances in Chemistry series no. 109—K. B. Bischoff (ed.), *Chemical Reaction Engineering*; no. 115—D. M Tassios (ed.), *Extractive and Azeotropic Distillation*; no. 116—L. H. Horsley, *Azeotropic Data*; no. 118—D. D. Reneau (ed.), *Chemical Engineering in Medicine*; no. 133—H. M. Hulburt (ed.), *Chemical Reaction Engineering—II*; no. 148—H. M. Hulburt (ed.), *Chemical Reaction Engineering Revisions*, American Chemical Society, Washington, DC

2. American Chemical Society Symposium series no. 22—L.F. Albright and C. Hanson, (eds.), *Industrial and Laboratory Nitrations*; no. 40—L. F. Albright and D. L. Crynes, *Industrial and Laboratory Pyrolyses*, J. R. Katzer (ed.), *Molecular Sieves*; no. 55—L. F. Albright and A. R. Goldsby (eds.), *Industrial and Laboratory Alkylations*; no. 56—P. R. Brooks and E. F. Hayes (eds.), *State-to-State Chemistry*, American Chemical Society, Washington, DC

3. *Advances in Chemical Engineering*, Academic Press, New York

4. J. Coulson and J. F. Richardson, *Chemical Engineering*, Pergamon, New York

5. H. W. Cremer (ed.), *Chemical Engineering Practice*, Butterworth, London

6. O. A. Hougan, *Chemical Process Principles*, Wiley, New York

7. American Institute of Chemical Engineers Monograph series and Symposium series, American Institute of Chemical Engineers, New York

8. P. H. Groggins, *Unit Processes in Organic Synthesis*, McGraw-Hill, New York

9. W. L. McCabe and J. C. Smith, *Unit Operations of Chemical Engineering*, McGraw-Hill, New York

10. E. S. Perry (ed.), *Separation and Purification*, Wiley, New York

11. S. Young, *Distillation Principles and Processes*, Macmillan, New York

12. T. K. Sherwood, *Absorption and Extraction*, McGraw–Hill, New York

13. T. K. Sherwood and R. L. Pigford, *Mass Transfer*, McGraw–Hill, New York

14. S. S. Zabrodsky, *Hydrodynamics and Heat Transfer in Fluidized Beds*, Massachusetts Institute of Technology Press, Cambridge, Mass.

15. J. R. Grace and J. M. Matseu (eds.), *Fluidization*, Plenum, New York

16. R. Prins and G. C. A. Schuit (eds.), *Chemistry and Chemical Engineering of Catalytic Processes*, Sitjhott and Morrdhoff, Germantown, Md.

17. Anon., *Centrifuges: A Guide to Performance Evaluation*, American Institute of Chemical Engineers, New York

18. M. G. Fontana and N. D. Greene, *Corrosion Engineering*, McGraw–Hill, New York

19. T. W. F. Russell and M. M. Denn, *Introduction to Chemical Engineering Analysis*, Wiley, New York

20. C. G. Hill, Jr., *An Introduction to Chemical Engine-*

ering Kinetics and Reactor Design, Wiley, New York

21. M. S. Peters and K. D. Timmerhaus, *Plant Design and Economics for Chemical Engineers*, McGraw–Hill, New York

22. R. M. Felder and R. W. Rousseau, *Elementary Principles of Chemical Processes*, Wiley, New York

VI. *Physical Chemistry*

1. *Annual Review of Physical Chemistry*, Annual Review, Palo Alto, Calif.

2. J. R. Partington, *An Advanced Treatise in Physical Chemistry*, Longman, New York

3. E. M. Loebl, *Physical Chemistry, A Series of Monographs*, Academic Press, New York

4. D. P. Craig and R. McWeeny (eds.), *Theoretical Chemistry, A Series of Monographs*, Academic Press, New York

5. H. S. Taylor (ed.), *Treatise on Physical Chemistry*, Van Nostrand, New York

6. A. Weissberger (ed.), *Physical Methods of Organic Chemistry*, Wiley, New York

7. F. Daniels and R. A. Alberty, *Physical Chemistry*, Wiley, New York

8. H. Eyring and D. Henderson, *Theoretical Chemistry: Advances and Perspectives*, Academic Press, New York

9. S. Glasstone, *Textbook of Physical Chemistry*, Van Nostrand, New York

10. W. J. Moore, *Physical Chemistry*, Prentice–Hall, New York

11. C. A. Coulson, *Shape and Structure of Molecules*, Oxford Press, London

12. L. Pauling, *Nature of the Chemical Bond*, Cornell Univ. Press, London

13. F. A. Cotton, *Chemical Applications of Group Theory*, Wiley, New York

14. R. B. Woodward and R. Hoffmann, *The Conservation of Orbital Symmetry*, Academic Press, New York

15. G. N. Lewis and M. Randall, *Thermodynamics*, McGraw–Hill, New York

16. F. T. Wall, *Chemical Thermodynamics. A Course of Study*, Freeman San Francisco

17. H. and E. M. Eyring, *Modern Chemical Kinetics*, Reinhold, New York

18. H. Eyring, *Basic Chemical Kinetics*, Wiley, New York

19. J. H. Hildebrand, *An Introduction to Molecular Kinetic Theory*, Reinhold, New York

20. K. J. Laidler, *Chemical Kinetics*, McGraw–Hill, New York

21. *Advances in Catalysis and Related Subjects*, Chemical Society (London)

22. B. C. Gates, J. R. Katzer, and G. C. A. Schmit, *Chemistry of Catalytic Processes*, McGraw–Hill, New York

23. C. Kittel, *Introduction to Solid State Physics*, Wiley, New York

24. Y. M. Paushkin (ed.), *Organic Polymer Semiconductors*, Rochester Institute of Technology, Rochester, N.Y.

25. J. Smit, *Magnetic Properties of Materials*, McGraw–Hill, New York

26. A. V. Adamson, *Physical Chemistry of Surfaces*, Wiley, New York

27. J. F. Danielli et al., eds., *Recent Progress in Surface Science*, Academic Press, New York

28. E. Matijevic (ed.), *Surface and Colloid Chemistry*, Wiley, New York

29. J. Alexander, *Colloid Chemistry*, Reinhold, New York

30. M. E. L. McBain and E. Hutchinson, *Solubilization and Related Phenomena*, Academic Press, New York

31. K. J. Mysels, *Introduction to Colloid Chemistry*, Wiley New York

32. P. Becher, *Emulsions, Theory, and Practice*, Reinhold, New York

33. T. Boublik and E. Hale, *Vapor Pressures of Pure Substances*, Elsevier, New York

34. J. Chu, *Vapor–Liquid Equilibrium Data*, Edwards, Ann Arbor, Mich.

35. R. R. Dreisbach, *Pressure–Volume–Temperature Relationships of Organic Compounds*, Handbook Pub., Sandusky, Ohio

36. L. H. Horsley, *Azeotropic Data*, American Chemical Society Advances no. 6, 35, and 116, American Chemical Society, Washington, DC

37. J. H. Hildebrand, *The Solubility of Nonelectrolytes*, Reinhold, New York

38. M. R. Rifi and F. H. Coritz, *Introduction to Organic Electrochemistry*, Dekker, New York

39. E. Yeager (ed.), *Techniques of Electrochemistry*, Wiley, New York

40. J. N. Pitts, Jr. (ed.), *Advances in Photochemistry*, Wiley, New York

41. A. Weissberger and B. W. Rossiter, *Physical Methods of Chemistry*, Wiley, New York

42. K. J. Klabunde, *Chemistry of Free Atoms and Particles*, Academic Press, New York

43. T. N. Rhodin and G. Ertl (eds.), *Nature of the Surface Chemical Bond*, North Holland Pub., Amsterdam

44. F. W. Sears and G. L. Salinger, *Thermodynamics, Kinetic Theory, and Statistical Thermodynamics*, Addison–Wesley, Cambridge, Mass.

45. F. J. Bockhoff, *Elements of Quantum Theory*, Addison–Wesley Cambridge, Mass.

46. A. Ben-Na'im, *Hydrophobic Interactions*, Plenum, New York

47. R. M. Pytkowicz (ed.), *Activity Coefficients in Electrolyte Solutions*, CRC Press, Boca Raton, Fla.

48. D. Bryce-Smith (ed.), *Photochemistry—A Review of the Literature*, Chemical Society, London

49. A. W. Adamson, *Textbook of Physical Chemistry*, Academic Press, New York

50. W. Gerrard, *Gas Solubilities*, Pergamon, New York

51. J. Gmehling, U. Onken, and W. Arlt, *Vapor Liquid Equilibrium Data Collection*, DECHMA, Frankfurt/Main.

52. G. Milazzo and V. K. Kharma, *Tables of Standard Electrode Potentials*, Wiley, New York

VII.   *Analytical chemistry*
  A.   General
1. C. N. Reilly, ed., *Advances in Analytical Chemistry and Instrumentation*, Wiley, New York
2. F. D. Snell and C. L. Hilton (eds.), *Encyclopedia of Industrial Chemical Analysis*, Wiley, New York
3. I. M. Kolthoff and P. J. Elving (eds.), *Treatise on Analytical Chemistry*, Wiley, New York
4. C. L. Wilson (ed.), *Comprehensive Analytical Chemistry*, Elsevier,New York
5. *Reagent Chemicals*, American Chemical Society
6. A. L. Beilby, *Modern Classics in Analytical Chemistry*, American Chemical Society
7. H. A. Laitinen and G. W. Ewing, *A History of Analytical Chemistry*, American Chemical Society, Washington, DC
8. H. Simmons and G. W. Ewing, *Progress in Analytical Chemistry*, Plenum, New York
9. J. Basset et al., *Vogel's Textbook of Quantitative Inorganic Analysis,* Longman, New York
10. B. S. Furniss et al. (eds.), *Vogel's Textbook of Practical Organic Chemistry*, Longman, New York
11. G. Svehla, *Vogel's Macro and Semimicro Qualitative Inorganic Analysis*, Longman, New York
12. F. Feigl and V. Anger, *Spot Tests in Inorganic Chemistry*, trans. by R. E. Oesper, Elsevier, New York
13. R. A. Day and A. L. Underwood, *Quantitative Analysis*, Prentice–Hall, New York
14. I. M. Kolthoff and E. B. Sandell, *Quantitative Chemical Analysis*, Macmillan, New York
15. J. Heyrovsky and J. Kuta, *Principles of Polarography*, Academic Press, New York
16. *State-of-the-Art of Thermal Analysis*, U.S. Government Printing Office, Washington, D.C.
17. T. S. Ma and R. C. Rittner, *Modern Organic Elemental Analysis*, Dekker, New York
18. J. S. Fritz and G. H. Schank, *Quantitative Analytical Chemistry*, Allyn & Bacon, Boston

19. *Annual Book of ASTM Standards*, American Society of Testing Materials, Philadelphia

20. R. Belcher and S. M. W. Anderson (eds.), *The Analysis of Organic Materials*, Academic Press, New York

B. Instrumentation

1. H. Bauer, G. D. Christian, and J. E. O'Reilly, *Instrumental Analysis*, Allyn & Bacon, Boston

2. A. J. Diefenderfer, *Basic Techniques in Electronic Instrumentation*, Saunders, Philadelphia

3. G. W. Ewing (ed.), *Topics in Chemical Instrumentation*, American Chemical Society, Washington, D.C.

4. C. K. Mann, T. J. Vickers, and W. M. Gulick, *Basic Concepts in Electronic Instrumentation*, Harper & Row, New York

5. C. K. Mann, T. J. Vickers, and W. M. Gulick, *Instrumental Analysis*, Harper & Row, New York

6. A. J. Senzel, *Instrumentation in Analytical Chemistry*, American Chemical Society, Washington, DC

7. H. A. Strobel, *Chemical Instrumentation: A Systematic Approach*, Addison–Wesley, Cambridge, Mass.

C. Chromatography

1. K. Blau and G. King, *Handbook of Derivatives for Chromatography*, Heyden, Philadelphia

2. E. J. Bonelli and H. McNair, *Basic Gas Chromatography*, Varian, Palo Alto, Cal.

3. R. L. Grob, *Modern Practice of Gas Chromatography*, Wiley, New York

4. E. L. Johnson, *Liquid Chromatography Bibliography*, Varian, Palo Alto, Cal.

5. E. L. Johnson and R. Stevenson, *Basic Liquid Chromatography*, Varian, Palo Alto, Cal.

6. J. G. Perry, R. Amos, and P. I. Brewer, *Practical Liquid Chromatography*, Plenum, New York

7. S. P. Cram, *High Resolution Gas Chromatography*, Academic Press, New York

8. G. Zweig and J. Sherma (eds.), *Handbook of Chromatography*, CRC Press, Boca Raton, Fla.

9. J. C. Giddings (ed.), *Advances in Chromatography*, Dekker, New York

10. T. R. Roberts, *Radiochromatography*, Elsevier, New York

11. C. Horvath (ed.), *High-Performance Liquid Chromotography*, Academic Press, New York

12. L. R. Snyder and J. J. Kirkland, *Introduction to Modern Liquid Chromatography*, Wiley, New York

13. T. Kremer and L. Boross, *Gel Chromatography: Theory, Methodology, Applications*, Wiley, New York

D. *Spectroscopy*

1. F. W. McLafferty, *Mass Spectral Correlations*, American Chemical Society, Washington, DC Advances 40, Washington, D.C.

2. J. L. Margrave (ed.), *Mass Spectrometry in Inorganic Chemistry*, American Chemical Society Advances 72, Washington, DC

3. A. Frigerio, *Recent Developments in Mass Spectrometry in Biochemistry and Medicine*, Plenum, New York

4. M. L. Gross, *High Performance Mass Spectrometry*, American Chemical Society, Washington, DC

5. R. J. Abraham and P. Lotus, *Proton and Carbon-13 NMR Spectroscopy, an Integrated Approach*, Heyden, Philadelphia

6. F. A. Bovey, *Nuclear Magnetic Resonance Spectroscopy: Principles and Applications in Organic Chemistry*, Academic Press, New York

7. W. Brügel, *Nuclear Magnetic Resonance Spectra and Chemical Structure*, Academic Press, New York

8. N. L. Alpert, W. F. Keiser, and A. H. Szymanski, *IR-Theory and Practice of Infrared Spectroscopy*, Plenum, New York

9. C. D. Craver (ed.), *The Coblentz Society Desk Book of Infrared Spectra*, The Coblentz Society, London

10. A. G. Brown, *X-Rays and Their Applications*, Plenum, New York

11. J. I. Steinfeld, *Laser Coherence and Spectroscopy*, Plenum, New York

12. *Analytical Methods for Flame Spectroscopy*, Varian, Palo Alto, Cal.

13. E. L. Wehry, *Modern Fluorescence Spectroscopy*, Plenum, New York

14. *Sadtler Standard and Commercial Spectra*, Sadtler Research Laboratories, Philadelphia

15. C. J. Pouchert, *The Aldrich Library of Infrared Spectra*, Aldrich Chemical, Milwaukee

16. J. G. Grasselli and W. M. Ritchey, *CRC Atlas of Spectral Data and Physical Constants for Organic Compounds*, CRC Press, Boca Raton, Fla.

17. E. Stenhagen, S. Abrahamson, and F. W. McLafferty (eds.), *Atlas of Mass Spectral Data*, Wiley, New York

18. N. S. Bhacca, L. F. Johnson, and J. N. Schoolery, *Varian NMR Spectra Catalog*, Varian, Palo Alto, Calif.

19. J. W. Robinson (ed.), *Handbook of Spectroscopy*, CRC Press, Boca Raton, Fla.

20. G. A. Webb (ed.), *Annual Reports on NMR Spectroscopy*, Academic Press, New York

21. M. M. Dorio and J. W. Freed, *Multiple Electron Resonance Spectroscopy*, Plenum, New York

22. H. W. Siesler and K. Holland-Moritz, *Infrared and Raman Spectroscopy of Polymers*, Dekker, New York

23. M. L. Martin and G. J. Martin, *Practical NMR Spectroscopy*, Heyden, Philadelphia

VIII. *Inorganic chemistry*

1. International Union of Pure and Applied Chemistry, *Nomenclature of Inorganic Chemistry*, Butterworth, London

2. M. E. Weeks, *Discovery of the Elements*, American Chemical Society, Washington, DC

3. A. J. Ihde, *The Development of Modern Chemistry*, Harper, New York

4. H. J. Emeleus and A. G. Sharpe (eds.), *Advances in Inorganic Chemistry and Radiochemistry*, Academic Press, New York

5. F. A. Cotton and G. Wilkinson, *Advanced Inorganic Chemistry. A Comprehensive Text*, Wiley, New York

6. H. J. Emeleus and A. G. Sharpe, *Modern Aspects of Inorganic Chemistry*, Wiley, New York

7. W. L. Jolly, *Principles of Inorganic Chemistry*, McGraw–Hill, New York

8. S. J. Lippard (ed.), *Progress in Inorganic Chemistry*, Wiley, New York

9. H. B. Jonassen and A. Weissberger, *Technique of Inorganic Chemistry*, Wiley, New York

10. F. A. Cotton and G. Wilkinson, *Basic Inorganic Chemistry*, Wiley, New York

11. J. C. Bailar, Jr., et al., *Comprehensive Inorganic Chemistry*, Pergamon, New York

12. M. J. Sienki and R. A. Plane, *Chemical Principles and Properties*, McGraw–Hill, New York

13. K. Niedenzu and H. Zimmer (eds.), *Annual Reports in Inorganic and General Synthesis*, Academic Press, New York

14. *Inorganic Syntheses*, Wiley, New York

15. A. F. Wells, *Structural Inorganic Chemistry*, Oxford, New York

16. R. J. Angelici, *Synthesis and Technique in Inorganic Chemistry*, Saunders, Philadelphia

17. E. I. Ochiai, *Bioinorganic Chemistry*, Allyn & Bacon, Boston

18. W. H. Lipscomb, *Boron Hydrides*, Benjamin, Menlo Park, Cal.

19. J. H. Simons (ed.), *Fluorine Chemistry*, Academic Press, New York

20. R. Stendel, F. C. Nachod, and J. J. Zuckerman, *Chemistry of the Non-Metals*, de Gruyter, Hawthorne, N.Y.

21. F. Basolo, J. F. Bunnett, and J. Halpern, *Transition Metal Chemistry*, American Chemical Society, Washington, DC

22. C. F. Bell, *Principles and Applications of Metal Chelation*, Oxford, London

23. E. Konig and S. Krener, *Ligand Field Energy Diagrams*, Plenum, New York

24. J. J. Zuckerman, *Organotin Compounds*, American Chemical Society, Washington, DC

25. W. Eitel, *Silicate Science*, Academic Press, New York
26. V. Gutmann, *Halogen Chemistry*, Academic Press, New York
27. A. G. Sharpe, *The Chemistry of Cyano Complexes of the Transition Metals*, Academic Press, New York
28. U. V. Rao (ed.), *Platinum Group Metals and Compounds*, American Chemical Society, Washington, DC
29. A. W. Langer (ed.), *Polyamine-Chelated Alkali Metal Compounds*, American Chemical Society, Washington, DC
30. R. B. King (ed.), *Inorganic Compounds with Unusual Properties*, American Chemical Society, Washington, DC

IX. *Organic chemistry*

A. *Nomenclature*

1. J. H. Fletcher, O. C. Dermer, and R. B. Fox, *Nomenclature of Organic Compounds: Principles and Practice*, American Chemical Society Advances in Chemistry 126, Washington, DC
2. R. S. Cahn and O. C. Dermer, *Introduction to Chemical Nomenclature*, Butterworth, London
3. A. M. Patterson, L. T. Capell, and D. F. Walker, *The Ring Index*, American Chemical Society, Washington, DC
4. International Union of Pure and Applied Chemistry, *Nomenclature of Organic Chemistry*, Butterworth, London
5. *Parent Compound Handbook*, Chemical Abstracts Service (See Chapter 7), Columbus, Ohio
6. J. E. Banks, *Naming Organic Compounds: A Programmed Introduction to Organic Chemistry*, Saunders, Phildelphia
7. International Union of Pure and Applied Chemistry, *Nomenclature of Organic Chemistry. Sections A through F*, Pergamon, New York

B. *General*

1. H. Kharasch (ed.), *Index to Reviews, Symposia Volumes and Monographs in Organic Chemistry*, Pergamon, New York

2. D. A. Lewis, *Index of Reviews in Organic Chemistry,* Chemical Society (London), London

3. J. B. Conant and A. H. Blatt, *The Chemistry of Organic Compounds,* Macmillan, New York

4. J. B. Hendrickson and G. S. Hammond, *Organic Chemistry,* McGraw–Hill, New York

5. P. Karrer *Organic Chemistry,* trans. by A. J. Mee, Elsevier, New York

6. R. T. Morrison and R. H. Boyd, *Organic Chemistry,* Allyn & Bacon, Boston

7. J. D. Roberts and M. C. Caserio, *Basic Principles of Organic Chemistry,* Benjamin, Menlo Park, Cal.

8. T. W. G. Solomons, *Organic Chemistry,* Wiley, New York

9. N. L. Allihger et al., *Organic Chemistry,* Worth, New York

10. J. M. and D. J. Cram, *The Essence of Organic Chemistry,* Addison–Wesley, Cambridge, Mass.

11. J. March, *Advanced Organic Chemistry,* McGraw–Hill, New York

12. A. Streitweiser, Jr., and C. Heathcock, *Introduction to Organic Chemistry,* Macmillan, New York

13. G. Gilman (ed.), *Organic Chemistry, An Advanced Treatise,* Wiley, New York

14. E. H. Rodd (ed.), *Chemistry of Carbon Compounds,* Elsevier, New York

15. S. H. Pine and J. B. Hendrickson, *Organic Chemistry,* McGraw–Hill, New York

16. F. A. Carey and R. J. Sundberg, *Advanced Organic Chemistry,* Plenum, New York

17. R. J. Fessenden, *Organic Chemistry,* Grant Press, Boston

C. *Physical organic*

1. V. Gold and D. Bethell, (eds.), *Advances in Physical Organic Chemistry,* Academic Press, New York

2. S. G. Cohen, A. Streitweiser, Jr., and R. W. Taft (eds.), *Progress in Physical Organic Chemistry,* Wiley, New York

3. M. J. S. Dewar and R. C. Dougherty, *PMO Theory of Organic Chemistry*, Plenum, New York

4. L. P. Hammett, *Physical Organic Chemistry: Reaction Rates, Equilibria, and Mechanisms*, McGraw–Hill, New York

5. J. Hine, *Structural Effects on Equilibria in Organic Chemistry*, Wiley, New York

6. E. S. Huyser, *Methods in Free Radical Chemistry*, Dekker, New York

7. H. E. Simmons and J. F. Bunnett, *Orbital Symmetry Papers*, American Chemical Society, Washington, DC

8. R. Zahradnik and P. Carsky, *Organic Quantum Chemistry Problems*, Plenum, New York

9. C. J. Ballhausen and H. B. Gray, *Molecular Electronic Structures: An Introduction*, Benjamin/Cummings, Menlo Park, Cal.

10. E. Buncel and T. Durst, *Comprehensive Carbanion Chemistry*, Elsevier, New York

11. W. F. Pryor, *Frontiers of Free Radical Chemistry*, Academic Press, New York

12. H. C. Brown, *The Nonclassical Ion Problem*, Plenum, New York

13. J. C. Stowell, *Carbanions in Organic Synthesis*, Wiley, New York

14. H. W. Wasserman and R. W. Murray, *Singlet Oxygen*, Academic Press, New York

15. G. A. Olah, *Carbocations and Electrophilic Reactions*, Wiley, New York

16. V. Gold and D. Bethell (eds.), *Advances in Physical Organic Chemistry*, Academic Press, New York

D. *Stereochemistry*

1. K. Mislow, *Introduction to Stereochemistry*, Academic Press, New York

2. H. B. Kagan (ed.), *Absolute Configurations of 6000 Selected Compounds with One Asymmetric Carbon Atom*, Academic Press, New York

3. H. B. Kagan (ed.), *Determinations of Configurations by Spectrometric Methods*, Academic Press, New York

4. W. Klyne and J. Buckingham, *Atlas of Stereochemistry, Absolute Configuration of Organic Molecules,* Oxford, London

5. B. Testa, *Principles of Organic Stereochemistry,* Dekker, New York

6. E. L. Eliel and N. L. Allinger, *Topics of Stereochemistry,* Wiley, New York

E. Organic functional chemistry

1. S. Patai (ed.), *The Chemistry of Functional Groups,* Wiley, New York

2. H. Bohme, *Iminium Salts in Organic Chemistry,* Wiley, New York

3. E. Kuhle, *The Chemistry of Sulfenic Acids,* Heyden, Philadelphia

4. S. Oae, *Organic Chemistry of Sulfur,* Plenum, New York

5. A. Senning, *Topics in Sulfur Chemistry,* Heyden, Phildelphia

6. E. E. Reid, *Organic Chemistry of Bivalent Sulfur,* Chemical Pub., New York

7. E. Block, *Reactions of Organosulfur Compounds,* Academic Press, Newe York

8. G. M. Kosolapoff and L. Maier (eds.), *Organic Phosphorus Compounds,* Wiley, New York

9. M. Grayson and C. J. Griffith (eds.), *Topics in Phosphorus Compounds,* Wiley, New York

10. J. R. Jones, *The Ionisation of Carbon Acids,* Academic Press, New York

11. A. A. Newman, *Chemistry and Biochemistry of Thiocyanic Acid and Its Derivatives,* Academic Press, New York

12. S. R. Sandler and W. Karo, *Organic Functional Group Preparations,* Academic Press, New York

13. I. Ugi (ed.), *Isonitrile Chemistry,* Academic Press, New York

F. Organometallics

1. P. M. Maitlis (ed.), *Organometallic Chemistry. A Series of Monographs,* Academic Press, New York

2. H. Alper, *Transition Metal Organometallics in Organic Synthesis*, Academic Press, New York

3. I. R. Compton, *Chemical Analysis of Organometallic Compounds*, Academic Press, New York

4. H. C. Brown, *Boranes in Organic Chemistry*, Cornell Univ. Press, Ithaca, NY

5. J. J. Zuckerman (ed.), *Organotin Compounds: New Chemistry and Applications*, American Chemical Society Advances in Chemistry 157, Washington, DC

6. K. J. Irgolic, *The Organic Chemistry of Tellurium*, Gordon & Breach, New York

7. E. J. Becker and M. Tsutsui (eds.), *Organometallic Reactions and Syntheses*, Plenum, New York

8. B. J. Wakefield, *Chemistry of Organolithium Compounds*, Pergamon, New York

9. R. B. King, *Organometallic Syntheses*, Academic Press, New York

10. J. P. Collman and L. S. Hegedus, *Principles and Applications of Organotransition Metal Chemistry*, University Science Books, Mill Valley, Cal.

11. F. G. A. Stone and R. West (eds.), *Advances in Organometallic Chemistry*, Academic Press, New York

12. E. Negishi, *Organometallics in Organic Synthesis*, Wiley, New York

13. G. Deganello, *Transition Metal Complexes of Cyclic Polyolefins*, Academic Press, New York

15. R. P. Houghton, *Metal Complexes in Organic Chemistry*, Cambridge Univ. Press, London

G. *Other topical areas*

1. L. F. and M. Fieser, *Reagents for Organic Synthesis*, Wiley, New York

2. R. Adams (ed.), *Organic Reactions*, Krieger Pub., Huntington, NY

3. C. A. Buehler, *Survey of Organic Synthesis*, Wiley, New York

4. W. G. Dauben, *Organic Reactions*, Wiley, New York

5. A. R. Katritzky (ed.), *Advances in Heterocyclic Chemistry*, Academic Press, New York

6. R. C. Elderfield (ed.), *Heterocyclic Compounds*, Wiley, New York

7. A. Weissberger (ed.), *Chemistry of Heterocyclic Compounds*, Wiley, New York

8. E. Guenther, *The Essential Oils*, Van Nostrand, New York

9. A. A. Newman (ed.), *Chemistry of Terpenes and Terpenoids*, Academic Press, New York

10. A. R. Pinder, *The Chemistry of the Terpenes*, Wiley, New York

11. J. L. Simonsen, *The Terpenes*, Cambridge Univ. Press, New York

12. R. S. Tipson and D. Horton (eds.), *Advances in Carbohydrate Chemistry*, Academic Press, New York

13. J. S. Glasky, *Encyclopedia of the Alkaloids*, Plenum, New York

14. T. K. Devon and A. I. Scott, *Handbook of Naturally Occurring Compounds*, Academic Press, New York

15. K. Nakanishi (ed.), *Natural Products Chemistry*, Academic Press, New York

16. P. Hodge and D. C. Sherrington, *Polymer-Supported Reactions in Organic Synthesis*, Wiley, New York

17. E. H. Pryde (ed.), *Fatty Acids*, American Oil Chemists' Society, Champaign, Ill.

X. Biochemistry

1. E. E. Snell et al. (eds.), *Annual Review of Biochemistry*, Stanford University Press, New York

2. S. Hwang and K. Kammermeyer, *Techniques of Chemistry*, Wiley, New York

3. A. Burger (ed.), *Medicinal Chemistry*, Wiley, New York

4. T. G. Cooper, *Tools of Biochemistry*, Wiley, New York

5. E. E. Conn and P. K. Stumpf, *Outlines of Biochemistry*, Wiley, New York

6. D. Glick, *Methods of Biochemical Analysis*, Wiley, New York

7. A. Kornberg (ed.), *Reflections in Biochemistry*, Pergamon, New York

8. R. W. McGilvery, *Biochemical Concepts*, Saunders, Philadelphia

9. L. J. Mullins, *Annual Review of Biophysics and Bioengineering*, Annual Reviews, Palo Alto, Cal.

10. D. Perlman (ed.), *Annual Reports on Fermentation Processes*, Academic Press, New York

11. G. E. Perlmann and L. Lorand (eds.), *Methods in Enzymology*, Academic Press, New York

12. H. Neurath and R. L. Hill (eds.), *Proteins*, Academic, Press, New York

13. E. Quagliariello, F. Palmieri, and T. P. Singer, *Horizons in Biochemistry and Biophysics*, Addison–Wesley, Cambrdige, Mass.

14. P. Ramwell, *The Prostaglandins*, Plenum, New York

15. R. Rivlin, *Riboflavin*, Plenum, New York

16. A. H. Rose, *Chemical Microbiology*, Plenum, New York

17. D. R. Sanadi (ed.), *Chemical Mechanisms in Bioenergenetics*, American Chemical Society, Washington, DC

18. F. F. Becker, *Cancer: A Comprehensive Treatise*, Plenum, New York

19. W. K. Stephenson, *Concepts in Biochemistry*, Wiley, New York

20. G. deStevens (ed.), *Medicinal Chemistry*, Academic Press, New York

21. L. B. Sandberg (ed.), *Advances in Experimental Medicine and Biology*, Plenum, New York

22. C. R. Cantor and P. R. Schimmel, *The Behavior of Biological Macromolecules*, Freeman, San Francisco

23. L. Stryer, *Biochemistry*, Freeman, San Francisco

24. M. J. Bull (ed.), *Progress in Industrial Microbiology*, Elsevier, New York

25. E. H. Lennette and A. Balows (eds.), *Manual of Clinical Microbiology*, American Society for Microbiology, Washington, D.C.

26. E.M. Walker, (ed.), *Structure and Biochemistry of Natrual Biological Systems*, Philip Morris, Richmond, Va

27. J. M. Clark, Jr., and R. L. Switzer, *Experimental Biochemistry*, Freeman, San Francisco

28. G. E. Schulz and R. H. Schirmer, *Principles of Protein Structure*, Springer–Verlag, Secaucus, N.J.

29. W. B. Pratt and R. W. Ruddon, *The Anticancer Drugs*, Oxford, New York

XI. *Polymer Chemistry*

A. *General*

1. H. F. Mark (ed.), *Encyclopedia of Polymer Science and Technology*, Wiley, New York

2. J. Brandrup and E. H. Immergut (eds.), *Polymer Handbook*, Wiley, New York

3. H. Mark et al. (eds.), *High Polymers*, Wiley, New York

4. A. Peterlin et al., (eds.), *Macromolecular Review*, Wiley, New York

5. A. D. Jenkins (ed.), *Progress in Polymer Science*, Pergamon, New York

6. Z. A. Rogovin (ed.), *Advances in Polymer Science*, Wiley, New York

7. H. J. Cantow et al. (eds.), *Advances in Polymer Science*, Springer–erlag, Secaucus, N.J.

8. W. Dawydoff, *Technical Dictionary of Higher Polymers*, Pergamon, New York

9. P. J. Flory, *Principles of Polymer Chemistry*, Cornell Univ. Press, Ithica, NY

10. F. W. Billmeyer, Jr., *Textbook of Polymer Science*, Wiley, New York

11. A. Ravve, *Organic Chemistry of Macromolecules*, Dekker, New York

12. M. L. Huggins, *Physical Chemistry of High Polymers*, Wiley, New York

13. H. I. Bolker, *Natural and Synthetic Polymers. An Introduction*, Dekker, New York

14. B. Vollmert, *Polymer Chemistry*, Springer–Verlag, Secaucus, N.J.

15. H. G. Elias, *Trends in Macromolecular Science*, Gordon & Breach, New York

16. E. Hans-George, *New Commercial Polymers*, Gordon and Breach, New York

17. H. S. Kaufman, *Introduction to Polymer Science and Technology. An SPE Handbook*, Wiley, New York

18. E. M. Pearce and J. R. Schaefgen, *Contemporary Topics in Polymer Science*, Plenum, New York

19. E. G. Richards, *An Introduction to the Physical Properties of Large Molecules in Solution*, Cambridge Univ. Press, England

20. H. R. Allcock and F. W. Lampe, *Contemporary Polymer Chemistry*, Prentice–Hall, New York

21. G. Scott (ed.), *Developments in Polymer Stabilisation*, Applied Science Pub., London

22. L. Lee (ed.), *Adhesion and Adsorption of Polymers*, Plenum, New York

23. J. F. Rabek, *Experimental Methods in Polymer Chemistry*, Wiley, New York

24. F. A. Bovey and F. H. Winslow (eds.), *Macromolecules: An Introduction to Polymer Science*, Academic Press, New York

25. D. C. Miles and J. H. Briston, *Polymer Technology*, Chemical Pub., New York

26. R. W. Whorlow, *Rheological Techniques*, Wiley, New York

27. J. F. McKellar and N. S. Allen, *Photochemistry of Man-Made Polymers*, Applied Science Pub., London

B. *Polymerization*

1. S. R. Sandler and W. Karo, *Polymer Synthesis*, Academic Press, New York

2. S. L. Aggarwal (ed.), *Block Polymers*, Plenum, New York

3. N. A. J. Platzer (ed.), *Polymerization and Polycondensation Processes*, American Chemical Society Advances in Chemistry 34 and 91, Washington, DC

4. D. Braun, *Techniques of Polymer Syntheses and Characterization*, Wiley, New York

5. E. M. Fettes (ed.), *Macromolecular Syntheses*, Wiley, New York

6. H. G. Elias, *Polymerization of Organized Systems*, Gordon & Breach, New York

7. I. Piirma and J. L. Gordon (eds.), *Emulsion Polymerization*, American Chemical Society Symposium 24, Washington, DC

8. T. Saegusa and E. Goethals (eds.), *Ring-Opening Polymerization*, American Chemical Society Symposium 59, Washington, DC

9. G. Odian, *Principles of Polymerization*, McGraw–Hill, New York

10. G. Natta and F. Danusso (eds.), *Stereoregular Polymers and Stereospecific Polymerizations*, Pergamon, New York

11. L. Reich and A. Schindler, *Polymerization by Organometallic Compounds*, Wiley, New York

12. J. Boor, Jr., *Ziegler–Natta Catalysts and Polymerizations*, Academic Press, New York

13. J. C. W. Chien (ed.), *Coordination Polymerization: A Memorial to Karl Ziegler*, Academic Press, New York

14. R. J. Cotter and M. Matzner, *Ring-Forming Polymerizations*, Academic Press, New York

15. S. R. Sandler and W. Karo, *Polymer Syntheses*, Academic Press, New York

16. D. C. Blackley, *Emulsion Polymerization. Theory and Practice*, Wiley, New York

17. R. J. Ceresa (ed.), *Block and Graft Polymerization*, Wiley, New York

18. A. Noshay and J. E. McGrath, *Block Copolymers. Overview and Critical Survey*, Academic Press, New York

19. J. Tsay, *Radiation-Induced Graft Polymerization of Styrene onto Cellulose Esters*, New York University Press, New York

20. *Advances in Emulsion Polymerization and Latex Technology*, (Lehigh University short course in two volumes) Bethlehem, Pa

21. R. N. Haward (ed.), *Developments in Polymerization*, Applied Science Pub., London

C. Specific polymers

1. H. D. Frank, *Polypropylene*, Gordon and Breach, New York

2. K. S. Kaufman, *The History of PVC*, Gordon and Breach, New York

3. M. Lewin, M. S. Atlas, and E. M. Pearce, *Flame Retardant Polymeric Materials*, Plenum, New York

4. J. G. Pritchard, *Poly(vinyl Alcohol). Basic Properties and Uses*, Gordon and Breach, New York

5. I. D. Rubin, *Poly(1-Butene): Its Preparation and Properties*, Gordon and Breach, New York

6. R. A. Wessling, *Polyvinylidene Chloride*, Gordon & Breach, New York

7. W. F. Christopher and D. W. Fox, *Polycarbonates*, Van Nostrand, New York

8. L. A. Wall, *Fluoropolymers*, Wiley, New York

9. F. E. Bailey and J. V. Koleske, *Poly(ethylene Oxide)*, Academic Press, New York

10. E. J. Vandenberg (ed.), *Polyethers*, American Chemical Society Symposium 6, Washington, DC

11. H. Lee (ed.), *Epoxy Resins*, American Chemical Society Advances in Chemistry 92, Washington, DC

12. E. Ott, H. M. Spurlin, and M. W. Grafflin (eds.), *Cellulose and Cellulose Derivatives*, Wiley, New York

13. N. M. Bikales and L. Segal, *Cellulose and Cellulose Derivatives*, Wiley, New York

14. W. M. Saltman (ed.), *Stereo Rubbers*, Wiley, New York

15. R. D. Deanin (ed.), *New Industrial Polymers*, American Chemical Society Symposium 4, Washington, DC

XII. *Industrial chemistry*

A. *General*

1. J. A. Kent (ed.), *Riegel's Handbook of Industrial Chemistry*, Van Nostrand, New York

2. F. A. Lowenheim and M. K. Moran, *Industrial Chemicals*, Wiley, New York

3. H. Bennett (ed.), *Chemical Formulary*, Chemical Pub., New York
4. *Preprints*, American Chemical Society Division of Organic Coatings and Plastics Chemistry, Washington, DC
5. *Annual Reviews of Industrial Chemistry*, American Chemical Society, Washington, DC
6. C. A. Price (ed.), *Reports on the Progress of Applied Chemistry*, Academic Press, New York
7. H. Bennett, *Chemical Specialties*, Chemical Pub., New York
8. C. A. Clausen and G. Mattson, *Principles of Industrial Chemistry*, Wiley, New York

B. *Adhesives*
1. I. Katz, *Adhesive Materials. Their Properties and Usage*, Foster, Long Beach, Cal.
2. E. P. McGuire, *Adhesive Raw Materials Handbook*, Podric, Mountainside, NJ
3. R. L. Patrick (ed.), *Treatise on Adhesion and Adhesives*, Dekker, New York
4. I. Skeist (ed.), *Handbook of Adhesives*, Van Nostrand, New York
5. J. Delmonte, *Technology of Adhesives*, Reinhold, New York
6. R. Houwink and G. Salomon (eds.), *Adhesion and Adhesives*, Elsevier, New York
7. R. S. R. Parker and P. Taylor, *Adhesion and Adhesives*, Pergamon, New York
8. D. L. Bateman, *Hot Melt Adhesives*, Noyes, Park Ridge, NJ
9. H. R. Dunning, *Pressure Sensitive Adhesives*, Noyes, Park Ridge, NJ
10. M. J. Satriana, *Adhesives Technology Annual*, Noyes, Park Ridge, NJ
11. *Adhesives for Industry*, El Segundo Technology Conference Papers, Society of Plastics Engineers, Calif.
12. Anon., *Adhesives Desk-Top Data Bank*, Cordura Pub., La Jolla, Cal.

13. K. W. Allen, *Adhesion*, Applied Science Pub., London

C. *Ceramics*

1. P. J. Adams, *Geology and Ceramics*, British Ceramic Society, London
2. C. F. Binns, *Lectures on Ceramics*, Alfred, Sherman Oaks, Cal.
3. P. P. Budnikov (ed.), *The Technology of Ceramics and Refractories*, Massachusetts Institute of Technology Press, Cambridge, Mass.
4. C. Z. Carroll-Porzynski, *Inorganic Fibers*, Academic, New York
5. J. E. Hove and W. C. Riley (eds.), *Ceramics for Advanced Technologies*, Wiley, New York
6. J. E. Hove and W. C. Riley (eds.), *Modern Ceramics; Some Principles and Concepts*, Wiley, New York
7. W. D. Kingery (ed.), *Introduction to Ceramics*, Wiley, New York

D. *Cosmetics*

1. M. S. Balsam and E. Sagarin (ed.), *Cosmetics: Science and Technology*, Wiley, New York
2. A. W. Middleton (ed.), *Cosmetic Science*, Butterworth, London
3. L. A. Greenberg and D. Lester, *Handbook of Cosmetic Materials*, Wiley, New York
4. R. G. Harry, *The Principle and Practice of Modern Cosmetics*, Chemical Pub., New York
5. A. W. Middleton (ed.), *Cosmetic Science*, Macmillan, New York

E. *Dyes and pigments*

1. *Colour Index*, Society of Dyers and Colorists, Bradford, England
2. *The Food and Color Additives Directory*, Hazleton Laboratories, Vienna, Va.
3. H. A. Lubs, *The Chemistry of Synthetic Dyes and Pigments*, Reinhold, New York
4. L. S. Pratt, *The Chemistry and Physics of Organic Pigments*, Wiley, New York

5.   K. Venkataraman, *The Chemistry of Synthetic Dyes*, Academic Press, New York

F.   *Explosives, propellants, space science*

1.   R. Assheton, *History of Explosives*, Institute of Makers of Explosives, New York

2.   F. P. Bowden and A. D. Yoffe, *Initiation and Growth of Explosives in Liquids and Solids*, Cambridge Univ. Press, Cambridge, Mass.

3.   M. A. Cook, *The Science of High Explosives*, Reinhold, New York

4.   W. S. Dutton, *One Thousand Years of Explosives, From Wildfire to the H-Bomb*, Holt, New York

5.   B. Kit and D. S. Evered, *Rocket Propellant Handbook*, Macmillan, New York

6.   J. R. Partington, *A History of Greek Fire and Gunpowder*, Barnes and Noble, New York

7.   R. Meyer, *Explosives*, Verlag-Chemie, Weinheim, West Germany

8.   T. L. Davis, *Chemistry of Powder and Explosives*, Wiley, New York

9.   R. T. Holzmann (ed.), *Advanced Propellant Chemistry*, American Chemical Society Advances in Chemistry 54, Washington, DC

10. C. Boyers and K. Klager (eds.), *Propellants Manufacture, Hazards, and Testing*, American Chemical Society Advances in Chemistry 88, Washington, DC

11. S. Glasstone, *Source Book of the Space Sciences*, Van Nostrand, New York

12. S. F. Sarner, *Propellant Chemistry*, Reinhold, New York

13. H. Burg and T. Almond, *Explosions: Cause, Prevention, Protection*, translated by W. Bartkhecht, Springer-Verlag, Secaucus, NJ

14. C. E. Gregory, *Explosives for North American Engineers*, Trans Tech, Rockport, Mass.

G.   *Fertilizers*

1.   R. A. Olson (ed.), *Fertilizer Technology and Use*, Soil Science Society of America, Madison, Wis.

2. S. L. Tisdale and W. L. Nelson, *Soil Fertility and Fertilizers*, Macmillan, New York

3. A. W. Flegmann, and R. A. T. George, *Soils and Other Growth Media*, Avi, Westport, Conn.

4. V. Sanchelli (ed.), *Chemistry and Technology of Fertilizers*, American Chemical Society, Washington, DC

5. F. R. Bear (ed.), *Chemistry of the Soil*, American Chemical Society, Washington, DC

6. V. Sanchilli (ed.), *Fertilizer Nitrogen*, American Chemical Society, Washington, DC

H. *Food science and technology*

1. E. O. Chichester (ed.), *Advances in Food Research*, Academic Press, New York

2. O. R. Fennema (ed.), *Principles of Food Science*, Dekker, New York

3. A. H. Johnson and M. S. Peterson (eds.), *Encyclopedia of Food Technology*, Avi, Westport, Conn.

4. J. B. Braverman, *Introduction to the Biochemistry of Foods*, Elsevier, New York

5. *Elements of Food Engineering*, Avi, Westport, Conn.

6. D. Pearson, *Chemical Analysis of Foods*, Chemical Pub., New York

7. A. W. and M. W. Blyth, *Foods: Their Composition and Analysis*, Van Nostrand, New York

8. *Recent Advances in Food Science*, Butterworth, London

10. R. J. Taylor, *Food Additives*, Wiley, New York

11. P. Koivistoien and L. Hyvönen (eds.), *Carbohydrate Sweeteners in Food and Nutrition*, Academic Press, New York

12. N. I. Mondy, *Experimental Food Chemistry*, Avi,

13. J. M. V. Blanshard and J. R. Mitchell, *Polysaccharides in Food*, Butterworth, London

14. P. Sherman (ed.), *Food Texture and Rheology*, Academic Press, New York

I. Paper

1. J. d'A. Clark, *Pulp Technology and Treatment for Paper*, Freeman, San Francisco

2. H. F. J. Wenzyl, *Chemical Technology of Wood*, Academic Press, New York
3. L. E. Wise, *Wood Chemistry*, Reinhold, New York
4. J. H. Ainsworth, *Paper, the Fifth Wonder*, Thomas, Kaukauna, Wis.
5. F. E. Brauns, *The Chemistry of Lignin*, Academic Press, New York
6. J. B. Calkin (ed.), *Modern Pulp and Papermaking*, Reinhold, New York
7. S. A. Rydkolm, *Pulping Processes*, Wiley, New York
8. J. P. Casey (ed.), *Pulp and Paper: Chemistry and Chemical Technology*, Wiley, New York
9. W. F. Reynolds (ed.), *Dry Strength Additives*, Technical Association of the Pulp and Paper Industry Press, Atlanta
10. H. F. Rance (ed.), *Handbook of Paper Science*, Elsevier, New York
11. J. Grant and J. H. Young (eds.), *Paper and Board Manufacture*, British Paper and Board Industry Federation, London

J. Petroleum

1. M. J. Astle, *The Chemistry of Petrochemicals*, Reinhold, New York
2. B. T. Brooks, *The Chemistry of Petroleum Hydrocarbons*, Reinhold, New York
3. B. T. Brooks and A. E. Dunstan, *The Science of Petroleum*, Oxford Univ. Press, New York
4. G. Egloff, *Physical Constants of Hydrocarbons*, Reinhold, New York
5. S. W. Ferris, *Handbook of Hydrocarbons*, Academic Press, New York
6. R. F. Goldstein and A. L. Waddams, *The Petroleum Chemicals Industry*, Spon, London
7. K. A. Kobe and J. J. McKetta, *Advances in Petroleum Chemistry and Refining*, Wiley, New York
8. G. A. Purdy, *Petroleum: Prehistoric to Petrochemicals*, McGraw–Hill, New York
9. J. G. Speight, *Chemistry and Technology of Petroleum*, Dekker, New York

10. P. B. Venuto and E. T. Habib, *Fluid Catalytic Cracking with Zeolite Catalysts*, Dekker, New York

11. A. Waddams, *Chemicals from Petroleum: An Introductory Survey*, Murray, London

K. *Pesticides*

1. S. C. Billings (ed.), *Pesticide Handbook*, Entomological Society, College Park, Md.

2. M. Sittig, *Pesticides Process Encyclopedia*, Noyes, Park Ridge, NJ

3. R. L. Metcalf and W. H. Luckmann, *Introduction to Insect Pest Management*, Wiley, New York

4. H. B. Scher, *Controlled Resease Pesticides*, American Chemical Society, Washington, DC

5. C. A. Stutte, *Plant Growth Regulators*, American Chemical Society, Washington, DC

6. J. R. Corbett, *Biochemical Mode of Action of Pesticides*, Academic, New York

7. F. Moriarty, *Organochlorine Insecticides: Persistent Organic Pollutants*, Academic, New York

8. L. J. Andus (ed.), *The Physiology and Biochemistry of Herbicides*, Academic Press, New York

9. D.E. H. Frear, *Chemistry of the Pesticides*, Van Nostrand, New York

10. D. E. H. Frear, *Pesticide Index*, College Science Pub., State College, Pa.

L. *Solvents and coatings*

1. A. K. Covington and T. Dickinson, *Physical Chemistry of Organic Solvent Systems*, Plenum, New York

2. I. Mellan, *Industrial Solvents Handbook*, Noyes, Park Ridge, NJ

3. *Raw Materials Index*, National Paint and Coatings Association, Washington, DC

4. R. R. Myers and J. S. Long, *Treatise on Coatings*, Dekker, New York

5. P. M. Fisk, *The Physical Chemistry of Paints*, Leonard Hill, London

6. Anon., *Paint Technology Manuals*, Reinhold, New York

7. D. H. Parker, *Principles of Surface Coating Technology,* Wiley, New York

8. H. F. Payne, *Organic Coating Technology,* Wiley, New York

9. M. Ash, *Formulary of Paints and Other Coatings,* Chemical Pub., New York

10. *Handbook of Organic Industrial Solvents,* Alliance of American Insurers, Chicago

11. M. T. Gillies (ed.), *Water-Based Industrial Finishes: Recent Developments,* Noyes Data Corp., Park Ridge, NJ

12. C. R. Martens, *Waterborne Coatings: Emulsion and Water-Soluble Paints,* Van Nostrand, New York

M. Surfactants

1. L. Chalmers and P. Bathe, *Household and Industrial Chemical Specialties,* Chemical Pub., New York

2. B. Levitt, *Oils, Detergents, Maintenance Specialties,* CRC, Boca Raton, Fla.

3. J. L. Moilliet, B. Collie, and W. Black, *Surface Activity,* Van Nostrand, New York

4. M. J. Schick, *Nonionic Surfactants,* Dekker, New York

5. K. Durham (ed.), *Surface Activity and Detergency,* Macmillan, New York

6. P. H. Elworthy (ed.), *Solubilization by Surface-Active Agents,* Barnes & Noble, New York

7. M. and I. Ash, *Encyclopedia of Surfactants,* Chem. Pub., New York

8. W. G. Cutler and R. C. Davis (eds.), *Detergency: Theory and Test Methods,* Dekker, New York

9. *McCutcheon's Detergents and Emulsifiers* (annual), MC Pub., Glen Rock, N.J.

10. K. L. Mittal (ed.), *Solution Chemistry of Surfactants,* Plenum, New York

N. Textiles

1. *Review of Textile Progress,* Society of Dyers & Colourists, London

2. *Encyclopedia of Textiles,* Prentice–Hall, New York

3. R. W. Moncrieff, *Man-Made Fibres,* Wiley, New York

4. J. W. Palmer, *Textile Processing and Finishing Aids—Recent Advances*, Noyes, Park Ridge, NJ

5. F. M. Buresh, *Nonwoven Fabrics*, Reinhold, New York

6. J. W. Hearle and R. H. Peters (eds.), *Fiber Structure*, Butterworth, London

7. K. P. Hess, *Textile Fibers and Their Uses*, Lippincott, Philadelphia

8. R. H. Peters, *Textile Chemistry*, Elsevier, New York

9. F. Happey, *Applied Fibre Science*, Academic Press, New York

10. I. Wingate (ed.), *Fairchild's Dictionary of Textiles*, Fairchild Pub., New York

2

ENCYCLOPEDIAS AND TREATISES

Although approaches to information are a matter of artistry to a large extent, there are a number of major reference works which every serious chemist should be aware of and should be able to use with skill and understanding. Among these major reference works are the following:

Gmelin's Handbuch der anorganischen Chemie
Beilstein's Handbuch der organischen Chemie
Houben-Weyl's Methoden der organischen Chemie
Comprehensive Organic Chemistry
Theilheimer's Synthetic Methods of Organic Chemistry
Kirk–Othmer Encyclopedia of Chemical Technology
Ullmann's Encycopädia der technischen Chemie
Encyclopedia of Polymer Science and Technology
The Merck Index
Unlisted Drugs Index-Guide
Chemical Economics Handbook

Gmelin's Handbuch der anorganischen Chemie

Leopold Gmelin (1788–1853), professor of chemistry at Heidelberg, published the first edition of his Handbuch der anorganischen Chemie over the period 1817–1819, and the third edition in 1830. In the first three editions, Gmelin reviewed all of chemistry, organic as well as inorganic. The fourth edition, which appeared between 1843 and 1866, covered only inorganic chemistry and was translated into English by the Cavendish Society. Through the sixth edition, which first appeared in 1872, the Handbuch was assembled by only a few collaborators on a part-time basis. The seventh edition was begun in 1905. The task of compiling the *Handbuch* became so large that in 1922 the German Chemical Society set up a full-time staff to work on the eighth edition. In 1946, the Gmelin Institute in Frankfurt/Main was placed under the Max Planck Society for the Advancement of Science in conjunction with the German Chemical Society for the preparation and publication of the eighth edition.

Gmelin's Handbuch covers the entire literature of inorganic chemistry, and strives for completeness. All data are critically evaluated. Information, arranged by each chemical element and then by its compounds, follows this order: analytical chemistry, atomic physics, ore preparation, chemical technology, electrochemistry, geochemistry, history, colloidal chemistry, coordination chemistry, corrosion and passivity, crystallography, economic deposits, metallurgy, mineralogy, physical properties, alloys, toxicity and hazards, and production statistics.

To assure that a given compound always will be located and indexed in the same place, the *Handbuch* uses the Gmelin "principle of last position," in which the elements are assigned serial numbers so that those which form anions have lower numbers than those which form cations. Thus, each compound is described in terms of the serial or system numbers of the element present. Within each serial or system number, information follows the sequence: history, occurrence, technology and preparation, physical properties, electrochemical behavior, chemical reactions, detection, and determination.

Examples of system numbers are as follows:

System Number	Element
1	Nobel Gases
2	H
3	O
4	N
5	F
6	Cl
7	Br
8	I
9	S
↓	↓
13	B
14	C
15	Si
16	P
↓	↓

32	Zn
33	Cd
↓	↓
41	Ti
↓	↓
46	Sn
↓	↓
52	Cr

In this serial arrangement, HCl is given the system number 6; $ZnCl_2$, 32; $CrCl_2$, 52; and $ZnCrO_4$, 52. Thus, the system number 32 represents zinc and all zinc compounds with elements numbered from 1 through 31.

The first volume of the eighth edition describes the element zinc and its compounds with elements numbered 1–31 in Gmelin. This volume, covering the total literature from the eighteenth century to the end of 1923, contains 329 pages. The supplement volume on zinc, which covers the literature from 1924 through 1949, contains 1025 pages, three times that of the eighth edition volume.

The enormous growth of the literature prompted the Gmelin Institute to decide against beginning the ninth edition and to invest its efforts instead in publishing supplements to the eighth edition. The first volume in the New Supplement series, *Inert Gas Compounds*, appeared in 1970, and did not follow the Gmelin classification. The second volume of the New Supplement series covers organochromium and organovanadium compounds. It is anticipated that organoiron compounds will require 20 volumes, of which eight will be for ferrocenes alone.

Although the volumes of the eighth edition were shelved by the Gmelin system numbers, they and the two supplemental series should be shelved together alphabetically by the chemical symbol of the element covered by each volume, so that volumes of the main, the supplement, and the new supplement on the same element and its compounds will be found together. A *Formula Index* was introduced in 1975, entirely in English, arranged alphabetically by the symbols of the elements; so far, 10 volumes of this index have been issued.

Beilstein's Handbuch der organischen Chemie

Friedrich Konrad Beilstein (1838–1906) is an outstanding example of the international nature of science in the nineteenth century. He was born in St. Petersburg to German parents, studied under Bunsen in Heidelberg, under Liebig in Munich, under Wöhler in Göttingen, and under Wurtz in Paris. Beilstein obtained his doctorate in 1858. In 1859 he was appointed as Löwig's assistant in Breslau, in 1860, as Wöhler's assistant in Göttingen, where he became an assistant professor in 1865; and in 1866, as professor at the Technological Institute of St. Petersburg. The last few years of his life he lived in Switzerland.

While at Göttingen, Beilstein began to accumulate notes on the literature of organic chemistry for his own use. After a 20-year accumulation of these notes, Beilstein published them in two volumes (divided into five sections) over the period 1881–1883. The second edition was published over the period 1886–1890, and the third over 1892–1899. The third edition, the last one published by Beilstein, consisted of four volumes, four supplements, and an index. The supplements were prepared by Paul Jacobson under the auspices of the Deutsche Chemische Gesellschaft, which assumed responsibility for *Beilstein's Handbuch* in 1896. The *Hauptwerk* (basic series) of the fourth edition, under the editorship of F. Richter, was issued by the Deutsche Chemische Gesellschaft. Succeeding supplements were issued by the Beilstein Institut, Frankfurt/Main.

The fourth edition of *Beilstein's Handbuch* differs considerably from the earlier three additions in size, scope, and system of arranging or classfying organic chemicals. The literature through 1909 was surveyed completely and every organic compound synthesized, analyzed, and characterized was included, as was any natural product which was investigated. The *Hauptwerk*, which covered some 200,000 organic chemicals and their derivatives in 27 volumes (plus two index volumes), was issued over the period 1919–1938. The first supplement (*I. Ergänzungswerk*), covering the literature from 1910 through 1919, began to appear in 1928, consists of 15 volumes (the last volume was issued in 1938), with contents matching those of the *Hauptwerk*. The second supplement (*II. Ergänzungswerk*), covering the literature from 1920 through 1929, consists of 27 volumes (the first was issued in 1941 and the last in 1955). The third supplement will cover the literature from 1930 through 1949 (Volume 1 appeared in 1958, Volume 6 in 1965), and the fourth, from 1950 through 1959. The third and fourth supplements are being issued currently, with Volumes XVII–XXVII, covering heterocyclic compounds combined for both

Each entry in Beilstein is described by the following features:

Constitution and configuration
Natural occurrence and isolation

Preparation and purification
Structure and physical properties
Chemical properties
Analysis
Salts and addition compounds

The Beilstein classification, as devised by Jacobson, Prager, Schmidt, and Stern, assigns to each chemical a definite place within a sequence of classes and subclasses labeled by system numbers and categorized under the following four divisions:

Acyclic

Alicyclic

Heterocyclic

Natural products not assigned in the above three divisions

Volumes I–IV (system numbers 1–449) cover the acyclics; Volumes V–XVI (system numbers 450–2358) the alicyclics; Volumes XVII–XXVII (system numbers 2359–4720) the heterocyclics; and Volumes XXX and above, natural products. Table 1 shows the distribution of system numbers in the various volumes of the *Hauptwerk*.

To use Beilstein expertly, which every chemist should be able to do, a complete understanding of the system plus searching experience is required. In addition to the first 47 pages of Volume I of the *Hauptwerk*, which, of course, is in German (in fine print), the following can be consulted for the use of *Beilstein's Handbuch*:

1. Deutschen Chemische Gesellschaft, *System der Organischen Verbindungen: Ein Leitfaden für die Benutzung von Beilstein's Handbuch der Organischen Chemie*, J. Springer, Berlin, 1929
2. E. H. Huntress, *J. Chem. Ed.* 15, 303–309 (1938).
3. E. H. Huntress, *A Brief Introduction to the Use of Beilstein's Handbuch der Organischen Chemie*, Wiley, New York 1938.
4. F. Richter, *J. Chem. Ed.* 15, 310–316 (1938).
5. O. Runquist, *A Programmed Guide to Beilstein's Handbuch*, Burgess Minneapolis, 1966.
6. J. E. H. Hancock, *J. Chem. Ed.* 45, 336–338 (1968).
7. O. Weissbach, *The Beilstein Guide*, Springer–Verlag, Berlin, 1976.

Until experience is gained, the user should be aware that the table of

TABLE 1. Distribution of the Contents of Beilstein's <u>Handbuch</u>

System Number	Volume Number	Stem Nuclei (functional groups)[a]
Acyclics		
1–151	I	Hydrocarbons −OH hydroxy compounds =O ketones, aldehydes =O + −OH hydroxy ketones and aldehydes
152–194	II	Carboxylic acids
195–322	III	Substituted, e.g., −OH carboxylic acids
323–449	IV	S, Se, and Te analogs of carboxylic acids −NH₂, −NHOH, −NHNH₂, and −N=NH −PH₂, −SiH₃, −HgOH, etc.
Alicyclics		
450–498	V	Hydrocarbons
499–608	VI	−OH hydroxy compounds, phenols
609–736	VII	=O ketones, aldehydes
737–890	VIII	=O + −OH hydroxy ketones and aldehydes
891–1050	IX	Carboxylic acids
1051–1504	X	Substituted, e.g., −OH carboxylic acids
1505–1591	XI	S, Se, Te analogs of carboxylic acids
1592–1739	XII	−NH₂
1740–1871	XIII	(−NH₂)ₓ di-, tri-, etc., amines
1872–1928	XIV	substituted amines, e.g., amino acids
1929–2084	XV	−NHOH, −NHNH₂
2085–2358	XVI	−N=NH, −PH₂, −SiH₃, etc.
Heterocyclics		
2359–2503	XVII	1 cyclic chalcogen (S, Se, Te) and −OH and =O derivatives
2504–2665	XVIII	1 cyclic chalcogen and other derivatives
2666–3031	XIX	2 or more chalcogens and derivatives[b]
3032–3102	XX	1 cyclic N
3103–3241	XXI	1 cyclic N, −OH and =O derivatives

TABLE 1. *(Continued)*

System Number	Volume Number	Stem Nuclei (functional groups)[a]
3242–3457	XXII	1 cyclic N, other derivatives
3458–3554	XXIII	2 cyclic N's[b] and −OH derivatives
3555–3633	XXIV	2 cyclic N's[b] and =O derivatives
3634–3793	XXV	2 cyclic N's[b] and other derivatives
3794–4187	XXVI	3 and 3+ cyclic N's[b] and derivatives
4188–4720	XXVII	Other heterocyclics and derivatives

[a]Other groups, such as halogens and nitro, are considered nonfunctional and thus will be placed at the parent compound. For example, p-nitrobenzaldehyde,

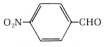

will be found as a derivative of benzaldehyde in Volume VII of the *Hauptwerk*.

[b]The heteroatoms may be in one or more rings of the molecule, e.g., each of the following is considered to have two cyclic N's and thus would be found in Volume XXIII.

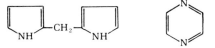

contents of each volume lists the classes of compounds it includes. The range of system numbers is shown on the spine of each volume. Each volume includes a name index (*Sachregister*) and, beginning with the third supplement, a formula index (*Formelregister*). The collective name and formula indexes, which appear in Volumes 28 (two parts) and 29 (three parts), issued in 1955 and 1957, are particularly helpful, since they combine the indexes of all volumes of the *Hauptwerk* and of the first and second supplements. Because of the multiplicity of names for many organic compounds, it is probably more efficient to use the formula index first. The name index gives preference to the Geneva nomenclature used in the *Hauptwerk*, except that prefixes are arranged in the order of increasing complexity rather than alphabetical. The alphabetical order for prefixed and IUPAC (International Union of Pure and Applied Chemistry) nomenclature will be used in the third and fourth supplements.

Houben–Weyl's Methoden der organischen Chemie

Now in the fourth edition, *Methoden der organischen Chemie* was initiated by Th. Weyl in 1909 and later taken over by J. Houben. From the very beginning, this treatise discussed experimental methods fully and critically with relevant examples. The fourth edition, begun in

1952, consists of 16 volumes in 35 parts plus subparts. Volumes of the fourth edition so far published are the following:

> Volume 1, Parts 1 and 2—General Laboratory Practice (1958 and 1959)
> Volume 2, Part 1—Analytical Methods (1953)
> Volume 3, Parts 1 and 2—Physical Methods (1955)
> Volume 4, Part 2—General Chemical Methods (1955)
>   Part 3—Three-Member Carbocyclics (1971)
>   Part 4—Four-Member Isocyclics (1971)
> Volume 5, Part 1a—Alkanes, Cycloalkanes (1970)
>   Part 1b—Alkenes, Cycloalkenes, Arylalkenes (1972)
>   Part 1c—Hydrocarbons (1970)
>   Part 1d—Polymers, Including Cyclics (1972)
>   Parts 3 and 4—Halogen Compounds (1962 and 1960)
> Volume 6, Part 2—Oxygen Compounds I (1963)
> Volume 7, Part 1—Oxygen Compounds II (1954)
>   Part 2a—Ketones (1973)
>   Part 4—Oxygen Compounds II (1968)
> Volume 8, Part 1—Oxygen Compounds III (1952)
> Volume 9, Part 1—Sulfur, Selenium, and Tellurium Compounds (1955)
> Volume 10, Part 1—Nitrogen Compounds I (1971)
>   Part 3—Nitrogen Compounds (1965)
> Volume 11, Part 1—Nitrogen Compounds II (1957)
>   Part 2—Nitrogen Compounds (1958)
> Volume 12, Parts 1 and 2—Phosphorous Compounds (1963 and 1964)
> Volume 13, Parts 1, 2a, 2b, 4—Organometallic Compounds (1964, 1970, 1973, 1974)
> Volume 14, Parts 1 and 2—Macromolecular Compounds (1961, 1963)
> Volume 15—Carbohydrates, Proteins, and Peptides
> Volume 16—Symbols, Nomenclature, Literature and Indexes

Comprehensive Organic Chemistry

The newest treatise of consequence to organic chemists is *Comprehensive Organic Chemistry. The Synthesis and Reactions of Organic Compounds,* edited by Sir Derek Barton and W. David Ollis and published in 1979 by Pergamon Press. This six-volume treatise was conceived by Sir Robert Robinson and developed by an editorial board of about 100 international organic chemists. The contents of the first five volumes reflect the current rapid development of modern organic chemistry and its relationship or interaction with biochemistry, inorganic chemistry, and other subject areas. Items for inclusion were based on what the editorial board considered to be important facets of modern organic chemistry and are presented with mechanistic treatments. The contents are as follows:

Volume 1, Part 1—Nomenclature and Stereochemistry

Part 2—Hydrocarbons

Part 3—Halo Compounds

Part 4—Alcohols, Phenols, Ethers, and Related Compounds

Part 5—Aldehydes and Ketones

Volume 2, Part 6—Amines and Related Compounds

Part 7—Nitro and Nitroso Compounds

Part 8—Imines, Nitrones, Nitriles, and Isocyanides

Part 9—Carboxylic Acids and Related Compounds

Part 10—Phosphorus Compounds

Volume 3, Part 11—Organic Sulfur Compounds

Part 12—Organic Selenium and Tellurium Compounds

Part 13—Organic Silicon Compounds

Part 14—Organic Boron Compounds

Part 15—Organometallic Compounds

Volume 4, Part 16—Azines

Part 17—Azoles and Other Nitrogen Systems

Part 18—Oxygen Systems

Part 19—Sulfur and Other Heteroatoms

Part 20—Mixed Heteroatoms

Volume 5, Part 21—Biological Chemistry

Part 22—Nucleic Acids

Part 23—Proteins: Amino Acids and Peptides

Part 24—Proteins: Enzyme Catalysis and Functional Proteins

Part 25—Lipid Chemistry

Part 26—Carbohydrate Chemistry

Part 27—Organic Macromolecules

Part 28—Bio-Organic Chemistry

Part 29—Biosynthetic Pathways from Acetate

Part 30—Biosynthesis

Volume 6—Formula, Subject, Author, Reaction, and Reagent Indexes

The formula index, which uses the Hill system, consists of about 20,000 molecular formulas (only carbon-containing compounds are indexed). The subject index uses IUPAC nomenclature, based on *IUPAC Nomenclature of Organic Chemistry*, sections H, Pergamon Press, (1979). The author index, which cites over 25,000 names from over 20,000 references, covers the literature up to mid-1978. The reagent index lists over 2500 organic and inorganic compounds, including those used as catalysts. At a price of $1250 plus mailing costs, *Comprehensive Organic Chemistry* is obviously for libraries. The write-ups are oriented to directing the reader to the recent literature, especially to reviews, but lacks historical and intellectual background.

Theilheimer's Synthetic Methods of Organic Chemistry

This treatise by W. Theilheimer first appeared in 1946. The first two volumes, written in German, were translated into English, and Volumes 3 and 4, also in German, were issued with English indexes. Subsequent volumes, issued annually, have been written in English. Each volume describes new and improved methods reported in the literature for the synthesis of organic compounds. The synthetic methods are arranged in a reaction classification order with reaction symbols noted on the top of each page to guide the searcher: the first part of the symbols denotes the chemical bonds formed during the reaction; the next symbol denotes the method, such as ring closure, ring contraction, rearrangement, addition, or elimination; the third symbol denotes the bonds changed or eliminated. An annual volume averages about 900 methods, and generally it is necessary to consult the original reference. Thus, the treatise is basically an annual index to synthetic methods. If one is mystified by the symbols, recourse is had to the annual and five-year cumulative indexes by subject (names of methods, chemical name, and reagents) and by formula.

Kirk–Othmer Encyclopedia of Chemical Technology

Since it was first issued between 1947 and 1956 in 15 volumes by Interscience–Wiley under the editorship of Raymond E. Kirk and Donald F. Othmer, this encyclopedia has gained a well deserved reputation as an outstanding source for background information. The second edition was issued over the period 1962–1972. The first volume of the third edition was issued in 1977, with subsequent volumes to be issued four per year until the 25 volumes planned are complete. The third edition has been completely revised and updated, with many new subjects added in the fields of energy, health, safety, toxicology, solid state chemistry, and composite materials. Chemicals will be identified with CAS registry numbers, and interim indexes will be issued until the index volume completes the set. For most Americans this encyclopedia has replaced *Ullmann's Encyclopädie der technischen Chemie* (third edition, 1951–1967).

Ullman's Encyclopädia der technischen Chemie

The first edition of F. Ullmann's encyclopedia appeared over the period 1914–1923. The second edition, in ten volumes which appeared from 1928 to 1932, was essentially a reprint of the first with the addition of an index volume. The third edition was issued between 1951 and 1967, and the fourth edition began to issue in 1972 with two volumes per year planned until Volume 25, the index volume, appears. Until the appearance of *Kirk–Othmer's Encyclopedia*, Ullmann's was the bible of chemical technology, and it still remains the work of choice for European and especially German chemical technology. The first six volumes of the current edition are relegated to general principles and methodology (thermodynamics, process engineering, physical and chemical analytical methods, pollution control, and safety) highly relevant to the interests and information needs of chemical engineers and plant chemists. The remaining volumes will consist of the alphabetic arrangement of subjects traditional to encyclopedias.

Encyclopedia of Polymer Science and Technology

This fairly comprehensive encyclopedia of 16 volumes plus supplements was first introduced in 1964, with Volume 1 using the style and format of the *Kirk–Othmer Encyclopedia*. The approximately 500 entries cover one or more of five aspects of polymer science and technology:

Chemical substances. Properties and preparation of monomers, polymerization methods, and characterization of polymers are covered. Natural polymers are discussed from the viewpoint of occurrence, isolation, reactions, and uses.

Polymer properties. Major ones, such as electrical and solution properties, are discussed separately from a theoretical viewpoint.

Methods and Processes. Entries are discussed on the basis of fundamentals and mechanisms.

Uses.   Broad use areas, such as aerospace, drilling-fluid additives, and laminates, are given full treatment.

General background.   Examples are classification of polymerization reactions, literature, and nomenclature.

Since the index volume, Volume 16, was issued in 1972, two supplements have appeared in 1976 and 1977.

The Merck Index

The Merck Index, an encyclopedia of chemicals, drugs, and biologicals, has been published by Merck and Co. since 1889. Originally, it was a 170-page alphabetical list of Merck products. It is now an internationally known, authoritative, 2000-page reference source containing capsule descriptions of about 10,000 chemicals, drugs, pesticides, and biologically active compounds, together with about 8000 chemical structures and a cross index of about 50,000 synonyms. The latest edition had a circulation of about 150,000 copies.

Unlisted Drugs Index–Guide

The *Unlisted Drugs Index–Guide,* published by Unlisted Drugs, Chatham, New Jersey, is a worldwide pharmaceutical reference directory and thesaurus containing some 130,000 drug entries with over 17,000 investigational drug codes (IDN). Trade names for the drugs, official and nonproprietary names, and acronyms are listed and related by synonym, product, and ingredients. Also included are a manufacturers' address directory (over 7000 entries) and short reviews of several hundred recent books on drugs.

Chemical Economics Handbook

The *Chemical Economics Handbook,* first published by the Stanford Research Institute in 1950, and supported by most chemical companies through subscription, consists of loose-leaf volumes of data sheets and reports with detailed coverage of the economic aspects of chemicals or groups of chemicals. Sections include information on status, outlook, manufacturing processes, producing companies, grades, statistics, consumption, price, etc. A *Chemical Economics Newsletter,* issued bimonthly, is part of the subscription.

3

NUMERICAL DATA COMPILATIONS

Numerical data on properties of chemicals occur in many articles in thousands of journals being published today. Even in the nineteenth century, when the number of journals was in the low hundreds and were thin in comparison with those of today, tables were compiled to secure or package the data in a conveniently accessible form, such as the *Landolt-Börnstein Tables*.

In 1965, the Office of Standard Reference Data polled the American Chemical Society (ACS) membership on needs for compilations of critically evaluated data. From the 100,000 members, 16,000 returns were received. About 300 data compilation activities were disclosed, and about 1600 chemical properties, for which the respondents often sought data in the literature, were identified. Some of the properties considered most essential were the following:

Boiling Point
Melting Point
Solubilities
Infrared Spectra
Thermodynamic Properties
Ultraviolet Spectra
Nuclear Magnetic Resonance Spectra
Specific Gravity and Density
Mechanical Properties
Free Energies
Equilibrium Constants
Viscosity
Heat Capacities
Refractive Index

The more important sources of data compilations on properties of chemicals, which are described in the following pages, are the following:

Landolt–Börnstein's Tables
International Critical Tables
National Standard Reference Data
API Research Project 44 and TRC Data
Center for Information and Numerical Data Analysis and Synthesis (CINDAS)
ASTM Data Banks
Cambridge Crystallographic Data Centre
Spectroscopic Data Banks
Single-Volume Handbooks

Landolt–Börnstein's Tables

The first edition of Landolt–Börnstein's Zahlenwerte und Funktionen aus Physik, Chemie, Astronomie, Geophysik und Technik appeared in 1883 with 281 pages in one volume. The second, third, and fourth editions, also in one volume, came out in 1894, 1905, and 1912, with 575, 875, and 1330 pages, respectively. The fifth edition, in eight volumes with 7457 pages, was issued over the period 1923–1936. The sixth edition, in 11 volumes with 8492 pages, was issued over the period 1950–1959. Thereafter only separate volumes covering specialized topics have been issued by Springer, Berlin. The contents of the four basic volumes and those in the New series are the following:

Volume 1—Atomic and Molecular Physics
    Part 1—Atoms and Ions
    Part 2—Molecular Structure
    Part 3—External Electron Ring
    Part 4—Crystals
    Part 5—Atomic Nucleus and Elementary Particles
Volume 2—Properties of Matter in Various States of Aggregation
    Part 1—Thermal Mechanical State
    Part 2—Equilibria (other than melting point)
    Part 2a—Vapor–Liquid Equilibria and Osmotic Pressure
    Parts 2b and 2c—Solution Equilibria

Part 3—Melting Point Equilibria and Interfacial Phenomena

Part 4—Calorimetry

Part 5a—Physical and Chemical Kinetics

Part 5b—Transport Phenomena, Kinetics, Homogeneous Gas Equilibria

Parts 6 and 7—Electrical Characteristics, Conductivity of Electron Systems

Part 8—Optical Constants

Parts 9 and 10—Magnetic Characteristics

Volume 3—*Astronomy and Geophysics*

Volume 4—*Basic Techniques*

Part 1—Mechanical Properties of Natural Materials

Part 2—Mechanical Properties of Metallic Materials: (a) Ferrous; (b) Heavy Metals; and (c) Light Metals

Part 3—Electrical, Optical, and X-Ray Techniques

Part 4a—Thermodynamic Properties of Gases, Liquids, and Solids

Part 4b—Thermodynamic Properties of Mixtures

New Series (tables of contents and introductions are in both German and English):

Group I—Nuclear Physics and Technology

Group II—Atomic and Molecular Physics

Group III—Crystal Structure and Solid State Physics

Group IV—Macroscopic Properties

Group V—Geophysics and Space Science

Group VI—Astronomy and Astrophysics

International Critical Tables

International Critical Tables, edited by E. W. Washburn, was published by McGraw–Hill over the period 1926–1933 in seven volumes plus an index. It covers the literature up to 1924 on physical constants and properties of importance in chemistry, physics, and engineering for which the data were examined and evaluated critically by many experts. The data are approached most easily through the excellent index.

The basis for the *International Critical Tables* was *Tables annuelles de constantes et données numerique de chemie, de physique, de biologie et de technologie*. *Tables annuelles*, initiated in 1910, was published by the International Union of Pure and Applied Chemistry (IUPAC), not as a critical compilation but as a collection of published numerical data, and up to 1936 the collection was quite comprehensive. Since 1936, IUPAC has published numerous volumes under the name *Physico-Chemical Selected Constants*. Each volume of this new series has been in a specific area and contains critically selected data.

National Standard Reference Data

The National Standard Reference Data System (NSRDS) of the National Bureau of Standards (NBS) was established in 1963 to make available critically evaluated data in the physical sciences. Towards this objective, NSRDS has generated close to 100 reference data compilations and an equal number of bibliographies and other publications, most of which have been printed by the U.S. Government Printing Office (GPO). The primary areas in which data on chemical properties are compiled are the following:

Atomic and Molecular
Thermodynamic and Transport
Solid State
Chemical Kinetics
Colloid and Surface
Nuclear
Mechanical

API Research Project 44 and TRC Data

The American Petroleum Institute (API) Project 44 was authorized in 1941 and began operations at the National Bureau of Standards to compile data on the physical, thermodynamic, and spectral properties of hydrocarbons and related compounds. During the 1950s, the project was housed at the Carnegie Institute of Technology, and through support of the Manufacturing Chemists Association, expanded to cover properties of all types of chemicals. Since 1966, the project has been associated with Texas A&M University under the name Thermodynamics Research Center (TRC). While still at the National Bureau of Standards, members of the project participated in the publication of NBS Circular 500, *Selected Values of Chemical Thermodynamic Properties*, a basic reference work. About ten years ago, TRC initiated the *International Data Series (IDS), Selected Data on Mixtures*. Each item in this publication presents the values of a specific property of a mixture as a function of composition and temperature, and each item is a one- or two-page article. New tables are issued at a rate of about 200 per year. Selected values of properties of chemical compounds are published in a continuing series that is a primary source of thermodynamics data.

The Central Abstracting and Indexing Service (CAIS) of the API produces three data bases which are online through the Systems Development Corporation's Orbit system: literature (APILIT), patents (APIPAT), and business data (P/E News) for the petroleum and petrochemical industries. APILIT is updated monthly with about 1500 items; APIPAT with about 700. Both have been available since 1964 for batch searching, and since 1974 for online searching for the 14 years of data input.

Center for Information and Numerical Data Analysis and Synthesis (CINDAS)

CINDAS at Purdue University is a specialized national center for the identification, compilation, critical evaluation, analysis and synthesis of numerical data on the physical properties of materials. It covers 14 thermophysical properties and 22 electronic, electrical, magnetic, and optical properties. Over the past 23 years, CINDAS has compiled well over 100,000 sets of experimental data from the literature and has evaluated these data in the generation of recommended reference data. These data have been assembled in an 80 volume "CINDAS Handbook Series on Material Properties". CINDAS has also published a 13 volume series called TPRC Data series, which has a total of 16,613 pages on 7414 materials covering 12,258 references. TPRC stands for Thermophysical Properties Research Center, a unit within CINDAS.

ASTM Data Banks

The American Society for Testing and Materials (ASTM) maintains four large data bases that supplement its standardization responsibilities: infrared spectroscopy, gas chromatography, mass spectrometry, and x-ray emission spectrography. The largest is the Infrared Spectral Index, an index of the significant absorption bands of well over 100,000 compounds. Every major collection in the world is included: Infrared Data Committee of Japan, Sadtler Catalog, Coblenz Society, API Research Project 44, etc., and abstracts from related literature. Infrared Spectral Index is available on magnetic tape and in book form, as are the other data bases.

Since 1925, ASTM has had a cooperative arrangement with the

American Society of Mechanical Engineers (ASME) for the collection of data on the properties of metals. A large number of data reports have been published on the properties of metals, from cryogenic to very high temperatures. A majority of these data tables are published in the American Society for Metals (ASM) *Metals Handbook.*

ASTM publishes extensive data tables on volume and weight corrections for a large number of commercial chemicals transported in containers and shipping vessels. Over many years ASTM has collected and published data on corrosion properties of metals and alloys.

Cambridge Crystallographic Data Centre

With financial support from the British Office for Scientific and Technical Information (OSTI), the data center was established in 1965 and staffed with laboratory scientists. The center is concerned with crystal and molecular structures obtained by x-ray and neutron diffraction for organic and organometallic compounds. The data are maintained as a computer-based file of bibliographic and numeric data for publication of the reference book series *Molecular Structures and Dimensions* and for various computer-based services. The first two bibliographic volumes in the *Molecular Structures and Dimensions* series covers the literature from 1935 to 1969; following volumes cover the literature on an annual basis. The bibliographic file is described by O. Kennard, D. G. Watson, and W. G. Town, in *Cambridge Crystallographic Data Centre. I. Bibliographic File, J. Chem. Doc.* 12, 14–19, 1972.

Spectroscopic Data Banks

Documentation of Molecular Spectroscopy, cosponsored by British and German organizations and published jointly by Butterworth and Verlag Chemie, consists of spectra on double edge punch cards (organic compounds on red cards, inorganic compounds on blue, and theory on yellow) giving up to ten strong bands. About 2000 cards are issued annually. Another set of cards is issued on NMR spectra. In addition, since 1966, *UV Atlas of Organic Compounds* has been published in a loose-leaf binder.

Among the large collections of spectral data are those issued by the Sadtler Research Laboratories in Philadelphia. These are on loose-leaf sheets for assembling in binders for infrared spectra—one for prism and another for grating, ultraviolet spectra, and NMR spectra. Included are indexes to the data published by the Coblenz Society, Varian NMR, and

JEOL (Japan Electronic Optics Laboratory) NMR, but the spectra from these three sources are not included.

The Coblenz Society Spectra (after W. W. Coblenz, who made many contributions in infrared spectroscopy in the early part of the twentieth century) has over 10,000 infrared spectra in its cumulative collection, to which it adds about 1000 high quality spectra annually. About 700 academic and industrial spectroscopists contribute to and monitor the collection.

As pointed out in the discussion on ASTM data banks, ASTM indexed infrared spectra in every major collection. The index covers well over 100,000 organic and inorganic compounds and is available on magnetic tape. The ASTM mass spectra file on over 8000 chemicals is available in printed and punched card form and is the basis for the Wiley *Atlas of Mass Spectral Data*.

Varian Associates' two-volume NMR Spectra Catalog lists spectra for over 700 chemicals with name, functional group, and chemical shift indexes. Japan Electron Optics Laboratory publishes its collection of NMR spectra under the title *High Resolution NMR Spectra*.

The Chemical Rubber Company (CRC) *Atlas of Spectral Data and Physical Constants for Organic Compounds* lists over 8000 compounds with their physical properties, up to four kinds of spectra, CAS registry numbers, and bibliographic information. The infrared, ultraviolet, NMR, and mass spectral data are given in tabular form.

The Aldrich Library of Infrared Spectra (by C. J. Pouchert, published by Aldrich Chemical Company, Milwaukee) lists some 10,000 spectra of the approximately 100,000 compounds in the Aldrich files. The spectra are arranged to illustrate the effect of functional groups, such as halogens and alcohols, on aliphatic and aromatic hydrocarbons. The formula index includes the chemical name, the Aldrich catalog number, and location of the spectrum for each compound.

Single-Volume Handbooks

The best known single volume handbooks are the following:

CRC Handbook of Chemistry and Physics
Perry's Chemical Engineering Handbook
Lange's Handbook of Chemistry

Each of these has undergone many editions, thus enabling the editors to reach a relatively high degree of accuracy and relevency.

The *CRC Handbook of Chemistry and Physics*, now reaching its 60th edition (1979) with 2500 pages of tabular data, has an interesting history. It was started by Arthur Friedman, who, as a student at Case School of Applied Science in Cleveland, made and sold rubber-coated aprons to students in various schools. To encourage the purchase of the aprons, he assembled a booklet of formulas, logarithms, and the periodic table to give away free with the aprons. As demand for the booklet increased, he kept expanding its contents until by 1914 he began to sell the *Handbook of Chemistry and Physics* as a book and the aprons without the bonus. Friedman's enterprise was named the Chemical Rubber Company and later changed to CRC Press (the last apron was produced in 1943).

COMPUTER-SEARCHABLE CHEMICAL DATA SYSTEMS

Although not as advanced or as readily available as bibliographic data bases, online computer-searchable chemical data bases have been assuming an increasingly important role in the storage and retrieval of numerical data and of the relationships between the structure and properties of chemicals. The most extensive computer-searchable collection of chemical data is the Chemical Information System (CIS).[1,2] The major components of the CIS online system are the following:

Mass Spectral Search System, with over 32,000 mass spectra

Carbon-13 Nuclear Magnetic Resonance, with about 8000 CNMR spectra

X-Ray Crystallographic Search System, with some 15,000 compounds from the Cambridge Crystal File and 24,000 from the NBS collection

X-Ray Powder Diffraction, with some 27,000 powder diffraction patterns

NIOSH RTECS Search System, a database created by the U.S. National Institute for Occupational Safety and Health (NIOSH) on the toxic effects of chemicals, published and updated in the NIOSH Registry of Toxic Effects of Chemical Substances (RTECS)

Structure and Nomenclature Search System (SANSS), based on the CAS Registry System

NMR Graphical Interactive Spectrum Analysis

Mathematical Modeling Systems

Conformational Analysis of Molecules in Solution

Merck Index, containing about 9000 chemicals

The development and organization of CIS has been under the direction of the National Institutes of Health and the Environmental Protection Agency. The system has about 300 subscribers, who access the data base through the communications network operated by Science Corporation, Washington, D.C.

Other online systems in the United States are the Sadtler system (described earlier in this chapter); PBM/STIRS[3], which contains over 41,000 spectra; and the MansLabs system, which contains thermochemical data on some 1800 inorganic compounds.[4]

A survey of 23 data banks was made by L.M. Rose[5] for the European Federation of Chemical Engineers.

REFERENCES

1. Heller, S. R. and G. W. A. Milne, *The NIH/EPA Chemical Information System,* Chapter 10 in the ACS Symposium series no. 84, 1978, ACS, Washington, D.C.

2. Milne, G. W. A., et al., *The NIH/EPA Structure and Nomenclature Search System, J. Chem. Inf. Comput. Sci.* 18, 181–186 (1978).

3. Stenhagen, E., S. Abrahamsson, and F. W. McLafferty (eds.), *Registry of Mass Spectral Data,* Wiley, New York, 1974.

4. Hawkins, D. T., "The MansLabs–NPL Materials Data Bank," *Online* 3 (2) 40–52 (1979).

5. Rose, L. M., "A Survey of Available Physical Property Data Banks," *ACHEMA,* Jahrb. I, 32 (1977/79).

PATENTS

HISTORICAL BACKGROUND

Patents as a literary form have no definite beginning. The term "patent" was derived from the Latin *litterae patentes*, meaning open letters, and the concept originated in the system whereby a sovereign or a governing body granted a privilege to a person or a group of persons to perform a service free of competition. Semantically, a patent today means essentially the same as it did in Florence in 1421, when the earliest record of an invention was granted a three-year monopoly for a hoisting gear fitted on a barge to load and unload marble being transported to building construction sites. The first law within the present patent concept was enacted in Venice in 1474, and over 100 patents were granted in Venice by 1550. From Florence and Venice, the patent concept was spread over Europe, initially by emigrating glass artisans from Venice who demanded patent protection—actually, monopoly—for introducing their skills and products, and then by governments seeking to encourage the introduction and growth of new industries. The first German patent was granted in 1484. France granted its first patent in 1543; in 1699, the French Royal Academy of Sciences was given the responsibility of examining patents when necessary for resolving disputed claims.

In 1315, England introduced monopoly rights, by which merchants and artisans were granted exclusive rights to regulate trade. The first industrial patent was granted in England in 1449; between 1561 and 1590, more than 50 patents were granted to encourage English industry. It was not until 1852, however, that a single Patent Office was given the responsibility for the granting of patents and that patents were required to be printed and published. It was not until 1872 that the British Patent Office employed scientifically trained examiners to process and examine patent applications; examination for novelty was initiated in 1905.

The first patent in colonial America was granted in 1641 by the Massachusetts General Court to Samuel Winslow for a method of making salt. The United States Constitution of 1789 empowered Congress "to promote the progress of science and useful arts by securing for limited times to authors and inventors the exclusive right to their respective writings and discoveries." In 1790, when Congress established the first U.S. Patent Act, which granted patents for 14 years, the administration was placed in the State Department, and the first board of examiners consisted of Thomas Jefferson, Secretary of State; Henry Knox, Secretary of War; and Edmund Randolph, Attorney General. The first United States patent was granted to Samuel Hopkins on July 31, 1790, for "a method of making potash and pearl ash." Fifty-seven patents were issued up to 1793, when a new act eliminated the examination and left questions of novelty, utility, and scope to the courts. The patents were available only in manuscript form in the State Department, which maintained a patent file arranged chronologically. The Patent Act of 1836 restored the requirement for examination and established a Patent Office.

In 1829, a subject list of U.S. patents was issued in which patents were segregated into 14 groups. The list was expanded to 16 groups in 1831 and to 22 in 1839. None of these had a logical relationship among the groups or classes, but within each group the patents were arranged chronologically and also alphabetically by the key words in the title. Up to 1836, a total of 10,000 patents had been granted; the number reached 80,000 by 1868.

French patents, which were printed beginning in 1811, and British patents, which were issued as printed patents in 1852, were available for searching in the Patent Office. French patents were listed alphabetically by key words in the title, as were the U.S. patents. British patents, however, were indexed chronologically and alphabetically by subject, as well as classified.

In 1868, the U.S. Patent Office published the booklet *Classification of Subjects of Inventions*, which described its 26 classes and their subdivisions. In 1872, the U.S. Patent Office expanded the number of classes to 145. The first 145 classes of today are the same as those used in 1872, and since then subsequent changes have been interclass changes, additions of new classes, or deletions of classes. By 1897, there were 215 classes, and some classes had as many as 200 alphabetically arranged subdivisions. The U.S. Patent Law of 1870 extended the life of patents to 17 years from the date of grant. In 1898, Congress directed the U.S. Patent Office to revise and perfect the patent classification system in accordance with written guidelines and detailed class and subclass titles and definitions.

The U.S. Patent Law now in effect was enacted July 19, 1952, and became effective January 1, 1953. A revision is now under consideration in Congress.

According to the U.S. Patent Law, patents may be granted for "any new and useful process, machine, manufacture, or composition of matter, or . . . improvements thereof." Chemical compositions, including mixtures, as well as new compounds, generally are the subject matter of "composition of matter" patents.

Because the American courts have defined a patent as "a creature of statute," the statute has been interpreted by the courts to exclude an abstract principle or idea, a method of doing business, a scientific theory, a function of machines, a law of nature, or a product of nature. Thus, patents are not a literature source for basic science. On the other hand, patents constitute a fertile literature source for new and useful chemicals and chemical compositions, processes for the production of chemicals, and apparatus and equipment for the manufacture of chemicals.

SOME PATENT-ISSUING COUNTRIES

Australia. Patents are announced in the *Australia Official Journal* approximately 18–24 months after filing of the complete specification. Following examination for novelty, an accepted application is assigned a six-digit number. Patents run for 17 years from date of grant.

Belgium. Belgian patents are laid open to public inspection three months after grant, which occurs 28 days after filing. The *Library Register*, a handwritten listing of all applications, is available 1–2 months after filing. Patents are classified alphabetically under the first letter of the applicant's name, and included in the listing is the International Patent Classification (IPC). The *Revue Gevers*, a monthly publication, lists all applications (about five months after filing) in IPC order with an alphabetical list of applicants. The average patent is about 20 pages. The majority of patents are in French; some are in Flemish, and a few in German. The *Recueil des Brevets*, issued monthly, contains abstracts in IPC order of patents about three to four years after the filing date. Patents run for 20 years from date of filing. A major advantage of Belgian patents is that those processed under a convention date become known earlier than those filed in other fast-publishing countries.

Canada. The *Patent Office Record*, issued weekly, lists all granted patents (usually several years from filing date) in patent number order with title and filing information (no abstract, summary, or claim). Patents run for 17 years from date of grant.

France. Patents generally are granted within eight to nine months from date of filing by non-French inventors. To enable French inventors to file in other countries, the period is advanced to one year. The *Bulletin Officel Lists*, issued weekly, gives filing details and classification of each application some 21 months after the first priority date. The *Bulletin Officel Gazette*, issued weekly, contains summaries of the patents arranged by IPC with filing details, usually about five weeks after the listing in the *Bulletin Officel Lists*. Because lack of novelty is not a reason for rejection, a relatively large number of French patents are without counterparts. Since 1960, however, pharmaceutical patents have been subjected to novelty examination, and these have been published in a separate weekly bulletin. Patents run for 20 years from date of application.

East Germany. Applications generally are published about one year after filing and are listed in the *Gazette*, which issues semimonthly, in patent number order, with titles and filing details. Patents run for 18 years from filing date.

West Germany. Patent applications, on acceptance, are published on a weekly schedule as *Offenlegungsschrifts* (usually 18 months from first priority date). Examined applications are published as *Auslegeschrifts*. Patents are announced in the weekly *Patentblatt* with filing details and IPC's, as well as with the German classification. Patents generally are limited to processes or new fields of application and run for 18 years from date of application.

Italy. Patents usully are granted within several months after filing, without examination for novelty. Photocopies are not available, however, for at least six months, and then with some difficulty and at a high cost. Printed specifications are available considerably later; they are not published in numerical or date order. Patents run for 15 years from date of application.

India. Patents filed out of convention in India issue early and are published in the weekly *Gazette of India*. Printed specifications are available several years after granting. Patents are not granted, however, in numerical order—the filing number becomes the final number. An average of about 100 patents per week appear in the gazette.

Israel. The *Israel Patents and Design Journal*, a monthly publication, lists applications with title, filing details, IPC's, and abstracts in application number order. Patents run for 20 years from date of filing.

Japan. An average of about 600 patents per week are issued, of which about one-third are related to chemistry (about one-sixth are granted to American inventors). Japanese patents have only one claim, although a subordinate claim is sometimes allowed. Applications are numbered serially as filed, with a new series beginning each year. On being granted, the patent is assigned a new six-digit number. Unexamined specifications are available in a bound gazette containing 100 patents arranged in open for public inspection (OPI) number order, each patent having filing details, Japanese classification, and IPC. The Japanese Patent Office issues a monthly bulletin listing the patents in OPI number order with titles, filing details, Japanese classification, and IPC, and a monthly *Patent Catalog* giving the final patent number of patents granted that month. Most references to Japanese patents are by the six-digit application number. Patents run for 15 years from the publication date.

Netherlands. Patents filed under "Convention" are open to inspection in Holland 18 months from the application or priority date. The application is assigned a seven-digit number and printed promptly. Novelty examination is made only by request of the applicant. A chemical is not patentable, only the process by which it is made, and thus the claims are process oriented. The *Netherlands Official Journal*, published each month in two parts, lists the patents some four to six weeks after applications are made public. The patents are arranged in IPC order with filing details; an index of IPC versus application number is provided. Patents run for 20 years from the date of application.

Soviet Union. Most Russian inventions are assigned to the state as author certificates. A small percentage of inventors, usually non-Russian, are granted patents. A granted application is assigned a six-digit number, and the claims (usually very narrow) are published in the weekly *Official Bulletin* in patent number order with filing details and claims; an index of IPC versus patent number and an index of application number versus patent number are provided. An average of about 150 patents are granted per week. Of these, the majority are mechanical, electrical, or electronics. Patents run for 15 years from date of application.

Switzerland. About 150 patents, issued weekly, are announced in German or French and occasionally in Italian in the semimonthly

Patentblatt, which lists the patents in IPC order with titles and filing details. Patents are published about six weeks after they are announced in the *Patentblatt,* and run for 18 years from filing date.

United Kingdom.   Patent specifications, very much like those in the United States, are detailed and informative. It normally takes more than two years for a specification to be accepted from the date the application is filed. The weekly *Official Journal* lists the new applications filed and the specifications accepted in serial number order with summaries or abridgments. Patents run for 16 years from date of filing.

United States.   About 1500 patents are granted weekly, of which about one-fifth are classified as chemical. These are announced in the weekly *Official Gazette of the United States Patent and Trademark Office,* in which the patents are in patent number order with titles, filing details, U.S. patent class, and IPC, with a relatively detailed abstract. Patents are granted within one to four years after filing and run for 17 years from date of granting. The *Official Gazette* includes indexes of applicants and assignees, classification of patent applications, and patentees. Table 2 lists patent office publications of various nations.

CONTENTS OF A PATENT

Although patents are written in a style pejoratively called "patentese," and in a manner that communicates the least amount of information possible, there is a uniformity required by the U.S. Patent Office that makes patents relatively easy to read and understand, especially by one "skilled in the art."

A patent is written to consist of the following parts:

1. Title. The title is generally short, but sufficiently long to spell out the invention's primary area, such as process, article, composition, or apparatus, and objective, for example, "Process for the Preparation of S-Triazolo [3,4-b]-Benzothiazoles" (U.S. Patent 3,937,713 issued February 10, 1976).
2. Introduction
    a.   Background information. Difficulties and problems in current practice are pointed out, such as those relating to efficiency, economics, complexity, hazards, and the like, which motivated the inventor to achieve the invention.

TABLE 2. Patent Office Publications of Various Nations

Nation	Publication
Australia	Australian Official Journal of Patents, Trademarks and Designs
Austria	Oesterreichisches Patentblatt
Belgium	Recueil des brevets d'invention
Canada	Canadian Patent Office Record and Register of Copyrights and Trademarks
Denmark	Dansk Patenttidende
Finland	Patenttilehti-Patenttidning
France	Bulletin Official de la propriete industrille et commerciale
Germany (West)	Patentblatt
	Aüszüge aus den Patentschriften
Great Britain	Abridgements of Specifications
	Official Journal (Patents)
Israel	Israel State Records—Patents and Design Journal
Italy	Bolletino dei brevetti per invenzoine, modelli e marchi
	Il Monitore industrial
Japan	Tokkyo Koho
Japan (unexamined patents)	Kokai Tokyuo Koho
Netherlands	Octrooiraad Nederland
	Bijblad bij industrieele eigendom
Norway	Norsk Tidende for det Industrielle Rettsvern
Soviet Union	Byulleten Byuro Ekspertizy i Registratsii Izobretenii Gosplana SSSR
Sweden	Svensk Patenttidning
Switzerland	Patentliste
United States	Official Gazette of the United States Patent Office

   b. Objects of the invention. This part, a continuation of the background information, discusses how the invention overcomes the disadvantages of the current practice, what problem the invention solves, and to what uses the invention will be applicable.

3. Detailed descriptions of the invention. This section begins with a generic statement of the invention in broad, general terms that include everything the patent embodies. A detailed description follows with as many sentences as there are steps, such as conditions of temperature, pressure, and time; catalysts; and proportions of reactants and catalysts. This detailed description generally is done first generically and then specifically.

4. Examples. These constitute illustrative and preferred embodiments of the invention in such a manner that one skilled in the art can obtain the same result. The examples usually proceed from very general to relatively specific directions, such as a generic range of ingredients and their proportions and the range of conditions, for example, temperature and pressure, to a specific ingredient and its amount and a specific temperature and pressure.

5. Claims. Whereas everything that precedes the claims in the specification should describe, explain, and disclose the invention, the claims define the invention's scope. Thus the claims, again proceeding from generic to specific, consider and include only operative elements that define the novelty, utility, and inventiveness of the patent. A claim using the term "comprising" is the most generic. Specific claims use the term "consisting of." Claims using the term "substantially, " such as for the amount or proportion of an ingredient, are broader than those not using the term.

Dates are important in the life of a patent, and in using the patent literature or in citing references, the following dates are significant:

Filing or Application Date.   This is the date that the specification is first submitted to a patent office.

Accepted or Allowed Date.   This is the date that the filed patent meets the statutory requirements of the patent office.

Laid Open to the Public.   This is the date that the application in text form or (in very few countries) printed document is made available to the public, and begins the period (usually two to four months) for others to oppose the granting of the patent, if they wish.

Priority Date or Convention Date.   In any of the seventy odd member nations of the International Convention for the Protection of Industrial Property, this is the earliest filing date of a given patent. A patent application filed in any convention nation within one year of the date of the earliest filing in another convention nation has the legal benefits of the earliest date with respect to priority.

Open to Public Inspection (OPI).   In many nations, and particularly in the United States, the OPI and the published date are identical. In the case of U.S. patents, this date is the same as the issue date of the Official Gazette of the United States Patent and Trademark Office, in which the granting of the patent is announced with filing information and an abstract.

Patent offices assign an application, file, or serial number to applications as received. The application number or a new number is assigned to specifications laid open to the public for possible opposition, and in some nations this number becomes the patent number. In other nations, such as the United States, a new number is assigned to the granted patent.

Applications for the same patent may be filed in many countries, often ten or more, and thus as many patents may be published on the same basic specification as filed. These corresponding patents are published, however, over a relatively long period, ranging from about six months from date of filing in Belgium to several years in the United Kingdom or the United States. It is advantageous to know how to find and obtain corresponding or equivalent patents, particularly when one is aware of a patent in a foreign language. Services such as Chemical Abstracts Service and Derwent have publications in which corresponding patents are listed.

Uniformity in the writing style and contents of patents is required by the Patent Office:

> The specification must include a written description of the invention or discovery and of the manner and process of making and using the same, and is required to be in such full, clear, concise, and exact terms as to enable any person skilled in the art or science to which the invention or discovery appertains, or with which it is most nearly connected, to make and use the same.
>
> The specification shall conclude with one or more claims particularly pointing out and distinctly claiming the subject matter which the applicant regards as his invention.
>
> The specification must set forth the precise invention for which a patent is solicited, in such a manner as to distinguish it from other inventions and from what is old. It must describe completely a specific embodiment of the process, machine, manufacture, composition of matter, or improvement invented, and must explain the mode of operation or principle whenever applicable. The best mode contemplated by the inventor of carrying out his invention must be set forth (Patent Act of 1952).

Although a patent is primarily a legal document, it is also an important and useful source of chemical technology. Over the years, patentese or patent language, especially for chemical patents, has evolved into a marriage of legal and technical phraseology. Initiation into an understanding and appreciation of patentese wording and linguistic structure takes time, and consequently the patent literature has not been consulted and utilized to its fullest potential. Awkward phrases, such as "characterized by (or in)," which had its origin in the translation of the German phrase *gekennzeichnet durch*, the repetition of information from part to part of each patent, and the consistently poor selection of titles are serious hurdles to those who are reading patents for the first time. However, because the language has a high degree of uniformity and the content of specifications is largely compartmentalized, patents can be read quickly with comprehension once one becomes accustomed to the style and form. A particularly good example of a highly stylized expression is the Markush claim, such as "a member selected from the group consisting of . . . " Sometimes a letter, such as R, X, Y, or Z, is used and defined as "a member of the group consisting of . . . " For example, R can stand for any alkyl group, X for a halogen, Y for an aromatic group, and Z for an olefin. Markush language is used generally to claim a class as a whole.

A basic legal document, the patent is an agreement between the inventor and a nation by which the inventor may practice and utilize his or her invention as a monopoly for a set number of years in return for disclosing the information that makes the invention possible and useful. Despite this agreement, however, inventors, in writing their specifications, disclose only the minimum amount of information necessary to obtain the patent, and patent office examiners try to elicit the maximum amount of information, especially in those nations that examine patents for novelty and utility.

Theoretically, a patent application is submitted only after sufficient work has been done to prove the utility and novelty of the invention as described fully and accurately in the specification. Unfortunately, reality does not always match theory, and a good number of patents are processed without an experimental basis. These "paper patents," when granted, have the same validity as any other patent until contested in a court of law.

Once a patent is granted, the invention may be used only by the inventor or assignees or by those with whom the inventor or assignees have entered into a license agreement. This monopoly does not exclude an experimentor from repeating the work or from using the information in the specification for purposes of research, so long as the results of the work do not involve the sale of a product.

SEARCHING PATENTS IN THE PATENT OFFICE

A thorough patent search to find out whether an invention is patentable, to determine whether a patent is an infringement, or to establish the validity of an existing patent is best done at the patent office of any country of interest. The unique feature of national patent offices is their classified files. In addition to copies of all U.S. patents, the Patent Office Search Center at Crystal Plaza, 2021 Jefferson Davis Highway, Arlington, Virginia, has available for public use over 120,000 volumes of scientific and technical books, over 90,000 bound volumes of scientific and technical journals, the official publications of foreign patent offices, and over 9.5 million foreign patents in bound volumes (currently, some 300,000 new foreign patents are added each year). Patents of some foreign countries are arranged both in numerical order and by the foreign country's patent classification system.

United States patents granted since 1836 may be searched by the public in the Search Room. The patents are arranged in one of thousands of classified shoes (compartments said to have been named from the original use of shoe boxes as containers). The U.S. Patent Office classification system consists of some 350 major classes (first line classes) and some 100,000 subclasses (main or first line subclasses, second line subclasses, and coordinate subclasses). The public may inspect the records and files of issued patents and other open records in the Record Room, which contains a set of U.S. patents arranged in numerical order. The Patent Office is open from 8 A.M. to 8 P.M., Monday through Friday.

In addition to the U.S. Patent Office, printed copies of U.S. patents, generally arranged numerically, are available in many libraries, such as the following:

Albany, N.Y.—State University of New York
Atlanta, Ga.—Georgia Institute of Technology
Boston, Mass.—Public Library
Buffalo, N.Y.—Public Library
Chicago, Ill.—Public Library
Cincinnati, Ohio—Public Library
Cleveland, Ohio—Public Library
Columbus, Ohio—Ohio State University
Detroit, Mich.—Public Library

Kansas City, Mo.—Linda Hall Library
Los Angeles, Calif.—Public Library
Madison, Wis.—State Historical Society of Wisconsin
Milwaukee, Wis.—Public Library
Newark, N.J.—Public Library
New York City, N.Y.—Public Library
Philadelphia, Pa.—Franklin Institute
Pittsburgh, Pa.—Carnegie Library
Providence, R.I.—Public Library
St. Louis, Mo.—Public Library
Stillwater, Okla.—Oklahoma Agricultural and Mechanical College
Sunnyvale, Calif.—Public Library
Toledo, Ohio—Public Library

The second most complete collection of foreign patents is in the New York City Public Library. The U.S. Patent Office also has on microfilm lists of the numbers of patents issued in each of its subclasses. These also have been made available to libraries. Searches of U.S. patents by the classification system is not something that can be done without considerable study and experience, which takes some time and effort. Because patents are arranged in the Patent Office Search Room in groups according to the class and subclass titles of the *Manual of Classification*, a searcher is able to find all patents in any field directly or consecutively in the order of historical development—but the searcher must know the *Manual of Classification*.

CLASSIFICATION SYSTEMS FOR PATENTS

The U.S. Patent Classification System was designed primarily to enable patent examiners to search for patentability. When Congress established the patent system, no provision was made, nor were methods available, for determining novelty and utility. In 1830, Congress authorized publication of a subject categorization of patents. This resulted in the listing of 16 groups of patents. These 16 groups were without an order, although subordinate titles were used. In 1837, a new subject list of 21 classes was published and expanded the following year to 22 classes. This list was used until 1868 when, taking advantage of indexing and classification developments in France and England, the U.S. list was expanded to 26 classes with primary and secondary subclasses introduced for many of the classes. In 1872, the system was expanded to 145 classes and became the framework on which the present system was built. Subsequent changes have been by adding new classes and by deleting, interchanging, and splitting classes.

By 1897 there were 215 classes, most of which were subdivided into alphabetically ordered subclasses (from 5 to over 200). In 1898, Congress authorized the Patent Office "to revise and perfect the classification by subject matter" and this process still continues. The revisions, however, have been uneven, and although essentially every class has been revised, each class reflects the stage of classification development at the time it was reclassified. The system must be an evolving one as classes are not created a priori, but by first analyzing the disclosures of patents as processed and then creating the divisions and subdivisions on the basis of the analyses. Each subclass of a class is defined to include, not to exclude, subject matter.

As mentioned earlier, utility is the principal classification basis. Utility means the function of a process or means, or the effect or product produced by such process or means. Thus, a chemical compound is classified by its structure or chemical constitution regardless of how it may be used or applied; mixtures or compositions, on the other hand, are classified by the disclosed application or use.

Since the total number of U.S. patents granted is now over the four million mark, it is quite understandable that maintaining a viable classification system is a Herculean task, particularly when one considers the number of known forms of energy, the number of known substances, the number of known mechanical and electrical elements, and all the possible combinations and permutations of these. The present classification is the primary basic tool, and to use this tool most effectively the searcher must become familiar with three aids:

Index to Classification

Manual of Classification

Class and Subclass Definitions

These documents are available from the Superintendent of Documents, U.S. Government Printing Office, Washington, D.C.

The *Index to Classification* is particularly useful to the novice because it lists alphabetically terms that pertain to arts, processes, machines, manufacturing, composition of matter, and so on, and cites by number the class and subclass of a particular subject matter.

The *Manual of Classification* is most useful to a knowledgeable searcher. It comprises a collection of the schedules: an array of the subclass titles and numbers arranged under a class title, a list of classes in numerical order, the main classes listed in alphabetical order, and the main classes listed by the Patent Office administrative examining groups.

The *Class and Subclass Definitions* are essential for a searcher to establish a field of search. Each definition consists of a statement of the scope with useful notes that supplement the definitions, give examples, and refer to other classes or subclasses. These search notes guide the searcher towards reaching a decision to include or exclude other subject matter. The definitions and notes are published in separate bulletins, for example, *U.S. Patent Office Classification Definitions, Class 260— Chemistry, Carbon Compounds, Revision 1, August 1967.*

The *Classification Key*, the British equivalent of the *Manual of Classification*, is available from the Patent Office Sales Branch, Orpington, Kent, England. The British classification system, modified extensively in 1963, is issued in 25 parts, corresponding to the Abridgement (abstracts) groups (of 25,000 patents each). Along with the *Key*, a necessary document is the *Reference Index to the Classification Key*, which defines the headings. The German classification system is described in the publication *Gruppeneinteilung der Patentklassen* and the subject index to the system, *Stichworterverzeichnis*, is available in an English edition from the U.S. Clearinghouse as TT65-50147.

The International Patent Classification (IPC), which was developed over many years, has some 35,000 divisions. It has replaced the classification systems of several nations, including Belgium, France, and Italy, and is used as a secondary system by most nations now, including the United States, the United Kingdom, Germany, and the Netherlands. Furthermore, the 40,000 subdivisions of the British and the 23,000 subdivisions of the German classifications have been undergoing modifications so that at least the major classes match the international system.

IPC divides the whole body of patent knowledge into eight sections (A–H, in which C is Chemistry and Metallurgy), then into subsections, such as C01 for Inorganic Chemistry and C07 for Organic Chemistry, then into classes, such as C07B for General Methods and Apparatus of Organic Chemistry and C07C for Acyclic and Carbocyclic Compounds, and then into subclasses, such as C07B1/00 for Organic Chemistry, General Methods and Apparatus, and Hydrogenation. Each subclass may be further divided into groups. The English version of IPC has been published by Morgan–Grampian Ltd., 30 Calderwood Street, Woolwich, London SE18 6QH, England.

IPC was developed cooperatively by European members of the 22-nation Committee for International Cooperation in Information Retrieval Among Examining Patent Offices (ICIREPAT), which functions through three groups: the Committee for Computerization, the Committee for Search Systems, and the Committee for Standardization. The International Patent Documentation Center (INPADOC) has been set up in Vienna, and the Patent Associated Literature (PAL) has been established by INSPEC (Information Service in Physics, Electrotechnology, and Computers) in London.

SOURCES FOR PATENT AWARENESS AND RETROSPECTIVE SEARCHING

Chemical Abstracts

Chemical Abstracts (CA) has recognized the importance of patents in the conduct of research and development and as a vital part of the chemical literature since 1907, the year it began publication. Although *Chemical Abstracts'* coverage of patents was not very good initially, the coverage has been expanded until now it monitors the patent literature of over 25 nations. The coverage is still somewhat selective in that all Belgian, British, French, West German, South African, and United States patents of chemical and chemical engineering content are covered, but patents from most of the remaining nations are covered only if they have been issued to inventors residing in the issuing nation. Thus the following nations' patents are covered in whole or in part:

Australia	Germany	Norway
Austria	Great Britain	Poland
Belgium	Hungary	Rumania
Canada	India	Soviet Union
Czechoslovakia	Israel	Spain
Denmark	Italy	Sweden
France	Japan	Switzerland
Finland	Netherlands	United States

In selecting patents for abstracting and indexing, *Chemical Abstracts* handles only those that contain new information, that is, the first issuing patent; equivalent patents, which have the same priority date and which carry the same application number, are listed in the *Chemi-*

Abstracts Patent Concordance. According to CAS studies, 32% of French and 22% of Belgian chemical patents are applied for by U.S. companies who also apply for corresponding U.S. patents. Whereas the U.S. patent will issue in two to four years, the Belgian and French patents usually will issue within a year.

Abstracting of patents in *Chemical Abstracts* is based on the examples in and claims of a patent. The abstract is written to give first the objective and scope; then an example of the reaction, apparatus, or composition is given in some detail; and finally, all compounds with their properties and uses are given either generically or specifically.

First-issued patents abstracted in *Chemical Abstracts* and the number of patent duplicates listed in the *Chemical Abstracts Patent Concordance* are shown in Table 3, along with the number of papers abstracted for the period 1963–1980:

Based on the contents of *Chemical Abstracts* over the period 1963–1980, the ratio of papers to first-issue patents was fairly constant at about 5.5. For the three years, 1974, 1975, and 1976, the ratio decreased

TABLE 3.   Abstracts of Papers, Books, and Patents and Number of Patent Duplicates in Chemical Abstracts 1963–1980

Year	Number of Abstracts			Patent Duplicates (Number)	Ratio of Paper to Patent Abstracts
	Papers	Books	Patents		
1963	141,016	4,200	26,240	8,400	5.4
1964	161,489	2,100	26,422	13,375	6.1
1965	165,770	2,200	29,225	19,312	5.6
1966	181,715	3,600	35,031	28,940	5.2
1967	202,684	3,100	36,797	26,766	5.4
1968	198,035	2,800	31,720	19,180	6.2
1969	210,344	2,600	39,424	33,026	5.3
1970	230,902	2,700	43,044	33,068	5.4
1971	262,127	3,500	43,405	41,129	6.0
1972	280,143	3,100	51,179	44,622	5.5
1973	269,711	2,600	48,683	35,544	5.5
1974	272,235	2,953	58,400	42,000	4.7
1975	317,472	6,291	68,400	62,000	4.7
1976	317,985	5,744	67,606	67,616	4.7
1977	348,059	6,637	55,441	68,088	6.3
1978	363,195	7,804	57,343	70,217	6.3
1979	370,771	7,378	58,738	78,854	6.3
1980 (est.)	400,533		61,998	72,937	6.5

to 4.7, and since then increased to over 6.3. Abstracts of patents increased at an average annual rate of 10.2% over the period 1971–1976 in contrast to 8.9% for the period 1966–1970, and have decreased by 9.4% since the 1975 peak. The number of equivalent patents cited in the *CA Patent Concordance*, which links equivalent patents from different countries to the *CA* abstract of the first-issued patent, grew at an average rate of 15.7% over the period 1971–1975 and 17.3% over the period 1966–1970. Since 1975, the number of patents abstracted has declined slightly.

Chemical Abstracts has been doing a better job in detecting and referencing patents and their equivalents in recent years than it did in earlier years. In addition, much of the increase has occurred because more nations, such as Japan and West Germany, are now publishing unexamined patent applications, and patents from these nations now comprise the larger percentage of first-issued patents abstracted in *Chemical Abstracts*. Although the U.S.S.R. has been a Convention member for over ten years, there has been no Soviet equivalent to any patent of the 25 nations covered by *Chemical Abstracts*.

Patent numbers are listed in *Chemical Abstracts' Numerical Patent Index* numerically in ascending order by country of issuance. The countries are listed alphabetically, and each patent number is linked with its CA abstract number.

Since 1980, Chemical Abstracts Service has drawn patent information for its publications and services from INPADOC's computer base of information on 8 million patents going back to 1968 and INPADOC's programs for linking patent documents issued by various nations on the same invention. Information on approximately 18,000 newly issued patent documents are added to the data base each week. CAS receives the additions weekly to update with the INPADOC backfile, to identify patents for abstracting in *Chemical Abstracts*, and to compile the *CA Patent Concordance*, which will be issued and available as part of the weekly, semiannual, and five-year collective indexes to *Chemical Abstracts* (the *CA Patent Concordance* no longer will be available in computer-readable form).

Derwent Publications Ltd.

The most extensive information service on patents issued throughout the world is that of Derwent Publications Ltd., Rochdale House, 128 Theobald Road, London WC1X 8RP, England. Founded in 1951, Derwent has issued about 3.5 million abstracts of different patents in its weekly *Patents Abstract Publications*. About one-fourth of Derwent's activities is directed to the documentation of pharmaceutical, agricultural, and pesticide journal literature, and three-fourths to the documentation of patents. Derwent's products fall into three major categories:

Patents Abstracts Publications.   Issued weekly, it completely covers all patents published by the British, Soviet, German, United States, and Belgian patent offices, with an approximately 100-word summary for each patent. Complete coverage of Belgian and U.S. patents was initiated in 1975; before then, the coverage was of only chemical patents. Only chemical patents are covered for patents published by the French, Japanese (both examined and unexamined), Netherlands, and South African patent offices.

Central Patents Index (CPI).   CPI is a coded card and magnetic tape service. The card service provides detailed abstracts of patents in the subject areas of polymers and plastics; pharmaceuticals; agricultural chemicals; foods and detergents; general chemicals; textiles and paper; printing and photographic; petroleum; chemical engineering, nucleonics and explosives; ceramics; and metallurgy. The card service is provided as a company code, as a manual code on cards or on microfilm, or as a punch code. The magnetic tape is issued in four parts: as a weekly minitape; as a manual code, company, and class tape; as a punch code search tape; and as a print tape. The abstracts are also available as bulletins by country or as bulletins by subject area. Basic patents are available as hard copies or on microfilm.

World Patents Index (WPI).   This index, issued weekly and quarterly, covers all published patents from 24 countries processed by Derwent. WPI is issued in four parts: general, mechanical, electrical, and chemical.

WPI and CPI are now online through Derwent and Systems Development Corporation (2500 Colorado Avenue, Santa Monica, Calif.) through the Tymshare network, and may be searched by patentee, Derwent classes, terms in the titles, international patent classification (IPC), priorities, patent number, and special Derwent index codes. Twelve major countries that have been covered in WPI since its beginning are Belgium, France, Japan, Netherlands, South Africa, and West Germany, each of which publishes patents within a few months after filing; and Canada, East Germany, the Soviet Union, Switzerland, the United Kingdom, and the United States, which publish patents considerably after filing, within several years for some. During 1975, the following 12 countries have been covered: Denmark, Finland,

Norway, Portugal, and Sweden, which publish patents reasonably soon after filing; and Argentina, Austria, Brazil, Czechoslovakia, Hungary, Israel, and Rumania, which issue patents considerably after filing.

TABLE 4. Average Number of Patents Covered Weekly During 1975r for Various Countries

Major Countries	Number of patents
Fast publishing	
Belgium	270
France	850
West Germany (unexamined)	1150
Japan (unexamined)	1000 (CPI only)
Netherlands (unexamined)	315
South Africa	130
Slow publishing	
Canada	400
East Germany	160
West Germany (examined)	405
Japan (examined)	260 (CPI only)
Netherlands (examined)	75
Soviet Union	750
Switzerland	250
United Kingdom	770
United States	1450
Minor Countries	
Fast publishing	
Brazil	150
Denmark	120
Finland	65
Norway	80
Portugal	45
Sweden	270
Slow publishing	
Argentina	80
Austria	150
Czechoslovakia	130
Hungary	45
Israel	50
Rumania	40

The weekly issues of *WPI* contain six indexes: basics by patentee and IPC, equivalents by patentee and IPC, concordance of equivalents to basics, and patent number. Quarterly cumulations are issued of the patentee and IPC's for the basic patents; the concordance is cumulated quarterly and annually.

The average number of patents covered weekly by Derwent during 1975 for each of the countries covered are given in Table 4.

IFI/Plenum Patent Service

The most extensive information service on U.S. patents is that of IFI/Plenum Data Company, 2001 Jefferson Davis Highway, Arlington, Virginia 22202. The *Uniterm Index to U.S. Chemical and Chemically Related Patents* covers U.S. patents from 1950 cumulatively to the current year. Patents are selected from the abstracts in the *Official Gazette*, and then purchased and examined by indexers for key words and descriptors. The number of key words, descriptors, or uniterms selected range from a low of five to over 150; the average is about 30–35 per patent. There are now over 350,000 patents in the index.

The *Uniterm Index* consists of two duplicate, dual alphabetical listings of uniterms. Under each uniterm appear, in ten columns, the IFI accession number for each patent for which the uniterm is relevant. The IFI six-digit accession number begins anew each year with 00001 and can go as high as 99999. The accession numbers are posted under the uniterms in those of the ten columns (0–9) with which the unit digit of the accession number corresponds. Patentee, assignee, and IFI accession number indexes are provided, and abstracts from the *Official Gazette* are arranged in patent number order with IFI accession numbers.

These indexes are also available on magnetic tape with search programs for searching on in-house computers. Demand searches may be requested from IFI/Plenum. This data base is also available by online terminal through the Lockheed DIALOG™ Information Retrieval Service. The IFI/Plenum data base is called CLAIMS™. Searchable areas of CLAIMS include U.S. patent classification code, assignee, patent number, title words, and uniterms. The record that appears in the CLAIMS CHEM file includes the seven-digit patent number (searched without commas), the accession number (the first two digits are the year code, and the following five digits the accession number), the U.S. class code, and a *CA* reference; each record carries the patent title, assignee by full text name and code number, foreign patent equivalents, cross references assigned by the U.S. Patent Office, priority date, types of claims in the patent (composition, device, or process), and list of terms.

Other Patent Reference Sources

In addition to *Chemical Abstracts*, whose coverage of patents was only fair from 1907 (the year it was first issued) until the 1920s (when it began to do a fine job with U.S. chemical patents; more recently it has been doing a superior job with patents from 22 countries), other abstracting journals are also of interest, especially for earlier years. *Chemisches Zentralblatt*, which began in 1830, covered only German chemical patents until about 1918; thereafter it covered patents from other nations as well. Unfortunately, this outstanding abstracting/indexing journal ceased publication in 1969.

Likewise *British Abstracts*, published between 1926 and 1953, did an outstanding job in covering patents issued in the United Kingdom.

Many chemical journals include sections that list or carry abstracts of patents. Examples are *Journal of Applied Chemistry, Chimie et Industrie, Chemiker-Zeitung, Zeitschrift fuer angewandte Chemie, American Dyestuff Reporter, Journal of the American Ceramic Society,* and *Petroleum Refiner.*

BIBLIOGRAPHY

Allcock, H. M., and J. W. Lotz, "Patent Intelligence and Technology," *J. Chem. Info. Comp. Sci.* 18, 65–69 (1978).

Asher, G., "International Patent Cooperation," *J. Chem. Doc.* 11, 14–18 (1971).

Baker, D. B., "Recent Trends in Growth of Chemical Literature," *Chem. Eng. News* 54, (20), 23–27 (1976) and 59, (22), 29–34 (1981).

Balent, M. Z., and J. M. Emberger, "A Unique Chemical Fragmentration System for Indexing Patent Literature," *J. Chem. Info. Comp. Sci.* 15, 100–104 (1975).

Berkman, R. G., "Utility in Chemical Patent Applications," *J. Chem. Doc.* 2, 140–143 (1962).

Bowman, W. H., "Importance of Patents and Information Services to Research Workers," *J. Chem. Info. Comp. Sci.* 18, 81–82 (1978).

Cattley, J. M., et al., "Inter-index Patent Searching by Computer," *J. Chem. Doc.* 6, 15–25 (1966).

Commissioner of Patents, U. S. Patent Office, *Classification Bulletins* issued periodically.

Cornog, J. R., and P. P. Ellis, "Patterns of Thinking in Searching Patent Applications by Manual and Machine-Assisted Methods," *J. Chem. Doc.* 5, 215–224 (1965).

Donovan, K. M., and B. B. Wilhide, "A User's Experience with Searching the IFI Comprehensive Database to U.S. Chemical Patents," *J. Chem. Info. Comp. Sci.* 17, 139–143 (1977).

Duffey, M. M., "Searching Foreign Patents," *J. Chem. Info. Comp. Sci.* 67, 126–130 (1977).

Fitting, J., et al., "Semiautomatic Coding of Steroid Markush Formulas," *J. Chem. Doc.* 14, 74–75 (1974).

Fitting, J., et al., "Plausibility Check of Chemical Coding by Computer Using a Modified Derwent Robins Program," J. Chem. Doc. 14, 75–79 (1974).

Fleischer, J., *Exploring U.S. Chemical Patent Literature*, 64–69, in Advances in Chemistry series no. 4, ACS, Washington, D.C., 1951.

Frome, J., "Generic Mechanized Search System," *J. Chem. Doc.* 2, 15–18 (1962).

Frome, J., and P. T. O'Day, "Practical Approach to Chemical Information Retrieval," *J. Chem. Doc.* 2, 48–54 (1962).

Frome, J., "The Effects of Information Storage and Retrieval Techniques and Computers on Problems of Patentability," *J. Chem. Doc.* 6, 66–71 (1966).

Garfield, E., "Patent Citation Indexing and the Notions of Novelty, Similarity, and Relevance," *J. Chem. Doc.* 6, 63–65 (1966).

Higgs, W. V., "British Patent Law and Practice," *J. Pat. Office Soc.* 41, 562–573 (1959).

Hurd, E. A., "Patent Literature: Current Problems and Future Trends," *J. Chem. Doc.* 10, 167–173 (1970).

Hyams, M., "Foreign Patents Documentation," *J. Chem. Doc.* 6, 101–123 (1966).

ICIREPAT 3rd Annual Meeting, Sept. 1963, Vienna, *Information Retrieval–Patent Offices*, Spartan, Baltimore, 1964.

IFI/Plenum News Releases, "CLAIMS™ Information on 350,000 U.S. Chemical Patents," *J. Chem. Info. Comp. Sco.* 15, 132 (1975).

Johns, T. M., and D. I. Ryno, "Patent Searching in a Pharmaceutical Company," *J. Chem. Info. Comp. Sci.* 18, 79–80 (1978).

Kaback, S. M., "A User's Experience with the Derwent Patent Files," *J. Chem. Info. Comp. Sci.* 17, 143–148 (1977).

Knight, L. F. W., "British Patent Office Practice," *J. Pat. Office Soc.* 47, 16–39 (1965).

Kohnke, E. L., and G. F. Lewenz, "Detecting Corresponding Patents from Different Countries," *J. Chem. Doc.* 1, (1) 41–43 (1961).

Lanham, B. E., "Chemical Patent Searches," *Ind. Eng. Chem.* 43, 2494 (1951).

Lawson, E. J., And E. A. Godula (Eds.), *Patents for Chemical Inventions*, Advances in Chemistry series no. 46, ACS, Washington, D.C., 1964.

Leibowitz, J., "Classification and Mechanization," *J. Chem. Doc.* 3, 161–164 (1963).

Liebesny, F., (ed.), *Mainly on Patents*, Archon, Hamden, Conn., 1972.

Marmor, A. C., "The Approach of the U.S. Patent Office and Trademark Office to Finding Prior Art," *J. Chem. Info. Comp. Sci.* 20, 6–9 (1980).

Marcus, I., "Agriculture and Food Technology in the Patent Office," *J. Chem. Doc.* 8, 225–228 (1968).

Marcus, M. J., "Patents and Information," *J. Chem. Info. Comp. Sci.* 18, 76–78 (1978).

Mayer, W. J., J. A. Angus, and P. Mariucci, "A Quick Systematic Method for Worldwide Patent Awareness," *J. Chem. Info. Comp. Sci.* 16, 76–77 (1976).

Maynard, J. T., "Chemical Abstracts as a Patent Reference Tool," *J. Chem. Info. Comp. Sci.* 17, 136–139 (1977).

Maynard, J. T., *Understanding Chemical Patents*, ACS, Washington, D.C., 1978.

McDonnell, P. M., "Technical Information Management in the U.S. Patent Office," *J. Chem. Doc.* 9, 220–224 (1969).

McDonnell, P. M., "Searching for Chemical Information in the Patent and Trademark Office," *J. Chem. Info. Comp. Sci.* 17, 122–125 (1977).

McGarvey, A. R., "Uniterm Index to U.S. Chemical Patents," *J. Chem. Doc.* 8, 23–25 (1968).

Mosher, E. H., "How Can the Chemist Help the Patent Attorney: Patent Background and Chemical Proprietorship," *J. Chem. Doc.* 1 (1), 29–31 (1961).

Newman, P., and E. I. Hoegberg, "What the Patent Attorney Needs from a Patent Information Point of View," *J. Chem. Info. Comp. Sci.* 18, 83–85 (1978).

Noone, T. M., "Trade Secret vs. Patent Protection," *Research Management*, May, 21–24 (1978).

Norton, H. M., "Challenges and Opportunities for Chemists in Patent Work," *J. Chem. Doc.* 2, 144 (1962).

O'Leary, P. T., et al.,"Computer Searching of Chemical Patents," *J. Chem. Doc.* 5, 233–237 (1965).

O'Leary, P. T., "Patent Information Activity of the Technical Information Retrieval Committee of the Manufacturing Chemists' Association," *J. Chem. Info. Comp. Sci.* 18, 63–65 (1978).

Payne, N. M., "Patent Terms in some Languages other than English," *J. Chem. Ed.* 25, 389–390 (1948).

Pfeffer, H. (ed.), ICIREPAT 4th Annual Meeting, Oct., 1964, *Information Retrieval Among Examining Patent Offices*, Spartan, Baltimore, 1966.

Pilch, W., and W. Wratschko, "INPADOC: A Computerized Patent Documentation System," *J. Chem. Info. Comp. Sci.* 18, 69–75 (1978).

Platau, G. O., "Documentation of the Chemical Patent Literature," *J. Chem. Doc.* 7, 250–255 (1967).

Rainer, H. B., "Criteria for the Chemist in Choosing a Career in Patent Work," *J. Chem. Doc.* 2, 144–147 (1962).

Rosa, M. C., "Outline of Practice Relative to Markush Claims," *J. Patent Office Society* 34, 324 (1952).

Rossmassler, S. A., "Patent Liaison—A Service to Industrial Management," *J. Chem. Doc.* 2, 150–152 (1962).

Rowlett, Jr., R. J., "Gleaning Patents with *Chemical Abstracts,*" *Chem. Tech.* 9, 348 (1979).

Schimmel, J., "How Can the Chemist Help the Patent Attorney: The Patent Office View," *J. Chem. Doc.* 1 (1), 32–33 (1961).

Schmitz, N. S., "The Proposed European Common Market Patent System and its Effect on United States Inventions," *J Chem. Doc.* 6, 10–14 (1966).

Schmitz, T. M., "Pitfalls to Avoid in Processing Patents," *J. Chem. Info. Comp. Sci.* 18, 61–62 (1978).

Schwartz, J. H., "Quantitative Characteristics of Patents, Inventions, and Innovations," *J. Chem. Doc.* 12, 6–8 (1972).

Simmons, G. W., "Centralized Abstracting of Petroleum Literature and Patents," *J. Chem. Doc.* 5, 166–169 (1965).

Singer, T. E. R., and Smith, J. F., "Patentese: A Dialect of English?" *J. Chem. Ed.* 44, 111–112 (1967).

Smith, J. F., "Patent Searching," in T. E. R. Singer (ed.), *Information and Communication Practice in Industry*, Reinhold, New York, 1958.

Smith, R. G., L. P. Anderson, and S. K. Jackson, "On-line Retrieval of Chemical Patent Information," *J. Chem. Info. Comp. Sci.* 17, 148–157 (1977).

Skolnik, H., "International Patent Cooperation," *J Chem. Doc.* 6 (4), (1966).

Skolnik, H., "Historical Aspects of Patent Systems," *J. Chem. Info. Comp. Sci.* 17, 119–121 (1977).

Superintendent of Documents, U.S. Government Printing Office, Washington, D.C.

    a.   *Development and Use of Patent Classification Systems* (1966).

    b.   *How to Obtain Information from United States Patents* (1962).

    c.   *Patents and Inventions - An Information Aid for Inventors* (1964).

    d.   *General Information Concerning Patents* (1969).

    e.   *Manual of Classification* (loose-leaf, issued periodically).

    f.   *Decisions of the Commissioner of Patents* (issued annually).

Terripane, J. F., "The Patent File and Trademark Office Technology Assessment and Forecast Program," *J. Chem. Info. Comp. Sci.* 17, 130–133 (1977).

Terrapane, J. F., "A Unique Source of Information," *ChemTech,* May, 272–276 (1978).

Turner, E. S., "Patents (Literature)," in Kirk–Othmer (eds.), *Encyclopedia of Chemical Technology,* Vol. 14, Wiley, New York, 1967.

Valance, E. H., "Understanding the Markush Claim in Chemical Patents," *J Chem. Doc.* 1 (2), 87–92 (1961).

Valance, E. H., "Patentability of Chemical Intermediates: the Nelson Case in Perspective," *J. Chem. Doc.* 3, 33–36 (1963).

Valicenti, A. K., "The Information Chemist's View of the Patent Information Needs of Research Workers and Patent Attorneys," *J. Chem. Info. Comp. Sci.* 18, 85–87 (1978).

Van dem Breemt, J. H., "Patents by Country of Origin of Invention," *Harvard Business Review* 45 (2), 57–62 (1967).

Van Oot, J. G., "Patents and Patent Guides on Microforms," *J. Chem. Doc.* 10, 9–13 (1970).

Vandenburgh, E. C., "Procedure and Practice in the German Patent Office," *J. Pat. Office Soc.* 38, 683–704 (1956).

Wade, W., "Patents for Technical Personnel," Advance House, Ardmore, Pa., 1957.

Wade, W., "Patents for Management," Advance House, Ardmore, Pa., 1961.

5

THE JOURNAL
LITERATURE

Although the achievement of writing made permanent records possible, information and knowledge could not be transmitted easily during the periods when clay was the writing surface or even when paper was invented and replaced papyrus, parchment, and vellum, for each of these allowed only one copy to be made with each writing, whether as an original or by copy scribes. The invention that made the big difference was that of Gutenberg's movable type in the 1440s; this made possible the large-scale publication of pamphlets and books. The advent of Gutenberg's printing press did not eradicate illiteracy overnight, but it did mark the beginning of the printed page for the many. Newspapers, introduced in the seventeenth century (the first printed newspaper was issued in Germany in 1609), were the first form of mass communication, one which was timely, widely available, and low cost.[6]

Progress in science and technology was quite pedestrian until the advent and growth of scientific and technological societies and of the journal literature for exchanging information. In the seventeenth century, natural philosophers, the predecessors of scientists, organized the first societies for exchanging information at regular meetings. The Royal Society was founded in 1662 in London, and the French Academie des Sciences in 1665 in Paris.[19,27,56,63,94,103,121]

Handwritten letters were the antecedent of the journal. Scientific communication, at the beginning of the seventeenth century, was through books, gazettes, and letters. Letters were the primary mechanism for telling friends of interesting experiments and the consequences or results of the experiments. Letters were distributed generally within a small group of like-minded scientists, who would study the contents with a minimum of criticism. It is not surprising that a large number of questions of priority arose, and the period was marked with many claims and counterclaims between advocates of the various groups of friends.

The first scientific journal, *Journal des sçavans*, was introduced as a weekly on January 5, 1665 by the French Academie des Sciences, primarily to disseminate news of its activities, list new books, publish obituaries of the famous scientists, and inform readers of current events that might affect the arts and sciences. Publication ceased in 1792 and began again in 1797. In 1816 the title was changed to *Journal des savants*. For many years the pages of the first scientific journal were dominated by the listing and reviewing of books.

The second journal appeared on March 6, 1665, and was called *Philosophical Transactions: Giving Some Account of the Present Undertakings, Studies, and Labours of the Ingenious in Many Considerable Parts of the World.* The editor was Henry Oldenburg (1617–1677), secretary of the Royal Society. As editor he was responsible for corresponding with European scientists, a responsibility that also was attached to his office of secretary, and Oldenburg was the supreme communication center until his death. The royal Society adopted the journal as its official organ in 1753.[79, 118]

The early journals of the seventeenth and eighteenth century more or less complemented rather than supplanted the publication of pamphlets and books, which remained the primary communication medium well into the nineteenth century. By the end of the eighteenth century, approximately 100 scientific journals had been introduced. By the end of the nineteenth century, there were well over 1000 scientific journals. Much of the impetus behind this proliferation of journals during the nineteenth century was the metamorphosis of natural philosophy into science and its disciplines such as chemistry, physics, biology, botany, and geology. Concomitant with the appearance of science (a word coined by William Whewell in 1840) and its disciplines was the organization of scientific societies. Chemists were among the first to have societies for their discipline, and many of the great national chemical soceities were formed during the nineteenth century.[24,26,33,83,93,109,119]

Societies such as the Royal Society and the Academie des Sciences covered the whole of science and served poorly the needs of the specialized sciences that were arising in the nineteenth century. Furthermore, too many members of these societies achieved membership for the honor and not for scientific contributions or for work that furthered science. The British Association for the Advancement of Science was formed in 1831 to counteract this lack, such as the establishment of rules for the use of symbols and numerals in chemical formulas. The American Association for the Advancement of Science was formed in 1848 to handle the needs of those working in various disciplines of science, such as geology and chemistry. The Royal Society of Arts, formed in England in 1754, established six committees, one of which became the Chemical Society (London) in 1841. The Chemical Society was incorporated by royal charter in 1848 with the objective: "for the general advancement of chemical science, as intimately connected with the prosperity of the manufactures of the United Kingdom." At its formation in 1841, the Chemical Society had 77 members (fellows); this increased to 551 by 1870.

The Chemical Society (London) was the first society organized exclusively for chemists and chemistry, and it still exists today. Its first publication was the Quarterly Journal, introduced in 1847 and renamed the Journal of the Chemical Society (London) when it became a monthly in 1861.[33]

To meet the needs of scientists in France for prompt publication of their scientific investigations, the Academie des Sciences introduced the weekly, Comptes rendus hebdomadaires des séances de l'académie des sciences, in 1835. Similar weekly publications were Nature in England (1869) and Science in the United States (1883), the latter becoming the official organ of the American Association for the Advancement of Science in 1895.

The Chemical Society of France was formed in 1855, and its publication, Bulletin de la société chimique de France, was introduced in 1858. The Deutsche Chemische Gesellschaft (German Chemical Society) was formed in 1866 by Hofmann, and its publication, Berichte der deutschen chemischen Gesellschaft, was introduced in 1867. The Russian Physical-Chemical Society and its journal, Journal of the Russian Physical-Chemical Society, were formed in 1869; in 1930 the journal was separated into two: Journal of General Chemistry and Journal of Physical Chemistry.

Other society publications of note are the following (year first issued is given in parentheses): Gazzetta chimica italia (1871), Journal of the American Chemical Society (1879), Journal of the Chemical Society of Japan (1880), Bulletin de la société chimique de Belgique (1887), Svensk Kemisk Tidskrift (1899), Chemisch Weekblad (Netherlands, 1903), Helvetica Chimica Acta (Switzerland, 1918), Journal of the Indian Chemical Society (1924), Acta Chemica Scandinavica (1947), and Australian Journal of Chemistry (1952).

During the nineteenth century, the number of journals in chemistry alone reached the point where chemists began to feel uncomfortable in trying to keep up-to-date with the evolving chemical journal literature. Pharmaceutisches Centralblatt was introduced in Germany in 1830 to cover papers in pure chemistry, and Science Abstracts first appeared in England in 1898. During its first year, 1907, Chemical Abstracts published some 12,000 abstracts from about 400 journals that the editor selected to cover the world's chemical journal literature. In 1977, *Chemical Abstracts* monitored approximately 12,000 journals published in over 150 nations, in more than 50 different languages, for the more than 350,000 abstracts of papers it published. According to the number of papers abstracted in *Chemical Abstracts* from 1971 through 1975, the journal literature grew at an average rate of 6.9%—a rate at which the literature would double within 11 years.[8-10,109]

From 1976 through 1980, the number of papers abstracted by *Chemical Abstracts* grew at an annual rate of 4.6%, a doubling rate of about 16 years, compared with 11 years for the 1971–1975 period, 8.5 years for the 1961–1970 period, and 8.8 years for the 1951–1960 period. In 1980, a record 475,739 abstracts of papers and patents were published in *Chemical Abstracts*, up 8.9% over 1979. *Chemical Abstracts* monitored 12,728 primary scientific and technical journals in 1980, of which 9401 had one or more articles that were selected for abstracting. Journal articles accounted for 73% of the abstracts in 1980. The average number of articles abstracted per journal in 1980 was 37.1 (347,289 divided by 9401).[9]

The *World List of Scientific Periodicals* includes over 100,000 separate titles. Furthermore, the number of pages printed per issue of most titles have increased steadily over recent years. The number of scientific and technical journals in chemistry, chemical technology, and allied fields, however, is probably somewhere between 20,000 and 40,000. Despite journal publishers' laments of rising costs and decreasing subscriptions, which they balance by increasing subscription charges, the birth of new journals has been outpacing the mortality rate. Actually, the picture is not as hopeless as it appears, for of the journals monitored by *Chemical Abstracts* in 1980, 90% of the abstracts came from 4145 journals, 75% from 1674, and 50% from 485.[8] Depending on the breadth of one's interest in chemistry or chemical technology, the number of journals of immediate need is still quite small and reasonably manageable.[7,30,42,104,108,119]

The form and function of chemical journals have changed perceptibly, although slowly, over the past 300 years, especially the past 75 years. More recently, some attention is being paid to potential changes, such as switching to miniprint or abridging long papers and relegating the originals to a microfilm edition, in an effort to reduce printing and mailing costs as well as to cater to the awareness needs of readers as opposed to their future reference needs. These changes are being made slowly and carefully.

Journals have evolved into a highly effective medium that attempts to meet the conflicting needs of scientists for communicating, recording, and establishing prestige and recognition. Science progresses primarily through the pages of an active journal literature. It is difficult to conceive of a growing and viable scientific discipline without the existence of journals.[4,13,46-48,54,64,65,67,68,88,107,112,117]

Chemisches Journal is credited as having been the first truly chemical journal. It was introduced in 1778, and renamed *Chemisches Annalen fuer die Freunde der Naturlehre* in 1784 under the editorship of Lorenz von Crell. It ceased publication at the end ـf 1803.

The oldest chemical journal still being published is *Annales de chimie*, which commenced publication in 1789, changed its name to *Annales de chemie et de physique* in 1816, and then, in 1914, divided into two separate journals, *Annales de chemie* and *Annales de physique*.

To organic chemists, *Annalen der Chemie*, has been one of the most significant journals covering experimental organic research for well over a century. Founded by Justus von Liebig in 1832 under the name *Annalen der Pharmacie*, the journal was renamed *Annalen der Chemie und Pharmacie* in 1840. On Liebig's death in 1873, its name was changed to *Justus Liebig's Annalen*, the name it still retains.

Another outstanding journal, the *Journal fuer praktische Chemie*, which appeared with this title under the editorship of Otto Linne Erdmann in 1834, was founded in 1798 as *Allgemeines Journal der Chemie*, by Alexander Nicolaus Scherer. Its name was changed to *Neues allgemeines Journal der Chemie* in 1804 when Gehlen became editor, and to *Journal fuer die Chemie, Physik, und Mineralogie* in 1807 to reflect Gehlen's interests, then to *Journal fuer die Chemie und Physik* when Johann S.C. Schweigger assumed the editorship in 1811.

During the last quarter of the eighteenth century, papers in chemistry and other disciplines read before the French Academie des Sciences were published in Rozier's journals, *Introduction aux observations sur la physique* (1773), *Observations et mémoires sur la physique, sur l'histoire naturelle et sur les arts et métiers* (1773-1793), and *Journal de physique, de chimie, de histoire naturelle et des arts* (1794-1823).

The *Chemical Journal* was founded in England by Nicholson in 1798. In 1814, it and the *Philosophical Journal* merged to become the *Philosophical Magazine*, which also absorbed Thomas Thompson's *Annals of Philosophy* (founded in 1813) in 1827.

German, French, and British journals dominated the whole of chemistry during the nineteenth century. Chemical journals, however, appeared in other nations, and those of note during the nineteenth century in the United States were the following:

Silliman's *Journal of Science* (1818)

Journal of the Franklin Intitute (1826)

Proceedings of the American Academy of Arts and Sciences (1846)

Chandler's *American Chemist* (1870)

Druggists' Circular and Chemical Gazette (1866)

American Gas Light Journal and Chemical Repertory (1868)

Proceedings of the American Chemical Society (1876)

Remsen's *American Chemical Journal* (1879)

Journal of the American Chemical Society (1879)

Science (1883)

Journal of Physical Chemistry (1896)

Journal of Analytical Chemistry (1887)

Table 5 lists the more important journals introduced in the seventeenth and eighteenth century, and Table 6, those introduced in the nineteenth century. Most of the earlier journals are no longer in existence, yet they remain important for historical purposes. Of the 38 journals listed in Table 5 as being the more important ones for chemists in the seventeenth century, only 15 continued into the twentieth century, of which only 10 retained their original names. During both the seventeenth and eighteenth centuries many journals were introduced, but most did not survive beyond their first issue or their first year. I found it very difficult to compile the list of journals in Tables 5 and 6 with any degree of confidence that the titles are accurate or that the list is an inclusive and exclusive representation of prestigious journals from the viewpoint of the chemists of that period. Indeed, even for today's output of journals, I doubt very much the validity of inclusive and exclusive census in terms of value and importance to chemists and to chemistry. It is even more difficult to take a census of the journals that count to chemists and to chemistry and chemical technology because of the great number of journals being published throughout the world, not to mention house organs and governmental serial publications, with the additional complication of adding those journals, such as mining, geology, mechanics, and entomology, which are peripherally of interest to many chemists and chemical engineers working in interdisciplinary areas. For example, in the area of medicinal chemistry alone there are an estimated 18,000 journals of medicinal and related interests according to Annan and Felter.[3] The National Lending Library of Science and Technology (Great Britain) reported in 1970 that it subscribed to 38,000 current titles.[1,2,11,12,14–21,24,25,56,63,73,78,85,93,97–99,102,121,122]

In view of the overwhelming number of journals published, we need

TABLE 5. Journals of the Seventeenth and Eighteenth Centuries

Year	Journal	Country
1665–	Transactions of the Royal Society	England
1665–1792 1797–	Journal des savants	France
1666–1790	Histoire de l'académie royale des sciences	France
1798–1815	Mémoires de l'institut national des sciences et arts	
1816–	Mémoires de l'académie royale des science de l'institut de France	
1679–1682	Philosophical Collections of the Royal Society of London	England
1710–	Sitzungsberichte der deutschen Akademie der Wissenschaften zu Berlin, Klasse fuer Mathematic und allgemein Naturwissenschaften	Germany
1710–1743	Miscellanea Berolinensia ad Incrementum Scientarium ex Scriptus Societes Regiae Scientarium	Germany
1745–1769	Histoire de l'académie royale des sciences et des belles-lettres de Berlin	
1770–1786	Nouveaux mémoires de l'académie royale des sciences et belles-lettres	
1786–1804	Mémoires de l'académie royale sciences et belles-lettres	
1804–	Abhandlungen der königlichen Akademie der Wissenschaften in Berlin	
1720–1760	Recueil des mémoires les plus interessants de chimie et d'histoire naturelle, contenus dans les actes de l'académie d'Upsala, et dans les mémoires de l'académie royale des sciences de Stockholm	Sweden
1726–1746	Commentarii Acadamiae Scientarium Imperialis Petropolitanae	Russia
1747–1775	Novi Commentarii Academiae Scientarium Imperialis Petropolitanae	
1777–1782	Acta Acadamiae Scientarium Imperialis Petropolitanae	
1783–1802	Nova Acta Academiae Scientarium Imperialis Petropolitanae	
1803–1822	Mémoires de l'académie imperiale des sciences de St. Petersbourg	
1728–1757	Raccolta d'opuscoli scientifici e fiologici	Italy
1755–1787	Nuova raccolta d'opuscoli scientifici e fiologici	

TABLE 5. *(Continued)*

Year	Journal	Country
1739–	*Handlinger Kongliga Svenska Vetenskaps-Academiens*	Sweden
1752–1755	*Observations sur l'histoire naturelle, sur la physique, et sur la peinture*	France
1756–1757	*Observations périodiques sur la physique l'histoire naturelle et les arts*	
1771–1772	*Introduction aux observations sur la physique, sur l'histoire naturelle, et sur les arts*	
1773–1823	*Journal de physique, de chimie, d'histoire naturelle, et des arts*	
1761–	*Kongelige Norske Videnskabers Selskabs, Det, Skrifter*	Norway
1769–	*Mémoires de l'académie des sciences, arts, et belles-lettres de Dijon*	France
1769–	*Transactions of the American Philosophical Society*	United States
1778–1781	*Chemisches Journal fuer die Freunde der Naturlehre, Artzneygelahrtheit, Haushaltungskunst und Manufacturen*	Germany
1781–1784	*Die neusten Entdeckungen in der Chemie*	
1784–1803	*Chemische Annalen fuer die Freunde der Naturlehre*	
1780–1802	*Almanach fuer Scheidekünstler und Apotheker*	Germany
1803–1819	*Taschenbuch fuer Scheidekunstler und Apotheker*	
1820–1829	*Trommsdorff's Taschenbuch fuer Chemiker und Pharmaceuten*	
1780–	*Memoirs of the American Academy of Arts and Sciences*	United States
1783–1784	*Chemische Archiv*	Germany
1784–1791	*Neues chemisches Archiv*	
1791–1798	*Neuestes chemisches Archiv*	
1783–	*Transactions of the Royal Society of Edinburgh*	Scotland
1794–1787	*Magazin fuer die höhere Naturwissenschaft und Chemie*	Germany
1785–1795	*Beiträge zu den chemischen Annalen von Lorenz Crell*	

TABLE 5. *(Continued)*

Year	Journal	Country
1785–1787	Magazin fuer Apotheker, Chemisten und Materialisten	
1788–1790	Repertorium fuer Chemie, Pharmacie, und Arzneimittelkunde	
1786–1787	Auswahl aller eigentkumlichen Abhandlungen und Beobachtungen in der Chemie	Germany
1788–1795	Bibliothek der neuesten physichen chemischen Literatur	Germany
1795–1802	Annalen der chemischen Literatur	
1788–1803	Sammlung der deutschen Abhandlungen der königlichen Akademie der Wissenschaften zu Berlin	Germany
1790–1802	Annali di chimica	Italy
1790–1794	Journal der Physik	Germany
1795–1797	Neues Journal der Physik	
1799–	Annalen der Physik	
1793–1817	Journal der Pharmacie fuer Aerzte und Apotheker	Germany
1817–1834	Neues Journal der Pharmacie	
1794–1815	Journal des mines	France
1816–	Annales des mines	
1795–1840	Berlinisches Jahrbuch fuer die Pharmacie	Germany
1795–1835	Procés-verbaux des séances de l'académia	France
1795–	Journal de l'école polytechnique	France
1795–1815	Beitrage zur chemischen Kentniss der Mineralkörper	Germany
1796–1815	Bibliothèque Brittannique, Sciences et arts	France
1816–1835	Bibliothèque universelle des sciences, belles-lettres, et arts	
1797–1813	Journal of Natural Philosophy, Chemistry, and the Arts	England
1814–	Philosophical Magazine (started 1788)	
1798–1803	Allgemeines Journal der Chemie	Germany
1803–1806	Neues allgemeines Journal der Chemie	
1806–1809	Journal fuer der Chemie, Physik, und Mineralogie	
1811–1833	Journal fuer Chemie und Physik (merged with Journal fuer praktische Chemie)	

TABLE 6. Journals of the Nineteenth Century

Year	Journal	Country
1800–1802	Archiv fuer die theoretische Chemie	Austria
1800–1801	Archiv fuer die thierische Chemie	Germany
1800–	Proceedings of the Royal Society (London)	England
1801–1805	Allgemeine chemische Bibliothek des Neunzehnten Jahrhunderts	Germany
1802–1813	Annales de muséum d'histoire naturelle	France
1815–1832	Mémoires de museum nationale d'histoire naturelle	
1803–1818	Archiv der Agriculturchemie fuer denkende Landwirthe	Germany
1806–1818	Afhandlingar i Fusik Kemi oc Mineralogi	Sweden
1807–1817	Mémoires de physique et de chimie de la société d'Arcueil	France
1808–1827	Giornale di fisica, chimica, et storia naturale	Italy
1810–1814	American Mineralogical Journal	United States
1810–	Memoirs of the Connecticut Academy of Arts and Sciences	United States
1813–1826	Annals of Philosophy (merged with Philosophical Magazine in 1827)	England
1813–1814	Memoirs of the Columbian Chemical Society	United States
1814–	Kongelige Danske Videnskabernes Selskab, Det, Oversitz over Selskabets Virksomhed	Denmark
1816–1830	Quarterly Journal of Science, Literature and Art	England
1817–1818	Nordische Blätter fuer Chemie	Germany
1819–1822	Allgemeine nordische Annalen der Chemie	
1823–1831	Magazine fuer die neuesten Erfahrungen (merged with Annalen der Pharmacie in 1832)	
1818–	American Journal of Science	United States
1818–1826	Edinburgh Philosophical Journal	Scotland
1826–1864	Edinburgh New Philosophical Journal	
1820–1928	Transactions of the Cambridge Philosophical Society	England
1820–1931	Dinglers Polytechnisches Journal	Germany
1821–1849	Jahresbericht über die Fortschritte der Chemie und Mineralogie	Germany
1821–1849	Asberdatteles om Framstegen i Physik och Chemi till Kong. Vet.-Akad.	Sweden
1822–1841	Jahresberichte über die Fortschritte der physischen Wissenschaften	Germany
1822–	Archiv der Pharmacie und Berichte der deutschen pharmazeutischen Gesellschaft	Germany

TABLE 6. (Continued)

Year	Journal	Country
1824–1832	Edinburgh Journal of Science (merged with Philosophical Magazine in 1832)	Scotland
1824–1835	Archiv fuer die gesammte Naturlehre	Germany
1824–1831	Bulletin des sciences mathematiques, astronomiques, physiques et chimiques	France
1824–1858	The Chemist	England
1825–1840	Laboratorium	Germany
1825–1876	Journal de chimie médicale, de pharmacie et de toxicologie (merged with Repertoire de pharmacie in 1876)	France
1826–	Journal of the Franklin Institute	United States
1826–	Belletin de la société industrielle de Mulhouse	France
1828–1933	Doklady Akademii Nauk Soyuza Sovetskikh, Sotsialisticheskikh Respublik	Soviet Union
1933–	Comptes rendus de l'académie des sciences de Russie	
1828–1833	Journal fuer technische und ökonomische Chemie	Germany
1829–	American Journal of Pharmacy	Germany
1831–1839	Gazetta eclettica di chemical farmaceutica	Italy
1832–1840	Annalen der Pharmacie	Germany
1840–1874	Annalen der Chemie und Pharmacie	
1874–	Liebig's Annalen der Chemie	
1832–	Bulletin de las classe des sciences, Académie royale de Belgique	Belgium
1833–1834	Gazetta eclettica di chimica technologia	Italy
1834–	Journal fuer praktische Chemie	Germany
1835–	Archiv der Pharmazie	Germany
1835–	Comptes rendus hebdomadaires des séances de l'académie des sciences	France
1835–	Sitzungsberichte der Mathmatischnaturwissenschaftlichen Klasse der bayerischen Akademie der wissenschaften zu Muenchen	Germany
1836–	Izvestiya Akademii Nauk Soyuza Sovetskikh Sotsialisticheskikh Republik	Soviet Union
1836–	Proceedings of the Royal Irish Academy	Ireland
1836–1842	Mechanic and Chemist	England
1837–1839	Répertoire de chimie et de physique	France
1838–	Proceedings of the American Philosophical Society	United States
1840–1852	Revue scientifique et industrielle	France

TABLE 6. (Continued)

Year	Journal	Country
1857–1863	Moniteur Scientifique (merged with Revue de Chimie Industrielle in 1927)	
1841–1843	Proceedings of the Chemical Society of London	England
1843–1848	Memoirs and Proceedings of the Chemical Society of London	
1849–1862	Quarterly Journal of the Chemical Society	
1862–	Journal of the Chemical Society	
1841–1843	Repertorium fuer organische Chemie	Germany
1841–1847	Annali di fisica, chimica e matematica	Italy
1847–1850	Annali di fisica, chimica e scienze affini	
1843–1859	Chemical Gazette	England
1860–1932	Chemical News	
1845–1851	Annuaire de Chimie	France
1845–1876	Scheikundige onderzoekingen gedaan in het laboratorium der Utrechtsche Hoogeschool	Netherlands
1845–	Archives des Sciences (Geneva)	Switzerland
1846–	Proceedings of the American Academy of Arts and Sciences	United States
1846–1883	Chemisch-Technische Mittheilungen der neuesten Zeit	Germany
1847–1848	Tekuo-kemisk Journal	Sweden
1847–	Atti della accademia nazionale dei Lincei, Memorie, di Scienze fisiche, mathematiche e naturali	Italy
1848–	Oesterrlichische Akademie der Wissenschaften Mathematischnaturwissenschaftliche Klasse, Sitzungsberichte	Austria
1849–1873	Tidsskrift voor wetenschappelijke Pharmacie	Netherlands
1857–	Zeitschrift des Vereins deutscher Ingenieure	Germany
1847–1926	Moniteur scientifique du Docteur Quesneville	France
1858–	Bulletin de la société chimique de France	France
1862–	Zeitschrift fuer analytische Chemie	Germany
1865–	Atti della accademia delle scienze di Torino	Italy
1866–	Archives néerlandaises des sciences exactes et naturelles (changed to Physica)	Netherlands
1868–	Transactions of the Royal Society of New Zealand	New Zealand
1868–	Chemisches Berichte	Germany
1869–	Nature	England
1869–1930	Journal of the Russian Physical-Chemical Society	Soviet Union

TABLE 6. (Continued)

Year	Journal	Country
1930–	Journal of General Chemistry and Journal of Physical Chemistry	
1871–	Gazetta chimica italiana	Italy
1871–	Oil, Paint, and Drug Reporter	United States
1872–	Paper Trade Journal	United States
1875–	Annales de la société scientifique de Bruxelles	Belgium
1876–	Anales de la sociedad cientifica argentina	Argentina
1876–	The Analyst	England
1876–	Chemiker Zeitung mit Chemie Börse	Germany
1877–	Chemiker Zeitung	Germany
1877–	Scientific Proceedings of the Royal Dublin Society	Ireland
1879–	Journal of the American chemical Society	United States
1880–	Journal of the Chemical Society of Japan	Japan
1882–	Transactions of the Royal Society of Canada	Canada
1882–	Journal of the Society of Chemical Engineers (London)	England
1882–	Recueil des travaux chimiques des Pays-Bas	Netherlands
1883–	Science	United States
1884–	Journal of the Society of Dyers and Colourists	England
1885–	Journal of the Faculty of Science, University of Tokyo	Japan
1887–	Zeitschrift fuer physikalische Chemie	Germany
1887–	Memorias y revista de la academia nacional de ciencias	Mexico
1887–	Bulletin des sociétés chemiques Belges	Belgium
1888–	Angewandte Chemie	Germany
1888–	Textile World	United States
1889–	Svensk Kemisk Tidskrift	Sweden
1889–	Bulletin international de l'academia polonaise des sciences et des lettres	Poland
1892–	Zeitschrift fuer anorganische und allgemeine chemie (now: Zeitschrift fuer anorganische Chemie)	Germany
1893–	Physical Review	United States
1895–	Farbe und Lack	Germany
1896–	Journal of Physical Chemistry	United States
1897–	Umschau in Wissenschaft und Technik	Germany
1898–	Proceedings of the American Society for Testing Materials	United States
1898–	Koninklijke Nederlandse Akademia van Wetenschappen, Proceedings	Netherlands

tools for finding out which journals exist and for assessing the value of journals in the various disciplines of science and technology to scientists and engineers working in various areas. (Some of these methods are discussed later in this chapter.) The outstanding tool for knowing journals exist and which libraries have them is the *Union List of Serials in Libraries of the United States and Canada*, a publication of the Library of Congress. The first edition, in 1927, listed 75,000 titles in 225 libraries. The second edition (1943–1953, with two supplements) listed 145,000 titles in 712 libraries. The third edition (1966, in five volumes) listed 156,000 titles in 956 libraries. Since 1955, the Library of Congress has compiled and issued monthly the *New Serial Titles—Classed Subject Index*, a cumulative supplement to the *Union List of Serials* from 1950 on, in which the entries are arranged by subject. In recent years, the number of new serials announced annually has averaged about 15,000 for all nations.

The *British Union Catalogue of Periodicals (BUCOP)* and supplements list over 150,000 periodicals in all subject areas from the seventeenth century on, giving title changes, complete reference data, and the names of libraries holding the journals. The British *World List of Scientific Periodicals* lists alphabetically over 60,000 journals published between 1900 and 1960. These two publications were merged and supplemented by the *Bucop Journal*, a quarterly introduced in 1964.

The Medical Library Center of New York issues the *Union Catalog of Medical Periodicals*, which lists over 15,000 titles.

In 1922, Chemical Abstracts Service introduced and published its *List of Periodicals Abstracted by Chemical Abstracts*. Revisions were issued every five years; annual supplements were issued in the intervening years. The 1969 publication, named the *CA Source Index*, was a much expanded, computer-produced version of the *List of Periodicals* that Chemical Abstracts Service had compiled first in 1918 and published since 1922 to help CA users identify and locate the primary publications cited in CA. The 1974 publication was named *Chemical Abstracts Service Source Index or CASSI, 1907–1974 Cumulative*. CASSI is an outstanding aid in identifying and locating primary journals, patents, reports, monographs, and conference proceedings cited in CA since 1907. It also includes the journals cited in *Chemisches Zentralblatt* from 1830 to 1940 and in *Beilstein's Handbuch der organischen Chemie* through 1965. Primary journals routinely monitored by CAS, Bio-Sciences Information Service, Engineering Index, Inc., and Original Article Tear Sheet Service of the Institute for Scientific Information are indicated. *CASSI* contains bibliographic and library holdings (by 398 major libraries) for 25,000 serials and 10,000 nonserials. Information associated with each entry includes:

1. Full title of the publication
2. Title abbreviation in bold face
3. CODEN (five letter identification code for each journal)
4. Translation of title except for French, German, and Spanish
5. History, frequency, and languages of the publication
6. Volume/year correlation
7. Publisher's address
8. Note of discontinuation
9. Editor

CASSI is kept current by the publication of CASSI Quarterly Supplements, which report bibliographic and library holdings information for publications added to the coverage since 1974 and changes and additions. The last quarterly issue each year is cumulative for the year. CASSI is available also in computer-readable form.

Other important publications which list journals are the following: Poole's Index to Periodical Literature, Ulrich's International Periodicals Directory, Fowler's Guides to Scientific Periodicals, Periodica Chimica, Periodical Publications in the (U.S.) Patent Office Library, and lists of journals covered by abstracting services, such as Science Citation Index, Pandex, Applied Science and Technology Index, Engineering Index, and Physics Abstract.

Through the use of these various tools and many reference books, I assembled Table 7, a list of chemical and related journals by subject areas.[3,8,12,14–26,29,31,33,35–39,42,44,49,51,52,62,69,76,87,92,111,113,114,120]

RANKING OF CHEMICAL JOURNALS

Many schemes have been advanced over the years for ranking journals, or at least for spotlighting the more important ones either generally or for specific disciplines of chemistry. The reliability of the various methods is difficult to establish with any degree of confidence. A priori we could assume that journals with a large number of subscriptions rank higher than those with a smaller number of subscriptions. On this basis Scientific American, with a subscription list of about 700,000, would be

TABLE 7. Chemical Journals by Subject Area

General

Accounts of Chemical Research—United States, 1968
Acta Chimica Scandinavica—Denmark, 1947
Annalen der Chemie (Liebigs Annalen)—Germany, 1832
Annales de chimie—France, 1789
Australian Journal of Chemistry—Australia, 1952
Bulletin of the Academy of Sciences of the U.S.S.R. (Izvestia Akademii Nauk SSSR)—Soviet Union, 1836
Bulletin de la Société Chimique de France—France, 1958
Bulletin of the Chemical society of Japan—Japan, 1926
Canadian Journal of chemistry—Canada, 1951 (Section B of Canadian Journal of Research, 1929–1950)
Chemical Reviews—United States, 1924
Chemisches Berichte—Germany, 1868
Chemiker-Zeitung mit Chemie Börse—Germany, 1877
Collection of Czechoslovak Chemical Communications—Czechoslavakia, 1929
Endeavor—England, 1942
Experientia—Switzerland, 1945
Fortschritte der chemischen Forschung—Germany, 1949
Gazzetta chimica italiana—Italy, 1971
Helvetica Chemica Acta—Switzerland, 1918
Journal of the American Chemical Society—United States, 1879
Journal of Chemical Education—United States, 1924
Journal of the Chemical Society—England, 1841 (In 1966, this journal was replaced by four separate ones, and in 1972 a fifth part was added by merger with the Transactions of the Faraday Society.)
Journal of the Chemical Society of Japan—1880
Journal of the Franklin Institute—United States, 1826
Journal of General Chemistry (Zhurnal Obshcheĭ Khimii)—Soviet Union, 1930
Journal of the Indian Chemical Society—India, 1924
Journal of Research of the National Bureau of Standards—United States, 1928
Monatshefte fuer Chemie und verwandte Teile anderer Wissenschaften—Austria, 1880
Nature—England, 1869
Naturwissenschaften—Germany, 1913
Quarterly Reviews—England, 1947
Recueil des travaux chimiques des Pays-Bas—Netherlands, 1882
Research—England, 1947
Science—United States, 1883
Scientia (Milan)—Italy, 1907
Svensk Kemisk Tidskrift—Sweden, 1889

TABLE 7. *(Continued)*

Transactions of the Faraday Society—England, 1905 (See *Journal of the Chemical Society*.)
Transactions of the Royal society—England, 1665
Uspekhi Khimii *(Progress of Chemistry)*—Soviet Union, 1932
Zeitschrift fuer anorganische und allgemeine Chemie—Germany, 1892
Zeitschrift fuer Naturforschung—Germany, 1946

Physics and Physical Chemistry

Acta Crystallographica—Denmark, 1948
Annalen der Physik—Germany, 1799
Annales de physique—France, 1915
Annals of Physics—United States, 1957
Applied Spectroscopy—United States, 1951
Atomics and Atomic Technology—England, 1950
Bulletin of the Chemical Society of Japan—Japan, 1926
Bulletin de la société chimiques de France—France, 1858
Canadian Journal of Physics—Canada, 1951
Colloid Journal *(Kolloidnyi Zhurnal)*—Soviet Union, 1935
Helvetica Physica Acta—Switzerland, 1928
Journal of the American Chemical Society—United States, 1879
Journal of Applied Physics—United States, 1929
Journal of Catalysis—England, 1962
Journal of the Chemical Society—England, 1841
Journal of Chemical Physics—United States, 1933
Journal de chimie physique et de physicochemie bielogique—France, 1903
Journal of Colloid Science—United States, 1946 (changed to *Journal of Colloid Interface Science* in 1966)
Journal of Physical Chemistry—United States, 1896
Journal of Physical Chemistry *(Zhurnal Fizicheskoi Khimii)*—Soviet Union, 1930
Journal of the Physical Society of Japan—Japan, 1946
Kolloid-Zeitschrift—Germany, 1906
Nucleonics—United States, 1945
Philosophical Magazine—England, 1798
Physica—Netherlands, 1933
Physics Today—United States, 1948
Proceedings of the Physical Society of London—England, 1874
Proceedings of the Royal Society—England, 1854
Progress of Physical Chemistry *(Uspekhi Fizicheskikh Nauk)*—Soviet Union, 1920
Reviews of Modern Physics—United States, 1928
Review of Physical Chemistry of Japan—Japan, 1925
Transactions of the Faraday Society—England, 1905
Zeitschrift fuer Kristallographie—Germany, 1877

TABLE 7. (Continued)

Zeitschrift fuer Physik—Germany, 1920
Zeitschrift fuer physikalische Chemie—Germany, 1887
Zeitschrift fuer physikalische Chemie (Frankfurt)—Germany, 1954

Inorganic Chemistry
Inorganic Chemistry—United States, 1962
Inorganic Chemica Acta—Italy, 1967
Inorganic Nuclear Chemistry Letters—England, United States, 1965
Journal of Inorganic Chemistry (Zhurnal Neorganicheskoi Khimii)—Soviet Union, 1956
Journal of Inorganic and Nuclear Chemistry—England, 1955
Zeitschrift fuer anorganische und allgemeine Chemie—Germany, 1892

Analytical Chemistry
Analyst—England, 1876
Analytica Chimica Acta—Netherlands, 1947
Analytical Chemistry—United States, 1929
Chimie analytique—France, 1896
Factory Laboratory (Zavodskaya Laboratoriya)—Soviet Union, 1935
Journal of Analytical Chemistry (Zhurnal Analiticheskie Khimii)—Soviet Union, 1946
Journal of the Association of Official Agricultural Chemists—United States, 1915
Journal of Chromatography—Netherlands, 1958
Journal of Electroanalytical Chemistry—Netherlands, 1959
Journal of Gas Chromatography—United States, 1962
Journal of High Resolution Chromatography and Chromatography Communications—Germany, 1978
Journal of Raman Spectroscopy—England, 1971
Journal of Thermal Analysis—England, 1972
Microchemical Journal—United States, 1957
Mikrochimica Acta—Germany, 1953
Organic Magnetic Resonance—England, 1967
Spectrochimica Acta—England, 1944
Talanta—England, 1958
Zeitschrift fuer analytische Chemie—Germany, 1862

Organic Chemistry
Acta Chemica Scandinavica—Denmark, 1947
Annalen der Chemie, Liebigs—Germany, 1832
Bulletin of the Academy of Sciences, U.S.S.R.—Soviet Union, 1836
Bulletin de la Société Chimique de France—France, 1858
Carbohydrate Research—Netherlands, 1965
Chemische Berichte—Germany, 1868

TABLE 7. *(Continued)*

Collection of Czechoslovak Chemical Communications—1929
Fortschritte der Chemie organischer Naturstoffe—Austria, 1938
Helvetica Chimica Acta—Switzerland, 1918
Journal of the American chemical Society—United States, 1879
Journal of the Chemical Society, Perkin Transactions—England, 1862
Journal of General Chemistry—Soviet Union, 1930
Journal of Heterocyclic chemistry—United States, 1964
Journal of Organic Chemistry—United States, 1936
Journal of Organometallic Chemistry—Netherlands, 1963
Journal fuer praktische Chemie—Germany, 1834
Monatshefte fuer Chemie—Austria, 1880
Pure and Applied Chemistry—England, 1960
Recueil des travaux chimiques des Pays-Bas—Netherlands, 1882
Soviet Journal of Coordination Chemistry (trans.)—Soviet Union, 1974
Synthesis—Germany, 1969
Tetrahedron—England, 1957
Tetrahedron Letters—England, 1959

Biochemistry

American Journal of Medical technology—United States, 1934
American Journal of Physiology—United States, 1898
Annales de l'institut Pasteur—France, 1887
Antibiotics and Chemotherapy—United States, 1951
Applied Microbiology—United States, 1953
Archives of Biochemistry and Biophysics—United States, 1942
Archives internationales de pharmacodynamie—Belgium, 1894
Arzneimittel-Forschung—Germany, 1951
Biochemical Journal—England, 1906
Biochemical Pharmacology—England 1958
Biochemische Zeitschrift—Germany, 1906
Biochemistry—United States, 1962
Biochimica et Biophysica Acta—Netherlands, 1947
Biokhimiya—Soviet Union, 1936
Biomechanical Engineering—United States, 1979
British Journal of Pharmacology and Chemotherapy—England, 1946
British Medical Journal—England, 1857
Bulletin de la société de chimie biologique—France, 1914
Comparative Biochemistry and Physiology—England, 1960
Comptes rendus des séances de la société de biologie—France, 1849
Endocrinology—United States, 1917
Endokrinologi—Germany, 1928
European Journal of Biochemistry—Germany, 1906
Helvetica Physiologica et Pharmacologica Acta—Switzerland, 1943
Hoppe-Seyler's Zeitschrift fuer physiologische Chemie—Germany, 1977

TABLE 7. (Continued)

Igaku to Seibutsugaku (Medicine and Biology)—Japan, 1945
Internationale Zeitschrift fuer Vitaminforschung—Switzerland, 1932
Journal of the American Medical Association—United States, 1883
Journal of Bacteriology—United States, 1916
Journal of Biological Chemistry—United States, 1905
Journal of Biochemistry—Japan, 1922
Journal of Biomechanical Engineering—United States, 1977
Journal de chimie physique et de physicochimie biologique—France, 1903
Journal of Experimental Biology—England, 1930
Journal of Laboratory and Clinical Medicine—United States, 1915
Journal of Pharmacology and Experimental Therapeutics—United States, 1909
Klinical Wochschrift—Germany, 1922
Lancet—England, 1823
Mikrobiologiya—Soviet Union, 1932
Pharmacological Reviews—United States, 1949
Proceedings of the Academy of Sciences, U.S.S.R., Biochemistry (Doklady Akademiya Nauk SSSR, Otdel Biokhimii)—Soviet Union, 1828
Proceedings of the Society for Experimental Biology and Medicine—United States, 1903

Polymer Science and Technology

Biopolymers—United States, 1963
British Plastics—England, 1929
British Polymer Journal—England, 1969
Bulletin of the Academy of Science, U.S.S.R., Chemical Science (Doklady Akademiya Nauk, SSSR, Otdel Khimmii)—Soviet Union, 1965
Chemiefasern—Germany, 1919
Chemistry of High Polymers (Kobunshi Kagaku)—Japan, 1944
Colloid and Polymer Science—Germany, 1974
Die Angewandte Makromolekulere Chemie—Germany, 1967
European Polymer Journal—England, 1965
Faserforschung und Textiltechnik—Germany, 1951
International Journal of Polymeric Materials—1971
Journal of Applied Polymer Science—United States, 1959
Journal of Cellular Plastics—United States, 1965
Journal of Macromolecular Chemistry—United States, 1965. A (Chemistry), B (Physics), C (Reviews), and D (Processing and Technology)
Journal of Polymer Science—United States, 1946. In 1963, Journal of Polymer Science was divided into three parts: A—General Papers, B—Letters, and C—Symposia. In 1966, it was divided into: A-1—Polymer Chemistry, A-2—Polymer Physics, and C—Polymer Symposia. In 1970, D became Volume 4 of the earlier Macromolecular Reviews series, and in 1972, it changed to

TABLE 7. *(Continued)*

Polymer Chemistry Edition, Polymer Physics Edition, Polymer Letters Edition, Polymer Symposia, and *Macromolecular Reviews.*
Journal of the Textile Institute—England, 1910
Koilloid Zeitschrift and Zeitschrift fuer Polmere—Germany, 1962
Kunstoffe—Germany, 1911
Kunstoffe - Plastics—Switzerland, 1954
Kunstoffe und Gummie—Germany, 1962
Macromolecules—United States, 1927
Makromolekulare Chemie—Germany, 1947
Modern Packaging—United States, 1927
Modern Plastics—United States, 1925
Plastics—England, 1937
Plastics and Polymers—England, 1932
Plastics Technology—United States, 1955
Polymer—England, 1960
Polymer Composites—United States (published quarterly by SPE)
Polymer Journal—Japan, 1970
Polymer Science U.S.S.R. (Vysokomolekularnye Soedineniya)—Soviet Union, 1959
Rubber Age—United States, 1917
Rubber Chemistry and Technology—United States, 1928
Rubber and Plastics Age—England, 1920
Soviet Plastics (Plasticheskie Massy)—Soviet Union, 1961
Soviet Rubber Technology (Kautchuk i Rezina)—Soviet Union, 1937
SPE Journal—United States, 1949
SPE Transactions—United States, 1961

Chemical Engineering and Chemical Technology

Acta Polytechnica—Sweden, 1947
Angewandte Chemie—Germany, 1888
American Society for Testing Materials, Bulletin—United States, 1921
American Society for Testing Materials, Proceedings—United States, 1898
Brennstoff-Warme-Kraft—Germany, 1949
British Chemical Engineering—England, 1956
British Journal of Applied Physics—England, 1950
Canadian Chemical Processing—Canada, 1917
Canadian Journal of Technology—Canada, 1950
Chemical Age—England, 1919
Chemical Engineering—United States, 1902
Chemical Engineering—Japan, 1937
Chemical and Engineering News—United States, 1923
Chemical Engineering Progress—United States, 1947
Chemical Engineering Science—England, 1951
Chemical Processing—United States, 1938

TABLE 7. *(Continued)*

Chemical and Process Engineering—England, 1920
Chemical Trade Journal—England, 1887
Chemical Week—United States, 1914
Chimia—Switzerland, 1947
Chemie-Ingenieur-Technik—Germany, 1928
Chimie et industrie—France, 1918
Chemiker-Zeitung mit Chemie Börse—Germany, 1876
Chemisch Weekblad—Netherlands, 1903
Chemische Industrie—Germany, 1949
Chemische Technik—Germany, 1949
ChemTech—United States, 1970
Engineering—England, 1866
Energy Resources Engineering—United States, 1979
European Chemical News—England, 1962
Génie chimique—France, 1955
Industrial Chemist and Chemical Manufacturer—England, 1925
Industrial and Engineering Chemistry, Fundamentals—United States, 1962
Industrial and Engineering Chemistry, Process Design and Development—
    United States, 1962
Industrial and Engineering Chemistry, Product Research and Development—
    United States, 1962
Industrie chimique—France, 1914
Industrie chimique belge—Belgium, 1930
International Chemical Engineering—United States, 1962
Journal of Applied Chemistry—England, 1951
Journal of Applied Chemistry (Zhurnal Prikladnoi Khimii—Soviet Union,
    1928
Journal of Chemical and Engineering Data—United States, 1956
Journal of the Chemical Society of Japan, Industrial Section—1938
Journal of the Society of Chemical Industry—England, 1882
Kunstoffe—Germany, 1911
*Proceedings of the Chemical Engineering Group, Society of Chemical
    Industry*—England, 1919
Transactions of the Institution of Chemical Engineers—England, 1923
Zeitschrift des Vereines deutscher Ingenieure—Germany, 1857

Industrial Chemistry

a. Agricultural Chemistry: Fertilizers, Pesticides, Soils

Acta Agricultura Scandinavica—Sweden, 1950
Advances in Agronomy—United States, 1949
Advances in Pest Control Research—United States, 1957
Agricultural and Biological Chemistry—Japan, 1955
Agricultural Chemicals—United States, 1946

TABLE 7. *(Continued)*

Agronomy Journal—United States, 1907
Annals of the Entomological Society of America—United States, 1908
Annual review of Entomology—United States, 1908
Australian Journal of Agricultural Research—1950
Bulletin of Entomological research—England, 1910
Commercial Fertilizer—United States, 1910
Contributions from Boyce Thompson Institute—United States, 1925
Crop Science—United States, 1961
Crops and Soils—United States, 1949
Entoma—United States, 1937
Entomologia, Experimentalis et Applica—Netherlands, 1958
Farm Chemicals—United States, 1894
International Pest Control—England, 1963
Japanese Journal of Applied Entomology and Zoology—1957
Journal of Agricultural and Food Chemistry—United States, 1953
Journal of Agricultural Science—England, 1905
Journal of the Association of Official Agricultural Chemists—United States, 1915
Journal of Economic Entomology—United States, 1908
Journal of the Science of Food and Agriculture—England, 1950
Journal of Soil Science—England, 1950
Pest Control—United States, 1933
Review of Applied Entomology—England, 1913
Soil Science—United States, 1916
Weed Research—England, 1961
Weed Science—United States, 1952
World Review of Pest control—England, 1962

b. Cellulose, Pulp, and Paper

Allgemeine Papier-Rundschau—Germany, 1921
Bulletin of the Association technique de l'industrie papetière—France, 1947
Bulletin of the Institute of Paper Chemistry—United States, 1930
Bulletin of the Textile Research Institute—Japan, 1928
Canadian Pulp and Paper—Canada, 1948
Das Papier—Germany, 1947
Chemiefasern—Germany, 1919
Forest Products Journal—United States, 1951
Holz ols Roh- und Werkstoff—Germany, 1937
Holzforschung—Germany, 1947
Indian Pulp and Paper—India, 1947
Journal of Forestry—United States, 1917
Journal of the Hokkaido Forest Products Research Institute—Japan, 1950
Journal of the Japanese Technical Association of the Pulp and Paper Industry—1947

TABLE 7. *(Continued)*

Journal of the Norwegian Paper, Pulp, Timber, and Wallboard Industries— Norway, 1947

La Papeterie—France, 1878

Paper and timber—Finland, 1921

Paper Industry—United States, 1919

Paper Industry—Soviet Union, 1926

Paper Maker and British Paper Trade Journal—England, 1891

Paper Trade Journal—United States, 1872

Papier und Druck—Germany, 1952

Pulp and Paper—United States, 1927

Pulp and Paper Magazine of Canada—Canada, 1903

Southern Pulp and Paper Manufacturer—United States, 1938

Svensk Papperstidning—Sweden, 1898

TAPPI—United States, 1918

Wood Science—United States, 1968

Zellstoff und Papier—Germany, 1952

c. Ceramics (Enamels and Glass); Cement (Concrete)

American Ceramic Society Bulletin—United States, 1922

Berichte Deutsche Keramische Gesellschaft—Germany, 1920

British Clayworker—England, 1893

Cement (Tsement)—Soviet Union, 1933

Cement and Lime Manufacture—England, 1928

Ceramic Age—United States, 1921

Ceramic Industry—United States, 1923

Ceramica—Italy, 1951

Ceramics—Japan, 1966

Ceramique Moderne—France, 1959

Concrete—United States, 1904

Enamelist Bulletin—United States, 1924

Glass—England, 1923

Glass and Ceramics (Stekla i Keramika)—Soviet Union, 1944

Glass Industry—United States, 1920

Glass Technology—England, 1960

Glastechnische Berichte—Germany, 1923

Industrie Ceramique—France, 1947

Journal of the American Ceramic Society—United States, 1918

Journal of the American Concrete Institute—United States, 1929

Journal of the British Ceramic Institute—England, 1964

Journal of the Ceramic Association of Japan—Japan, 1893

Journal of the Society of Glass Technology—England, 1917

Keramische Zeitschrift—Germany, 1948

Klai en Keramiek—Netherlands, 1951

Magazine of Concrete Research—England, 1949

TABLE 7. *(Continued)*

Nuovo Cimento—Italy, 1855
Physics and Chemistry of Glasses—England, 1960
Popular Ceramics—United States, 1949
Proceedings of the British Ceramic Society—England, 1964
Silicates Industriels—Belgium, 1929
Transactions of the British ceramic Society—England, 1901
Zement-Kalk-Gips—Germany, 1948

d. Cosmetics

American Perfumer and Aromatics—United States, 1906
Drug and Cosmetic Industry—United States, 1926
Industries de la parfumerie—France, 1946
International Perfumer—England, 1951
Journal of the Society of Cosmetic Chemists—United States, 1947
Perfumery and Essential Oil Record—England, 1910
Proceedings of the Scientific Section of the Toilet Goods Association—United
    States, 1944
Seifen - Öle-Fette-Wachse—Germany, 1874
Soap, Perfumery and Cosmetics—England, 1928

e. Environmental Chemistry

Chemosphere—Chemistry, Physics and Biology as Focused on Environmental
    Problems—England, 1972
Critical Reviews in Environmental Control—United States, 1970
Environment Reporter—United States, 1980
Environmental Science and Technology—United States, 1967
Journal of Environmental Sciences—United States, 1959
Science of the Total Environment—Netherlands, 1972

f. Explosives

Explosifs—Germany, 1948
Explosives Engineer—United States, 1923
Explosivstoffe—Germany, 1952
Mémorial des l'artillerie francaise—France, 1921
Memorial des poudres—France, 1882
Mémorial des services chimiques de l'état—France, 1882
Sprengtechnik Zeitschrift fuer die Wissenschaft, Technik und Wirtschaft der
    Sprengstoff und Züdmittel—Germany, 1952

g. Food Industries

American Brewer—United States, 1868
American Dairy Review—United States, 1939
American Journal of Enology and Viticulture—United States, 1950
American Miller and Processor—United States, 1873
American Soft Drink Journal—United States, 1905
American Society of Brewing Chemists, Proceedings—United States, 1941

TABLE 7. *(Continued)*

Association of Food and Drug Officials of the United States—United States, 1937
Bakers' and confectioners' Journal—United States, 1895
Baking Industry—United States, 1887
British Food Journal and Hygienic Review—England, 1899
Candy Industry and Confectioners Journal—United States, 1944
Cereal Chemistry—United States, 1924
Citrus Industry—United States, 1920
Coffee and Tea Industries and the Flavor field—United states, 1878
Confectionery Manufacture—England, 1955
Dairy Industries—England, 1936
Die Milchwissenschaft—Germany, 1946
Fermentatio—Belgium, 1939
Food and Drug Packaging—United States, 1959
Food Research—United States, 1936
Food Technology—United States, 1947
Ice Cream Review—United States, 1917
Journal of Agricultural and Food Chemistry—United States, 1953
Journal of the American Leather Chemists Association—United States, 1906
Journal of Animal Science—United States, 1942
Journal of the Association of Official Agricultural Chemists—United States, 1915
Journal of Dairy Research—England, 1929
Journal of Dairy Science—United States, 1917
Journal of Food Science—United States, 1936
Journal of the Science of Food and Agriculture—United States, 1950
Memoirs of the Research Institute of Food Science—Japan, 1951
Modern Packaging—United States, 1927
Poultry Science—United States, 1908
Quick Frozen Foods—United States, 1938
Rice Journal—United States, 1898
Wallerstein Laboratories Communications—United States, 1937
Zeitschrift fuer Lebensmittel Untersuchung und Forschung—Germany, 1882

h. Petroleum
Bulletin of the American Association of Petroleum Geologists—United States, 1917
Bulletin of the Geological Society of America—United States, 1899
Bulletin of the Japanese Petroleum Institute—Japan, 1959
Erdöl und Kohle—Germany, 1948
Geophysics—United States, 1930
Hydrocarbon Processing and Petroleum Refiner—United States, 1922
L'Industrie der Petrole—France, 1957
Journal of Energy Resources Technology—United States, 1979

TABLE 7. (Continued)

Journal of the Institute of Petroleum—England, 1914
Journal of Petroleum Technology—United States, 1949
Lubrication Engineering—United States, 1945
Oil and Gas Journal—United States, 1902
Petroleum—England, 1939
Petroleum Chemistry—Soviet Union, 1961
Petroleum Engineer—United States, 1929
Petroleum Processing—United States, 1946
Petroleum Refiner—United States, 1922
Proceedings of the American Petroleum Institute—United States, 1920
Society of Petroleum Engineers, Journal—United States, 1961
World Oil—United States, 1916
World Petroleum—United States, 1930

i. Protective Coatings and Inks

American Ink Maker—United States, 1923
American Paint Journal—United States, 1916
Chimie des Peintures—Belgium, 1938
Coatings—United States, 1937
Deutsche Farben Zeitschrift—Germany, 1947
Farbe und Lacke—Germany, 1895
Industrial finishing—United States, 1924
Journal of the American Oil Chemists' Society—United States, 1924
Journal of the Oil and Colour Chemists' Association—England, 1918
Oil, Paint and Drug Reporter—United States, 1871
Organic Finishing—United States, 1939
Paint—England, 1931
Paint Technology—England, 1936
Peintures, Pigments, Vernis—France, 1924

j. Textiles

American Dyestuff Reporter—United States, 1917
Bulletin de l'institut textile de France—France, 1947
Canadian Textile Journal—Canada, 1974
Chemiefasern—Germany, 1919
Faserforschung und Textiltechnik—Germany, 1950
Journal of Serviculture Science of Japan—Japan, 1930
Journal of the Society of Dyers and Colourists—England, 1884
Journal of the Society of Textile and Cellulose Industry—Japan, 1946
Journal of the Textile Institute—England, 1910
Melliand Textilberichte—Germany, 1947
Modern Textiles Magazine—United States, 1925
Rayonne et fibres synthétique—France, 1945
Reyon, Zellwolle, und andere Chemiefasern—Germany, 1919
Technology of the Textile Industry—Soviet Union, 1960

TABLE 7. *(Continued)*

Textil Rundschau—Switzerland, 1945
Textile Age—United States, 1937
Textile Bulletin—United States, 1933
Textile Industry—Soviet Union, 1941
Textile Institute and Industry—United States, 1963
Textile Organon—United States, 1930
Textile Research Journal—United States, 1930
Textile world—United States, 1888

k. Toxicology (see Agricultural Chemistry and Biochemistry earlier in this table)

Acta Pharmacoligica et toxicologia—Denmark, 1945
Advances in Chemical Toxicology—United States, 1963
American Medical Association Archives of Industrial Health—United States, 1950
American Journal of Hygiene—United States, 1921
Journal of Economic Entomology—United States, 1908
Journal of the Institution of Sanitary Engineers—England, 1905
Journal of the Royal Sanitary Institute—England, 1876
Journal of the Water Pollution Control Federation—United States, 1928
Journal of Wildlife Management—United States, 1937
Pesticides Monitoring Journal—United States, 1967
Pharmacology and Toxicology—Soviet Union, 1957
Toxicology and Applied Pharmacology—United States, 1959
World Review of Pest Control—England, 1962

the highest ranking scientific journal in the world. Scientific society journals, such as the American Chemical Society's *Chemical and Engineering News* and the American Association for the Advancement of Science's *Science*, which members receive automatically with payment of dues, also would be among the top ranking journals. These three journals are outstanding in their well written review articles and excellent news reporting, but they are not outstanding scientifically.

Tabulation of abstracts in *Chemical Abstracts* has been used frequently for preparing lists of significant journals. None of these studies attempted to separate or to evaluate the abstracts in terms of the quality of the contributions.

From 1907 through 1920, *Chemical Astracts* cited 178,000 papers, an average of 12,700 papers per year over the 14-year period. Over the following 10 years (1921–1930), 233,000 papers were cited, an average of 23,300 per year. From 1931 through 1940, the number of papers cited averaged 40,500 per year for a total of 405,000. During the next 10 years, 1941–1950, which indcluded the World War II years, the average dropped to 3300 per year for a total of 334,000 papers. In 1946, the 40 years of abstracting by Chemical Abstracts Service had resulted in a cumulative total of 1,000,000 abstracts. From 1951 through 1960, a total of 772,000 papers were abstracted, an average of 77,000 per year. By the end of this decade, in 1960, the cumulative total of abstracts of papers reached 2,000,000. During the next 10 years, 1961 through 1970, the average per year increased to 175,000 per year for a total of 1,750,000; the three millionth abstract was printed in 1967. During the 1970s, the annual average has been between 383,000 (1971–1975) and 500,000 (1976–1980); the four millionth abstract was printed in early 1972, less than five years since the three millionth, and eleven years since the two millionth. Baker[9] predicts the nine millionth abstract will appear in 1981. The number of papers abstracted currently (over the past five years, 1976–1980) is increasing at a 7% average annual rate.[9,10,44,62,82,94–99,105,114]

Journal articles represent 73% of the items cited in Chemical Abstracts (1980) as compared with 69% in 1975 and 75% in 1970. The number of conference proceedings articles abstracted increased from 4600 in 1970 to about 32,000 in 1975 and 35,000 in 1980; and the number of technical reports abstracted increased from 7200 in 1975 to over 16,000 in 1980. With the journal's rising production costs, increasing adoption of page charges, and long delays between receipt of papers and their publication, more and more papers will find their way into proceedings and symposia volumes. This trend has lowered the technical quality of papers.[7,27,40,47,48,68,75,80,88,90,107]

Table 8 gives the national origin of authors of journal articles abstracted in Chemical Abstracts over the period 1951–1980, and Table 9 shows the languages of the papers abstracted in Chemical Abstracts from 1961 through 1975; in addition to the major languages, "others" in the table include about 50 different languages.[9]

In the publication of Chemical Titles in 1961, Chemical Abstracts Service inventoried the journals they monitored for abstracting in Chemical Abstracts for Volumes 56–61 (1962–1964), inclusive. For the most productive 1000 journals in this period, 250 journals produced 50% of the abstracts, 1000 produced 75%, a second 1000 added only 10%, and a third 1000 contributed only 5% more. Interestingly, no volume of Chemical Abstracts contained abstracts from more than 5500 of the

TABLE 8.   Abstracts in Chemical Abstracts by National Origin of Authors, 1951–1980

Nation	Percent of Abstracts						
	1980	1975	1970	1965	1960	1956	1951
United States	26.2	25.8	27.4	28.5	27.1	28.4	36.6
Soviet Union	19.0	24.6	23.6	20.7	19.1	13.5	6.3
Japan	10.4	7.3	7.2	7.3	7.8	10.4	9.1
Germany (E & W)	7.0	6.8	6.5	8.5	7.8	8.4	7.9
United Kingdom	5.9	6.4	6.2	6.7	7.7	7.5	9.6
France	4.2	4.1	4.1	4.5	5.0	6.0	6.2
India	3.4	2.7	2.7	2.2	2.2	—	—
Canada	2.6	2.7	2.4	2.0	1.9	—	—
Italy	2.4	2.1	2.7	2.7	3.2	4.1	3.3
Others	18.9	17.5	17.2	16.9	18.2	21.7	24.3

TABLE 9.   Languages of Papers Abstracted in Chemical Abstracts 1961–1975

Language	Percent of Abstracts				
	1980	1975	1970	1965	1961
English	64.7	59.7	56.4	52.0	43.3
Russian	17.8	23.3	22.6	20.0	18.4
German	4.0	4.8	6.6	9.8	12.3
French	2.0	3.0	4.0	5.1	5.2
Japanese	5.2	3.0	3.4	4.0	6.3
Polish	1.1	1.2	1.1	1.9	1.9
Italian	0.8	0.7	1.4	1.9	2.4
Others	4.4	4.3	4.5	5.3	10.2

11,000 journals monitored during this period. The top ranking chemical journals in this study are listed in Table 10.[14]

According to Fischer,[36] 45% of abstracts relevant to analytical chemistry was in the analytical chemistry section of the 1965 Chemical Abstracts. Brooks and Smythe[23] estimated that over the 60-year period 1910–1970, only 40% was in the analytical chemistry section; they also estimated that the percentage of analytical papers fell within 5.6–7.5% of the total papers abstracted in Chemical Abstracts. Table 11 gives the

TABLE 10. Top Chemical Journals in Chemical Abstracts, 1962–1964

Rank	Journal Title
1	Nature
2	Dokl. Akad. Nauk SSSR
3	Compt. rend.
4	J. Am. Chem. Soc.
5	J. Chem. Phys.
6	J. Org. Chem.
7	Biochim. Biophys. Acta
8	Phys. Rev.
9	J. Chem. Soc.
10	Zh. Obshch. Khim.
11	Kogyo Kaguku Zasshi
12	J. Phys. Chem.
13	Anal. Chem.
14	Zh. Neorgan. Khim.
15	Zh. Eksperim i Teor. Fiz.
16	Biochem. J.
17	Zh. Fiz. Khim.
18	Proc. Soc. Exptl. Biol. Med.
19	Izv. Akad. Nauk SSSR Ser. Khim.
20	J. Appl. Phys.
21	Acta Chem. Scand.
22	Zh. Prikl. Khim.
23	Bull. Chem. Soc. Japan
24	Bull. soc. chim. France
25	Boll. soc. Ital. Biol. Sper.
26	Naturwissenschaften
27	Chem. Ind. (London)
28	Chem. Ber.
29	Can. J. Chem.

TABLE 11. National Origin of Analytical Papers, 1910–1970

Country	Percent of Papers						
	1910	1920	1930	1940	1950	1960	1970
Soviet Union	1.0	—	5.7	30.8	12.8	22.9	28.4
United States	28.9	25.3	18.8	25.0	19.9	20.7	17.7
Japan	1.0	—	2.6	2.9	5.0	7.7	7.7
Germany	31.9	19.9	26.3	10.5	6.7	4.8	6.1
United Kingdom	17.6	12.3	10.5	7.1	12.0	6.0	5.9
France	10.3	21.0	14.5	3.8	9.2	3.1	2.6
Italy	—	—	1.8	2.5	2.3	2.5	1.0

TABLE 12.   Languages in Which Analytical Papers Were Published, 1910–1970

	Percent of Papers						
Language	1910	1920	1930	1940	1950	1960	1970
English	50.6	40.4	32.8	34.1	35.4	34.2	30.3
Russian	1.0	—	5.7	30.8	17.8	22.9	28.4
German	32.9	21.7	27.6	12.6	9.2	6.7	8.1
Japanese	1.0	—	2.6	2.9	5.0	7.7	7.7
French	12.4	21.0	16.7	4.2	11.7	3.5	3.6
Italian	—	0.5	1.8	2.5	2.3	2.5	1.0

national source of the analytical papers, and Table 12 the language in which the papers were published (compared Table 12 with Table 9). Table 13 lists the number of articles and pages for the leading analytical journals from 1950 to 1970.

The following 13 journals, in alphabetical order, accounted for 30% of the 18,500 papers in analytical chemistry abstracted in the 1970 *Chemical Abstracts*:

Analytica Chimica Acta

Analytical Biochemistry

Analytical Chemistry

Japan Analyst

Journal of Electroanalytical Chemistry

Journal of the AOAC

Mikrochimica Acta

Nukleonika

Talanta

The Analyst

Zavodskaya Laboratoriya

Zeitschrift fuer Analytische Chemie

Zhurnal po Analiticheskoi Khimii

By counting abstracts in Section 78 (Inorganic Chemicals and Reactions) of the 1970 *Chemical Abstracts*, Woodburn[120] reported that 1260 abstracts were of articles from 235 journals but 609 came from only 12 journals; 26 journals accounted for 10 or more inorganic papers in 1970.

TABLE 13. Total Articles and Pages of Four Analytical Journals

Year	Analytical Chemistry		Analyst		Zeitschrift fuer Analytische Chemie		Zavodskaya Laboratoriya	
	Articles	Pages	Articles	Pages	Articles	Pages	Articles	Pages
1950	499	1593	142	693	58	1000	—	—
1955	690	2026	151	912	200	3200	—	—
1960	782	1930	184	928	220	3250	620	1400
1965	624	1812	128	760	252	3000	710	1450
1970	539	1880	163	1048	244	4800	705	1500

TABLE 14. Ranking of Inorganic Chemistry Journals

Journal (Nation[a]) (Language[b])	1970	1962	1958
Zh. Neorgan. Khim. (U.S.S.R.) (R)	1	1	1
J. Inorg. Nucl. Chem. (U.K., U.S.) (E)	2	3	8
Inorg. Chem. (U.S.) (E)	3	15	—
J. Chem. Soc. (U.K.) (E)	4	5	4
Chem. Communications (U.K.) (E)	5	—	—
Z. anorg. allgem. Chem. (G) (G)	6	4	3
Inorg. Nucl. Chem. Letters (U.K., U.S.) (E)	7	—	—
Bull. Chem. Soc. Japan (J) (E)	9	20	18
J. Am. Chem. Soc. (U.S.) (E)	9	2	2
Compt. rend. (F) (F)	10	6	6
Izvestiya Akad. Nauk SSSR (U.S.S.R.) (R)	11	—	—
Inorg. Chim. Acta (It) (It)	12	—	—
Dissertation Abstracts (U.S.) (E)	13	7	7
Bull. soc. chim. France (F) (F)	14	10	17
J. Indian Chem. Soc. (In) (E)	15	13	10
Total journals ranked	121	115	115

[a] G = Germany, J = Japan, F = France, It = Italy, In = India.

[b] R = Russian, E = English, G = German, F = France, It = Italian.

Table 14 gives Woodburn's ranking of the journals in 1970 and that of Trimble[114] in 1962 and in 1958.

In 1958, 22 journals (8%) accounted for 59% of the abstracts in Section 6. As Inorganic Chemistry did not appear until February, 1962, its impact and importance could not show up until the Woodburn study.[120]

Schwartz and Powers[99] counted the abstracts of biochemical articles published in the biological chemistry section of *Chemical Abstracts* for every tenth year from 1910 to 1960 for each journal in which the article was published, and rated the journals for each decade as shown in Table 15.

Languages in which the articles were published in the above study are shown in Table 16 (compare with Tables 9 and 12).

To determine the significant journals in the history of chemistry, chemical education, and chemical information science, J. B. Ayers[8] tabulated the sources of the abstracts in Section 1 of *Chemical Abstracts* for the period 1962–1969 and in Section 20 for 1979. In 1969, 41.5% were related to history, 38.5% to education, and 20.0% to information science. In 1979, the figures were 41.8%, 48.3%, and 9.9%, respectively. Tables 17, 18 and 19 list the journals in descending order of citations.

References cited in papers have gained popularity as a measure of a journal's importance, especially since the introduction of *Science Citation Index*. This measure is based on two assumptions: that all references are equal and that the journals examined are the most important ones for the study. The quality factor is lacking, just as it is in the other methods for evaluating a journal's importance. The reference citation method is very much weighted in favor of review journals and of journals which contain some review papers, and such journals generally are found high on the list of most cited journals. In general, journals with a high number of subscribers tend to fare well in lists of most cited journals.

In 1927, Gross and Gross[45] tabulated the references cited in the papers of the 1926 issues of *Journal of the American Chemical Society* to rank the importance of the cited journals. Since then, many papers have used the method of counting citations as a measure of journal importance. Martyn and Gilchrist[73] used the 'impact factor," the mean number of citations to articles in a given journal by papers published in other journals, obtained by dividing the number of times the journal is cited by the number of articles published by the journal in a given period. The impact factor was first proposed in 1963;[39] the average impact factor was found to be 1.9 in a 1965 study by ISI of 1963 papers. The *Journal of Molecular Biology* scored 7, meaning that for the 168 papers, each was cited an average of seven times; the *Journal of Biological Chemistry* had an impact factor of about 3.

Based on the 1969 *Science Citation Index*, ISI published in 1972 a list of the 50 most frequently cited journals,[6] from which the ranking given in Table 21 was taken. Another ISI study of the 1969 *Science Citation Index*[6] yielded the list given in Table 22, the ranking of journals most cited in *J. Am. Chem. Soc.*

TABLE 15. Rating of Biochemical Journals, 1910–1960

Journal	1960 Number	1960 Rank	1950 Number	1950 Rank	1940 Number	1940 Rank	1930 Number	1930 Rank	1920 Number	1920 Rank	1910 Number	1910 Rank
Nature	936	1	277	4	112	13	—	—	—	—	—	—
J. Biol. Chem.	661	2	524	2	401	2	266	2	202	2	18	16
Biochem. et Biophys. Acta	635	3	96	22	—	—	—	—	—	—	—	—
Proc. Soc. Exptl. Biol. Med.	607	4	598	1	587	1	55	23	—	—	20	13
Am. J. Physiol.	385	5	235	7	187	6	218	3	110	3	39	7
Compt. rend. soc. biol.	365	6	391	3	326	3	104	12	43	13	284	1
Diss. Abstr.	361	7	228	8	—	—	—	—	—	—	—	—
Biochem. J.	342	8	243	6	193	5	140	8	39	16	18	16
Arch. Biochem. Biophys.	312	9	192	9	—	—	—	—	—	—	—	—
Compt. rend.	274	10	128	18	—	—	129	11	77	5	84	4
Endocrinology	252	11	138	16	258	4	—	—	—	—	—	—
Boll. soc. ital. biol. sper.	88	—	254	5	144	9	202	4	—	—	—	—
Klin. Wochschr.	212	13	106	19	80	24	162	5	—	—	—	—
Biochem. Z.	—	—	—	—	97	20	474	1	205	1	201	2
Z. Immunitätsforsch	—	—	—	—	—	—	160	6	90	4	—	—
Z. physiol. Chem., Hoppe-Seyler's	—	—	—	—	87	22	138	9	34	20	184	3
Munch. med. Wochschr.	—	—	—	—	—	—	—	—	54	7	51	5

TABLE 16. Major Languages in Articles in Biochemistry Journals

Language	1960 Number	1960 Percent	1950 Number	1950 Percent	1940 Number	1940 Percent	1930 Number	1930 Percent	1920 Number	1920 Percent	1910 Number	1910 Percent
English	15,310	52.5	7,308	56.9	6,138	55.4	2,892	40.5	1,492	48.1	263	14.0
German	3,125	10.7	1,331	10.4	1,457	13.2	2,234	31.3	895	29.8	920	49.1
French	2,610	8.9	1,435	11.2	932	8.4	639	8.9	355	11.4	467	24.9
Japanese	2,168	7.4	334	2.6	439	4.0	283	4.0	47	1.5	—	—
Italian	1,645	5.6	837	6.5	557	5.0	475	6.7	122	3.9	166	3.4
Russian	1,522	5.2	512	4.0	639	5.8	144	2.0	—	—	—	—
Spanish	429	1.5	435	3.4	—	—	110	1.5	—	—	—	—
Polish	299	1.0	—	—	—	—	—	—	—	—	—	—
Dutch	—	—	—	—	—	—	—	—	60	1.9	—	—
Total Languages	46		21		27		22		17		17	

TABLE 17. History of Chemistry Journals, 1962–1969

Journal	Articles, 1962–1965		Articles, 1966–1969		Articles, 1969		Articles, 1979	
	Number	Percent	Number	Percent	Number	Percent	Number	Percent
Chem. Eng. News	282	20.4	359	21.5	110	24.0	86	9.2
J. Chem. Ed.	29	2.1	39	2.3	13	2.8	26	2.8
Chymia	20	1.5	43	2.6	—	—	—	—
Kagaku No Ryoiki	17	1.2	21	1.3	—	—	—	—
Chem. Weekblad	10	0.8	21	1.3	9	2.0	0	0
Ann. Sci.	9	0.7	19	1.1	—	—	—	—
Isis	8	0.6	17	1.0	—	—	—	—
Others	999	72.7	1154	68.9	326	71.2	798	88.0
Total	1374		1673		458		930	

TABLE 18. Education Journals

Journal	Articles, 1962–1965		Articles, 1966–1969		Articles, 1969		Articles, 1979	
	Numbers	Percent	Numbers	Percent	Numbers	Percent	Numbers	Percent
J. Chem. Ed.	438	47.1	674	39.5	147	34.6	284	26.5
Sch. Sci. Dev.	138	14.8	192	11.2	50	11.8	46	4.3
Khim. Shk.	29	3.1	97	5.7	68	16.0	100	9.3
Chem. Eng. News	77	8.4	27	1.6	—	—	—	—
Educ. Chem.	19	2.0	73	4.3	16	3.8	38	3.5
Chemistry	25	2.7	46	2.7	—	—	—	—
Others	205	21.9	595	35.0	144	33.8	605	56.5
Total	931		1704		425		1073	

TABLE 19. Chemical Information Science Journals

Journal	Articles, 1962–1965		Articles, 1966–1969		Articles, 1969		Articles, 1979	
	Number	Percent	Number	Percent	Number	Percent	Number	Percent
J. Chem. Doc. (J. Chem. Info. Comput. Sci.)	229	44.8	217	30.2	62	28.1	64	29.1
Am. Doc.	43	8.4	21	2.9	—	—	—	—
Advances in Chemistry	10	2.0	19	2.6	14	6.3	0	0
Noch. Dok.	8	1.6	10	1.4	—	—	—	—
Chem. Eng. News	10	2.0	1	0.1	—	—	—	—
Others	210	41.2	450	62.8	145	65.6	156	70.9
Total	510		718		221		220	

TABLE 20. Languages of the Articles in History, Education, and Information Science

Language	History			Education			Information Science		
	1962–1965	1966–1969	1979	1962–1965	1966–1969	1979	1962–1965	1966–1969	1979
	Percent	Percent	Percent	Percent	Percent	Percent	Percent	Percent	Percent
English	53.2	64.1	56.7	88.7	76.5	53.7	85.0	65.1	62.7
German	12.6	9.9	12.6	2.3	4.9	13.8	6.2	6.6	4.1
Russian	10.2	5.6	11.0	4.1	7.5	16.4	3.1	12.8	20.0
French	6.2	4.5	4.8	1.0	1.5	1.7	0.2	4.6	0.5
Japanese	4.7	2.9	3.8	1.0	1.8	3.1	2.0	0.3	5.0
Others	13.1	13.0	11.1	2.9	7.8	11.3	3.5	10.6	7.7

TABLE 21. ISI List of Most Cited Journals

Rank	Journal Title
1	*J. Am. Chem. Soc.*
2	*Phys. Rev.*
3	*J. Biol. Chem.*
4	*Nature*
6	*J. Chem. Soc.*
7	*Science*
8	*Biochim. et Biophys. Acta*
9	*Proceedings, Natl. Acad. of Sci. (U.S.)*
10	*Biochem. J.*
11	*Lancet*
12	*Phys. Rev. Letters*
13	*Compt. rend.*
14	*Am. J. Physiology*
15	*J. Org. Chem.*
16	*J. Applied Physics*
20	*Proceedings of the Royal Soc. (London)*
23	*J. Phys. Chem.*
24	*Ber.*
29	*Anal. Chem.*
32	*Biochem.*
44	*Trans. Faraday Soc.*
48	*Angewandte Chemie*

Pinski[91] introduced three journal measures:

Influence weight = Total references to a journal ÷ Total references from the journal to other journals

Influence per publication = Influence weight × References per publication

Total influence = Influence per publication × Number of publications

The citation matrix for the 107 chemical journals studied by Pinski was taken from the tapes of *Science Citation Index*, 1973. Table 23 lists the top journals by these influence measures, ranked by total influence under each of eight groups.

TABLE 22. Journals Most Cited in the Journal of the American Chemical Society

Rank	Journal Title
1	J. Am. Chem. Soc.
2	J. Chem. Soc.
3	J. Chem. Phys.
4	J. Org. Chem.
5	Tetrahedron Letters
6	Chem. Com.
7	Inorg. Chem.
8	J. Phys. Chem.
9	Ber.
10	Can. J. Chem.
11	Angewandte Chemie
12	Tetrahedron
13	Trans. Faraday Soc.
14	Ann.
15	J. Biol. Chem.
16	Bull. Chem. Soc. Japan
17	Helvetica Chim. Acta
18	Anal. Chem.
19	Acta. Crystall.
20	Accounts of Chem. Res.
21	Chem. Rev.

PUBLICATIONS OF SCIENTIFIC AND TECHNICAL SOCIETIES AND TRADE ASSOCIATIONS

As science emerged from alchemy, information was disseminated by visits or by correspondence among those who carried out investigations. This period was also marked by incunabula, that is, books and manuscripts. During the seventeenth century, as interest in natural philosophy grew, people of like interests began to form informal groups to discuss their work. These gradually evolved into more formal associations, such as learned societies. Many were short-lived, such as the Accademia dei Lincei and the Accademia del Cimento in Italy between 1600 and 1660. Ever since the French Academie des Sciences introduced its Journal des scavans in 1665 and the Royal Society (London) introduced its Philosophical Transactions a few months later, also in 1665, scientific and technical societies and trade associations have played a vital role in the communication of scientific knowledge with their journals.[21,22,27,42,56,63,82-85,93-97,109,121]

TABLE 23. Ranking of Journals by Total Influence

Journal	Influence Weight	References per Paper	Influence per Paper	Number of Papers	Total Influence
General Chemistry					
J. Am. Chem. Soc.	2.20	24.5	53.8	1813	97,612
J. Chem. Soc.	1.41	14.4	20.4	2962	60,277
Chem. Ber.	1.53	17.2	26.4	436	11,489
Can. J. Chem.	0.76	17.8	13.6	615	8,339
Bull. Chem. Soc., Japan	0.48	12.6	6.1	1013	6,189
Acta Chem. Scand.	0.99	12.6	12.5	492	6,160
Bull. soc. chim. France	0.40	19.5	7.9	708	5,572
Helv. Chim. Acta	1.10	16.8	18.4	273	5,016
Chem. Rev.	0.71	209.0	148.6	27	4,011
Ann.	0.97	16.2	15.7	239	3,748
Accnt. Chem. Res.	1.18	44.5	52.5	63	3,306
Rec. trav. chim.	1.66	13.2	21.9	136	2,973
Coll. Czech. Chem. Com.	0.43	11.8	5.1	499	2,535
Zh. Obs. Kh.	0.44	11.2	4.9	478	2,366
Chem. Soc. Rev.	1.05	79.5	83.2	22	1,831
J. Chem. Ed.	0.61	5.5	3.3	427	1,426
Monats. Chem.	0.46	11.5	5.3	216	1,136
Physical Chemistry					
Acta Cryst.	2.58	11.1	28.6	796	22,805
J. Phys. Chem.	1.52	18.9	28.7	639	18,358
J. Mol. Spect.	2.38	13.7	32.6	200	6,520
Spect. Acta	1.55	15.3	23.7	245	5,809
Z. Phys. Chem.	1.21	11.6	14.0	274	3,847
Ber. Bun. Ges.	1.24	16.7	20.6	168	3,462

TABLE 23. Ranking of Journals by Total Influence

Journal	Influence Weight	References per Paper	Influence per Paper	Number of Papers	Total Influence
Theor. Chim.	1.32	19.5	25.7	126	3,241
J. Quan. Spect.	1.87	13.2	24.7	131	3,233
J. Electrochem. Soc.	0.69	11.3	7.8	395	3,069
Faraday Dis.	3.17	19.6	62.1	41	2,545
J. Chim. phys.	0.69	15.1	10.4	223	2,330
Z. Krist.	2.28	10.5	23.9	85	2,030
Analytical Chemistry					
Anal. Chem.	0.75	20.9	15.6	603	9,401
J. Chromat.	0.53	10.7	5.6	631	3,553
J. AOAC	1.04	5.1	5.3	321	1,692
Anal. Chim. Acta	0.51	8.9	4.5	344	1,555
J. Chrom. Sci.	0.94	11.9	11.2	118	1,317
Z. anal. chem.	0.76	6.4	4.9	249	1,210
Analyst	0.82	9.7	7.9	131	1,039
Organic Chemistry					
J. Org. Chem.	0.78	17.0	13.3	1266	16,812
Tetrahedron Lett.	1.20	8.5	10.1	1406	14,229
Tetrahedron	0.67	18.6	12.5	552	6,894
J. Organomet. Chem.	0.24	21.6	5.2	798	4,126
Carbohydrate Res.	0.22	14.7	3.3	361	1,195
Zh. Org. Kh.	0.18	10.8	2.0	489	973
J. Hetero. Chem.	0.29	11.0	3.2	229	733
Synthesis	0.14	18.5	2.6	197	512
Inorganic and Nuclear Chemistry					
Inorg. Chem.	0.87	19.9	7.2	677	11,651

J. Inorg. Nuc.	0.47	12.1	5.6	632	3,546
Z. anorg. Chem.	0.86	12.6	10.8	280	3,027
Zh. Neorg. Kh.	0.33	7.6	2.5	589	1,467
Inorg. Nucl.	0.48	7.3	3.5	263	923
Coord. Chem. Res.	0.16	176.8	27.6	26	719
Chemical Engineering					
Angew. Chem.	1.64	25.1	41.1	295	12,122
Ind. Eng. Chem.	1.53	10.4	16.0	236	3,774
Chem. Ind. London	1.36	6.2	8.4	282	2,377
J. Am. Oil Chemists	0.61	11.7	7.2	151	1,084
J. prak. Chem.	0.51	12.0	6.1	155	949
J. Appld. Chem.	0.66	8.7	5.7	94	536
Chem. ind.	0.26	15.0	3.9	101	395
Polymer Chemistry					
J. Poly. Sci.	0.54	12.0	6.4	897	5,741
Makromol. Chem.	0.38	12.2	4.7	294	1,367
Vyso. Soed.	0.20	8.5	1.7	665	1,137
Macromol. Chem.	0.39	16.9	6.6	152	1,003
J. Appl. Poly.	0.29	10.3	3.0	318	944
Polymer	0.37	12.4	4.6	127	589
J. Macro. Sci.	0.14	20.5	2.9	151	436
Eur. Polym. J.	0.19	12.7	2.5	134	331
Polymer J.	0.15	14.6	2.2	114	255
Polym. Eng. Sci.	0.18	11.7	2.2	64	138

TABLE 24. Some U.S. Scientific, Technical, and Professional Societies and Their Publications

American Academy of Arts and Sciences, 280 Newton St., Brookline, Mass. 02146: Founded during the American Revolution.

Daedulus—quarterly (1846). History, culture, and science related to world affairs.

American Academy of Forensic Sciences, 44 Medical Dr., Salt Lake City, Utah 84113: Founded 1948.

Journal of Forensic Sciences—quarterly (1955).

American Association for Cancer Research, 7701 Burholme Ave., Phila., Pa. 19111: Founded 1907.

Cancer Research—monthly (1941).

American Association for Textile Technology, Inc., 101 W. 21st St., New York, N.Y. 10001: Founded 1934.

Modern Textiles—monthly (1956).

American Association for the Advancement of Science, 1515 Massachusetts Ave., N.W., Washington, D.C. 20005: Founded 1847.

Science—weekly (1801).

Science Books: A Quarterly Review (1965).

American Association of Cereal Chemists, Inc., 1821 University Ave., St. Paul, Minn. 55104: Founded 1915.

Cereal Chemistry—bimonthly (1934).

Cereal Science Today—monthly (1956).

American Association of Clinical Chemists, Ardmore Station, Winston-Salem, N.C. 27103: Founded 1948.

Clinical Chemistry—monthly (1955).

American Association of Textile Chemists and Colorists, Research Triangle Park, N.C. 27709: Founded 1921.

Textile Chemist and Colorist—monthly (1969).

The American Ceramic Society, Inc., 4055 N. High St., Columbus, Ohio 43214: Founded 1899.

Journal of the American Ceramic Society—monthly (1918).

American Chemical Society, 1155 16th St., N.W., Washington, D.C. 20036: Founded—1876.

Analytical Chemistry—monthly (1929).

Journal of the American Chemical Society—biweekly (1879).

Biochemistry—biweekly (1962).

Journal of Medicinal Chemistry—monthly (1958).

Inorganic Chemistry—monthly (1962).

Journal of Organic Chemistry—biweekly (1936).

Journal of Agricultural and Food Chemistry—bimonthly (1953).

Journal of Chemical and Engineering Data—quarterly (1956).

Macromolecules—bimonthly (1968).

Accounts of Chemical Research—monthly (1968).

Chemical Reviews—bimonthly (1901).

Journal of Physical Chemistry—biweekly (1897).

148

TABLE 24. *(Continued)*

Journal of Chemical Information and Computer Sciences—quarterly (1961).

Industrial and Engineering Chemistry—
   Fundamentals—quarterly (1962).
   Process Design and Development—quarterly (1962).
   Product Research and Development—quarterly (1962).
Environmental Science and Technology—monthly (1967).
Chemical and Engineering News—weekly (1923).
Chemistry—monthly (1928) (changed to *SciQuest* in 1979).
Chemical Technology—monthly (1970) (changed to *CHEMTECH* in 1979).

American Concrete Institute, 22400 W. Seven Mile Rd., Detroit, Mich. 48219: Founded 1905.
   Journal of the American Concrete Institute—monthly (1905).

American Dairy Science Association, 113 Neil St., Champaign, Ill., 61820: Founded 1906.
   Journal of Dairy Science—monthly (1918).

American Federation of Information Processing Societies, Inc., 210 Summit Ave., Montvale, N.J. 07645: Founded 1961.
   Proceedings of the Joint Computer Conferences—semiannual (1963).

American Institute of Aeronautics and Astronautics, 1290 Avenue of the Americas, New York, N.Y. 10019: Founded 1963.
   AIAA Journal—monthly (1963).

American Institute of Biological Sciences, Inc., 3900 Wisconsin Ave., N.W., Washington, D.C. 20016: Founded 1947.
   BioScience—semimonthly (1951).

American Institute of Chemical Engineers, 345 E. 47th St., New York, N.Y. 10017: Founded 1908.
   Chemical Engineering Progress—monthly (1905).
   AIChE Journal—bimonthly (1955).
   International Chemical Engineering—quarterly (1961)

The American Institute of Chemists, Inc., 79 Madison Ave., New York, N.Y. 10016: Founded 1923.
   The Chemist—monthly (1925).

American Institute of Industrial Engineers, Inc., 345 E. 47th St., New York, N.Y. 10017: Founded 1948.
   Industrial Engineering—monthly (1969).

American Institute of Mining, Metallurgical and Petroleum Engineers, Inc., 345 E. 47th Street, New York, N.Y. 10017: Founded 1871.
   Mining Engineering—monthly (1949).
   Journal of Metals—monthly (1949).
   Journal of Petroleum Engineering—(1949).

The American Institute of Nutrition, 9650 Rockville Pike, Bethesda, Md. 20014: Founded 1928.
   Journal of Nutrition—monthly.

TABLE 24. *(Continued)*

American Institute of Physics, Inc., 335 E. 45th Street, New York, N.Y. 10017: Founded 1931.
>   *Review of Scientific Instruments*—monthly (1931).
>   *Journal of Chemical Physics*—semimonthly (1918).

The American Leather Chemists Association, Campus Station, Cincinnati, Ohio 45221: Founded 1903.
>   *Journal*—monthly (1906).

The American Microchemical Society, 170 Tabor Rd., Morris Plains, N.J. 07950: Founded 1935.
>   *Microchemical Journal*—quarterly (1956).

Americal Oil Chemists' Society, 35 E. Wacker Dr., Chicago, Ill. 60601: Founded 1909.
>   *Journal*—monthly (1924).

American Petroleum Institute, 1801 K St., N.W., Washington, D.C. 20006: Founded 1919.
>   *Petroleum Today*—quarterly (1960).

American Pharmaceutical Assocn., 2215 Constitution Ave., N.W., Washington, D.C. 20037: Founded 1852.
>   *Journal*—monthly (1940).
>   *Journal of Pharmaceutical Sciences*—monthly (1912).

The American Philosophical Society, 104 S. 5th St., Phila., Pa. 19106: Founded 1769.
>   *Transactions*—annual (1910).
>   *Proceeding*—bimonthly (1857).

American Society for Information Science, 1140 Connecticut Ave., N.W., Washington, D.C. 20036: Founded 1937.
>   *Journal*—bimonthly (1950).

American Society for Metals, Metals Park, Ohio 44073: Founded 1913.
>   *Metal Progress*—monthly (1869).

American Society of Agronomy, Inc., 677 S. Segoe Rd., Madison, Wis. 53711: Founded 1907.
>   *Agronomy Journal*—bimonthly (1909).

American Society of Biological Chemists, 9650 Rockville Rd., Bethesda, Md. 20014: Founded 1906.
>   *Journal of Biological Chemistry*—semimonthly (1905).

Association of Official Analytical Chemists, Box 540 Benjamin Franklin Station, Washington, D.C. 20044: Founded 1884.
>   *Journal*—bimonthly (1919).

Federation of Societies for Paint Technology, 121 S. Broad St., Philadelphia, Pa. 19107: Founded 1922
>   *Journal of Paint Technology*—monthly (1929).

Institute of Food Technologists, 221 N. LaSalle St., Chicago, Ill. 60601: Founded 1939.
>   *Food Technology*—monthly (1947).

TABLE 24. *(Continued)*

Journal of Food Science—bimonthly (1936).
National Association of Corrosion Engineers, 2400 W. Loop South, Houston, Tex. 77027: Founded 1943.
  Corrosion—monthly (1945).
The Society for the History of Technology, Case Western Reserve University, Cleveland, Ohio 44106: Founded 1958.
  Technology and Culture—quarterly (1960).
Society of Cosmetic Chemists, 50 E. 41st St., New York, N.Y. 10017: Founded 1945.
  Journal—monthly (1950).
Society of Plastics Engineers, Inc., 656 W. Putnam Ave., Greenwich, Conn. 06830: Founded 1941.
  Journal—monthly (1945).
  Polymer Engineering and Science—bimonthly (1961).
The Society of the Sigma Xi, 155 Whitney Ave., New Haven, Conn. 06510: Founded 1886.
  American Scientist—bimonthly (1913).
Textile Research Institute, P.O. Box 625, Princeton, N.J. 08540
  Journal—monthly (1930).

Table 24 lists the publications of some U.S. scientific and technical societies and trade associations. Table 25 lists the publications of some international and other national scientific and technical societies and their publications.

TRENDS IN JOURNAL PUBLICATION

Despite the fact that the introduction of new journals exceeds the demise of older ones and that approximately 30,000 scientific and technological journals are published currently, there are many problems facing both the journal publishers and their clientele.

Inflationary forces have plagued publishers with rising costs of paper, printing, postage, and labor, which, in turn, have been passed on to subscribers. Foreign journal subscriptions, over the past few years, have had a far greater inflation because of currency exchanges unfavorable to American libraries. A survey by Clasquin and Cohen[30] of 294 journals (123 in physics, 149 in chemistry, and 22 in both) showed an average price of $165.71 for physics journals and $148.81 for chemistry journals in 1976. Relative to 1967 prices of $48.55 for physics and $50.23 for chemistry journals, the average cost of physics journals in 1976 was greater by a factor of 3.41 and that of chemistry journals by 2.96; the

TABLE 25. Some International and Other Nationl Scientific and Technical Societies and Their Publications

---

UNESCO

United Nations Educational, Scientific and Cultural Organization, 7/9 Place de Fontenoy, Paris 7e, France. Founded in 1945, one of the objectives of UNESCO under its Natural Sciences programs is the transfer of scientific and technical information. Reports are issued on needs for such information, the use of computers in information processing, the establishment of a world network, and documents and publications of interest.

Bulletin for Libraries—monthly

ICSU

International Council of Scientific Unions, 7 Via Cornelio Celso, Rome 00161, Italy. Founded in 1931, it succeeded the International Research Council, founded in 1919, as coordinator of international efforts in various branches of science and technology. One of these efforts is centered in the International Union of Pure and Applied Chemistry (IUPAC). Founded in 1919, IUPAC has made major contributions in the field of nomenclature. IUPAC publishes the following:

Pure and Applied Chemistry
Comptes Rendus
Information Bulletin

ETC

European Translation Centre, Doelenstraat 101, Delft, The Netherlands. Founded in 1960, ETC is an international clearinghouse for translations in science and technology, especially from Slav, Chinese, and Japanese languages into Western languages. ETC draws from a pool of over 120,000 translations, and its catalogs refer to over 500,000 translations available elsewhere.

World Index of Scientific Translations (1967)

Argentina

Asociacion Quimica Argentina (Argentine Chemical Association). Founded in 1912.

Anales de la Asociacion Quimica Argentina
Industria y Quimica

Australia

Royal Australian Chemical Institute. Founded 1917.

Proceedings—monthly
Reviews of Pure and Applied Chemistry—quarterly

TABLE 25. *(Continued)*

Belgium

Sociéte Royale des Sciences. Founded 1835.
 Bulletin—bimonthly
 Memoires—annually

Brazil

Associacao Brasileira de Quimica (Brazilian Chemical Association). Founded in 1922.
 Anais, Boletini—monthly
 Revista—bimonthly

Bulgaria

Bulgarian Academy of Sciences. Founded 1869.
 Comptes Rendus, Spisanie—monthly

Canada

Royal Society of Canada. Founded 1882.
 Canadian Pharmaceutical Association. Founded 1907.
 Canadian Pharmaceutical Journal—monthly.
Royal Canadian Institute. Founded 1849.
 Transactions
National Research Council of Canada. Founded 1916.
 Canadian Journal of Chemistry
 NRC Review

China

Chinese Academy of Sciences. Founded 1928.
 Science Monthly
 Acta Scientia Sinica—quarterly
Chinese Chemical Society. Founded 1932.
 Chemical Bulletin

Czechoslovakia

Czechoslovak Academy of Sciences. Founded in 1952
 Collection of Czechoslovak Chemical Communications

Finland

Chemical Society of Finland. Founded 1891.
 Finska Kemistsamfundets Meddelanden
 Suomen Kemistiseuran Tiedonantoja
Finnish Chemical Society. Founded 1919.
 Suomen Kemistilenti—monthly.

TABLE 25. *(Continued)*

***

France

L'Institut de France. Founded 1795.
    Société de Chimie Biologique. Founded 1914.
        Bulletin—monthly
    Société de Chimie Industrielle. Founded 1917.
    Société Chimique de France. Founded 1857.
        Bulletin—monthly

Germany

Gesellschaft Deutscher Chemiker. Founded 1946.
    Angewandte Chemie—monthly
    Chemie-Ingenieur-Technik—monthly
    Chemische Berichte—monthly
Verein der Zellstoff- und Papier-Chemiker und Ingenieure. Founded 1905.
    Das Papier
Chemisches Gesellschaft in der DDR. Founded 1953.
Germany Academy of Sciences. Founded 1700.

Great Britain

The Royal Society. Founded 1660.
    Philosophical Transactions
    Proceedings
British Association for the Advancement of Science. Founded 1831.
    The Advancement of Science—quarterly.
British Society for the History of Science. Founded 1946.
    British Journal for the History of Science—semiyearly
The Biochemical Society. Founded 1911.
    The Biochemical Journal—biweekly
Chemical Society. Founded 1841.
    Journal of the Chemical Society
    Chemical Communications
    Annual Reports
    Quarterly Reviews
    Current Chemical Papers
    Chemistry in Britain
Faraday Society. Founded 1903.
    Transactions—monthly
    Discussions—semiyearly
    Symposia—annual
Oil and Colour Chemists' Association. Founded 1918.
    Journal—monthly
Royal Institute of Chemistry. Founded 1877.
    Chemistry in Britain—monthly
    Education in Chemistry—bimonthly

TABLE 25. *(Continued)*

Society for Analytical Chemistry. Founded 1874.
    The Analyst—monthly
    Analytical Abstracts—monthly
    Proceedings—monthly
Society of Chemical Industry. Founded 1881.
    Chemistry and Industry—weekly
    Journal of Applied Chemistry—monthly
    Journal of the Science of Food and Agriculture—monthly
    Annual Report on the Progress of Applied Chemistry
The Institute of Chemical Engineers. Founded 1922.
    Transactions—monthly
    The Chemical Engineer—monthly
The Plastics Institute. Founded 1931.
    Transactions and *Journal*—bimonthly
Society of Dyers and Colourists. Founded 1884.
    Journal—monthly
Society of Glass Technology. Founded 1916.
    Glass Technology—bimonthly
    Physics and Chemistry of Glasses—bimonthly
Textile Institute. Founded 1910.
    Journal of the Textile Institute—monthly

Hungary

Hungarian Academy of Sciences. Founded 1825.
    Acta Chimica—16 issues per year
    Acta Biochimica et Biophysica—quarterly
Hungarian Chemical Society. Founded 1907.
    Magyar Kemiai Folyoirat—monthly

India

Indian Chemical Society. Founded 1924
    Indian Journal of Applied Chemistry—bimonthly
    Journal of Indian Chemical Society—monthly
National Academy of Sciences. Founded 1930.
    Proceedings, A; Physical Sciences—monthly
    Proceedings, B; Biological Sciences—monthly

Ireland

Royal Irish Academy. Founded 1786.
    Proceedings, Section B (Biology, Chemistry, and Geology)—monthly
The Institute of Chemistry of Ireland. Founded 1950.
    Proceedings—monthly

Israel

Israel Academy of Sciences and Humanities
    Proceedings—monthly

TABLE 25. *(Continued)*

Association for the Advancement of Science in Israel. Founded 1953.
    Proceedings of Congress of Scientific Societies—monthly
Biochemical Society of Israel. Founded 1958.
Israel Chemical Society. Founded 1952.
National Council for Research and Development
    Israel Journal of Chemistry—bimonthly

Italy

Accademia Nazionale Dei Lincei. Founded 1603.
    Rendiconti della Classe di Scienze Fisiche—monthly
Società Chimica Italiana. Founded 1919.
    Gazetta Chimica Italiana—monthly
    Annali di Chimica—monthly
    La Chimica e l'Industria—monthly

Japan

Japan Academy. Founded 1879
    Proceedings—monthly
Japanese Biochemical Society. Founded 1926.
    Journal of Biochemistry—monthly
The Society of Polymer science. Founded 1951.
    Chemistry of High Polymers—monthly
Japan Society of Analytical Chemists. Founded 1952.
    Japan Analyst—monthly
Japanese Chemical Abstracting Society. Founded 1926.
Chemical Society of Japan. Founded 1878.
    Kagaku to Kogyo—monthly
    Nippon Zassi—monthly
    Kogyo Kagaku Zassi—monthly
    Bulletin—monthly
Japan Oil Chemist Society. Founded 1954.
    Journal—monthly
Government Chemical Industrial Research Institute. Founded 1900.
    Hohkoku—monthly
Textile Research Institute
    Bulletin—semimonthly

Mexico

Academia Nacional de Ciencias. Founded 1884.
    Revista—bimonthly
Instituto Mexicano de Ingenieros Quimicos. Founded 1950.
    Revista—bimonthly

The Netherlands

Royal Netherlands Chemical Society. Founded 1903.

TABLE 25. *(Continued)*

Chemisch Weekblad—weekly
Recueil des travaux chimiques des Pays-Bas—monthly.

New Zealand

The Royal Society of New Zealand. Founded 1867.
Transactions—monthly
Proceedings—annual

Norway

Norwegian Chemical Society. Founded 1893.
Tidsskrift for Kjemi—monthly

Poland

Polish Biochemical Society. Founded 1958.
Postephy Biochemii—quarterly
Polish Chemical Society. Founded 1919.
Roczniki Chemii—monthly

Romania

Society of Physical and Chemical Sciences. Founded 1964.
Revista di Fizica si chimia, seria A, B—monthly

South Africa

South African Chemical Institute. Founded 1912.
Journal—biannually
The South African Industrial Chemist—monthly

Spain

Asociacion Nacional de Quimicos de Espana. Founded 1945.
Quimica e Industria—bimonthly

Sweden

Swedish Institute for Textile Research Founded 1943.
Meddelanden fran Svenska Textilforsknings-institutet

Turkey

The Chemical Society of Turkey. Founded 1919.
Kimya ve Sanayi (Chemistry and Industry)—quarterly

Soviet Union

Academy of Sciences of the U.S.S.R. Founded 1725.
All-Union Council of Scientific and Engineering Societies. Among its 21 scientific and engineering societies are D. I. Mendeleev All-Union Chemical Society, Scientific, and Engineering Society of the Oil and Gas Industry. Numerous publications.

consumer price index, by comparison, rose by a factor of 1.70 over this 10-year period.

According to Brown,[25] the inflationary index for chemistry and physics journals was higher than for journals in other subjects, as shown in Table 26.

A more direct picture of the appreciation of journal subscription prices is given in Table 27. These journals were selected because of their high value to and popularity with scientists in an industrial research and development environment. It is to be noted that the journals issued by the AAAS and the American Chemical Society are priced relatively low in comparison to the subscription prices of commercial publishers, such as Wiley (*J. Poly. Sci.*) and Pergamon (*Tetrahedron*). The inflationary index for these nine journals based on 1973 is shown in Table 28.

The inflationary index is not a completely fair measure of a journal's subscription price increase. A better measure would be the subscription price per page, providing the words per page is constant. For example, between 1959 and 1969, the subscription price of 20 physics journals increased by 202%, and during this same period the number of pages in these journals increased by 147%.[74]

Increasing subscription prices, warranted or not, have resulted in decreasing subscriptions by individuals and by libraries. Since the early 1970s, most library budgets have experienced a budgetary squeeze, that is, advances in budgets have not paralleled the increasing costs of books and journals. Indeed, many budgets have been reduced, and, consequently so have the number of duplicate subscriptions, and marginal journals have been canceled. Libraries have begun to depend on photocopies of journal articles obtained through loans from such libraries as

TABLE 26.   1976 Inflationary Index of Journals in Different Areas

Subject	Average Price ($)	Inflationary Index[a]
Chemistry and Physics	86.72	354.2
Medicine	47.47	244.9
Engineering	31.87	317.7
Business and Economics	16.98	225.2
Political Science	13.09	211.8
Fine and Applied Arts	12.42	185.1
History	11.94	215.6
Literature and Language	11.60	215.6

[a]Relative to consumer price index of 100 for 1967 and 170.5 for 1976. The inflationary index was derived using the following formula: (1976 price/1967 price) × 100.

TABLE 27.   Prices of Selected Chemical Journals, 1973–1978

Journal	Price ($)					
	1973	1974	1975	1976	1977	1978
J. Chromatography	392	429	624	699	715	923
Liebig's Annalen	134	188	179	187	184	194
Chem. Ber.	166	239	242	244	241	288
Tetrahedron[a]	360	360	798	798	1083	1083
J. Am. Chem. Soc.	66	66	88	112	112	136
J. Org. Chem.	60	60	80	104	104	104
J. Poly. Sci.[b]	350	375	400	425	450	485
J. Chem. Soc.[c]	640	660	684	790	895	—
Science	20	30	40	50	50	60

[a]Multiple-year subscription price.

[b]Price for the five-part package.

[c]Price for the six-part package.

the National Library of Medicine and the Center for Research Libraries in Chicago. What effect the new copyright law, which became effective January 1, 1978, will have on library budgets and interlibrary loans must await the future. One thing is clear: whatever affects a library's ability to enter subscriptions eventually must affect the publisher.[50,68,70,75,88,107]

Journal publishers, especially the learned societies, have reacted to some of the growing problems.[118] To counter the increasing receipt of papers, some journals have been divided into parts or separates. For example, the Canadian Journal of Research, which was introduced in 1929 with Volume 1, changed to a two-part journal in 1941, part A/B being Physical and Chemical Sciences and part C/D Botanical and Zoological Sciences; then in 1951, it was issued in six parts (A, Physical Science; B, Chemical Science; C, Botanical Science; D, Zoological Science; E, MedicalScience; and F, Technology); in 1956, each of these became independent journals with titles like Canadian Journal of Chemistry.

The American Chemical Society (ACS) is undoubtedly the outstanding publisher of scientific and technological journals in the world, with its stable of 21 society journals, two divisional journals, and a variety of publications from Chemical Abstracts Service.[109] It began in 1876 with a single publication, Proceedings of the American Chemical Society, with a 500 print order. In 1879, the name was changed to Journal of the

TABLE 28.   Inflationary Index of Journals in Table 27

Journal	Inflationary Index[a]
J. Chromatography	235
Liebig's Annalen	145
Chem. Ber.	173
Tetrahedron	301
J. Am. Chem. Soc.	206
J. Org. Chem.	173
J. Poly. Sci.	139
J. Chem. Soc.	140
Science	300

[a]The inflationary index was derived using the following formula: (1978 price/1973 price) ×
100.

American Chemical Society (JACS), and the journal began to appear monthly. The Journal of Analytical and Applied Chemistry merged with JACS in 1893. The second ACS journal, Chemical Abstracts, appeared in 1907. The third, Journal of Industrial and Engineering Chemistry, which appeared in 1909, was renamed Industrial and Engineering Chemistry (I & EC) in 1922, and, in 1923, began to be issued in two parts: Industrial and News. In 1924, Chemical Reviews was taken over by ACS. The Journal of Chemical Education was started in 1924 as a publication of the ACS Division of Chemical Education, and Rubber Chemistry and Technology was issued in 1928 by the ACS Division of Rubber Chemistry.

In 1929, the Analytical Edition of Industrial and Engineering Chemistry was established, and in 1933 ACS took over the publication of the Journal of Physical Chemistry (founded in 1896 by W. D. Bancroft of Cornell University). The Journal of Agricultural and Food Chemistry was established in 1953, and in 1955 ACS acquired the Journal of Organic Chemistry (first introduced in 1936).

In 1956, the three parts of Industrial and Engineering Chemistry became three separate journals: Industrial and Engineering Chemistry, Chemical and Engineering News, and Analytical Chemistry. Also in 1956, ACS introduced the Journal of Chemical and Engineering Data. The American Chemical Society introduced the Journal of Chemical Documentation in 1961[101] (which was renamed in 1975 Journal of

Chemical Information and Computer Sciences), and *Biochemistry* and *Inorganic Chemistry* in 1962.

ACS acquired the *Journal of Medicinal and Pharmaceutical Chemistry* in 1961 and renamed it *Journal of Medicinal Chemistry* in 1963.

In 1962 *Industrial and Engineering Chemistry* spawned three new journals: *I & EC Fundamentals, I & EC Process Design and Development,* and *I & EC Product Research and Development.*

Chemistry, which was founded in 1927 as *Chemistry Leaflet,* was acquired by the ACS in 1944 (its name was changed to *Sci Quest* in 1979). *Environmental Science and Technology* was introduced in 1965, *Accounts of Chemical Research* in 1967, and *Macromolecules* in 1968.

In 1970, *Industrial and Engineering Chemistry* ceased publication and was replaced with *Chemical Technology* in 1971 (now *CHEMTECH).* As a consequence of a cooperative program of the National Bureau of Standards, the American Institute of Physics, and ACS, the *Journal of Physical and Chemical Reference Data* was introduced in 1972. In 1975, all ACS research journals were issued also on microfiche and microfilm.

Until the 1950s, journal publishers undertook no research and development toward new publishing methods. The American Chemical Society initiated a research project in 1957 to investigate new developments in the graphic arts, such as the Photon photocomposition device, with the final goal being computer-assisted photocomposition.[64] The feasibility of this objective was realized in 1966 with the production of the *Journal of Chemical Documentation,* the first journal to be produced by computer-aided typesetting. Other journals produced by this method were *Journal of Chemical and Engineering Data* and the quarterlies *I & EC Product Research and Development* and *I & EC Process Design and Development.* All ACS publications were produced by photocomposition by 1976. Development work continues in the area of typewriter composition of journals, miniprint pages, and new formats, such as a dual journal: one journal with the full paper and one with a synopsis (two pages or less) of the full paper.[65–67, 100]

Although the American Chemical Society has decided for the time being not to publish a synopsis or dual journal, other organizations are now using this approach. With the January 1974 issue, *Chemie-Ingenieur-Technik* began the first synopsis journal by the Gesellschaft Deutscher Chemiker (West German Chemical Society), Verein Deutsche Ingenieure, and Deutsche Gesellschaft fuer Chemisches Apparatwesen as joint publishers of the biweekly. The synopsis in this journal, although generally one page, is rather detailed. The full manuscript is available only on Microfiche.

In 1977, the Chemical Society (London) introduced its *Journal of*

Chemical Research, which prepares synopses of the manuscripts it accepts. The synopses are published in the journal, and readers who wish to acquire the original paper are sent, on request, the microfilm, microfiche, or microprint form. The Société Chimique de France and the Société de Chimique-Physique also have been planning to publish a synopsis journal.[5,27,40,58,59]

The synopsis journal may not be the final answer, but it does succeed in reducing materially the cost of producing a journal by at least one-half to one-quarter. Furthermore, it reduces materially the number of words that must be read to maintain current awareness of the evolving literature. Libraries benefit by having the archival journal in microfilm form, as the microfilm can be stored in 5% of the space required by the hard copy journal.[57,67,80,112] Microform readers and printers, unfortunately, are not yet of the quality that encourages reading for any extended time. Although we may expect improvements to be made, it is doubtful whether microform readers will ever equal the ease of reading hard copy journals. Yet we do know from the many studies made of the reading habits of scientists and engineers that relatively few articles in any issue of a journal are read by an individual. With this in mind, it is quite apparent that the hard copy journal is not an efficient or effective communication medium for current awareness purposes. The synopsis journal is a decided improvement and its future looks promising—providing we learn to write good synopses from the reader's viewpoint.[10]

Despite the apparent health today of journal publishing, this enterprise faces an uncertain future that can adversely affect communication of scientific and technological information. The synopsis journal can be an effective answer to the problem if it can be associated with a service that is able to distribute the full original paper in a form and price range similar to those of U.S. patents. The time has come to consider this solution.

REFERENCES

1. Adomaitis, V., "The Chemical and Related Technical Literature of Lithuania," *J. Chem. Doc.* **4**, 244–246 (1964).
2. Alverson, R. A., "An Evaluation of the Pesticide Literature—Problems, Sources, and Services," *J. Chem. Doc.* **4**, 204–208 (1964).
3. Annan, G. L., and J. W. Felter, (eds.), *The Handbook of Medical Library Practice*, Medical Library Association, 1970, Chicago.
4. Anon., "Which Way Now for Journals?", *Nature* **262**, 731 (1976).

5. Anon., "Synopsis Journal Idea Catching on in Europe," *Chem. Eng. News*, April 14, 14–15 (1975).

6. E. Garfield, "A Basic Journal Collection," *Current Contents*, Jan. 12 and Feb. 2 (1972), Institute for Scientific Information, Philadelphia.

7. Arverson, M. H., "Economic Aspects in the Dissemination of Chemical Knowledge," *J. Chem. Doc.* **1** (3), 1–3 (1961).

8. Ayers, J. B., "The Journals of Chemical History, Education, and Documentation," *J. Chem. Doc.* **11**, 12–13 (1971), and "Journals and Conference Proceedings of Chemical History, Education, and Documentation," *J. Chem. Info. Comput. Sci.* **21**, 71–72 (1981).

9. Baker, D. B., "Recent Trends in Growth of Chemical Literature," *Chem. Eng. News* **54** (20), 23–27 (1976) and **59** (22), 29–34 (1981).

10. Baker, D. B., F. A. Tate, and R. J. Rowlett, Jr., "Changing Patterns in the International Communication of Chemical Research and Technology," *J. Chem. Doc.* **11**, 90–99 (1971).

11. Barr, K. P., "Estimation of the Number of Currently Available Scientific and Technical Periodicals," *J. Doc.* **23**, 110 (1967).

12. Barrett, R. I., and M. A. Barrett, "Journals Most Cited by Chemists and Chemical Engineers," *J. Chem. Ed.* **34**, 35 (1957).

13. Belknap, R. H., "How to Improve Scientific Communication," *J. Chem. Doc.* **2**, 133–135 (1962).

14. Bernays, P. M., K. L. Coe, and J. L. Wood, "A Computer-Based Inventory of *Chemical Abstracts*," *J. Chem. Doc.* **5**, 242–249 (1965).

15. Boig, F. S., and P. W. Howerton, "History and Development of Chemical Periodicals in the Field of Organic Chemistry, 1877–1949," *Science*, **115**, 25 (1952).

16. Boig, F. S., "Domestic and Foeign Periodicals in the Field of Organic Chemistry. A Statistical Analysis," *Science* **110**, 107 (1949).

17. Boig, F. S., and P. W. Howerton, "History and Development of Chemical Periodicals in the Field of Analytical Chemistry: 1877–1950," *Science*, **115**, 555 (1952).

18. Boig, F. S., "Domestic and Foreign Publications in the Field of Analytical Chemistry. A Statistical Analysis," *Chemist-Analyst* **38**, 3 (1949).

19. Bonn, G. S., *Literature of Science and Technology*, McGraw–Hill, 1966.

20. Bonn, G. S., "Science-Technology Periodicals," *Library J.* **88**, 954 (1963).

21. Bourne, C.P., "The World's Technical Journal Literature: An Estimate of Volume, Origin, Language, Field, Indexing, and Abstracting," *Am. Doc.*, April, 159–168 (1962).

22. Bottle, R. T., Ed., *The Use of Chemical Literature*, Butterworth, London, 1969.

23. Brooks, R. R., and L. E. Smythe, "The Progress of Analytical Chemistry 1910–1970," *Talanta* **22**, 495–504 (1975).

24. Brown, C. H., *Scientific Serials, Characteristics and Lists of Most Cited Publications in Mathematics, Physics, Chemistry, Geology, Physiology, Botany, Zoology, and Entomology*," Association of College and Reference Libraries, Chicago, 1956 (ACRL Monograph No. 16).

25. Brown, N. B., "Price Indexes for 1976 U.S. Periodicals and Serials," *Library J.* **101**, 1600–1603 (1976).

26. Burman, C. R., *How to Find Out in Chemistry*, Pergamon, New York, 1965.

27. Cahn, R. S., *Survey of Chemical Publications*, The Chemical Society (London), 1965.

28. Canham, G. W. R., "Information Problems of an Inorganic Chemist," *J. Chem. Doc.* **12**, 5–6 (1972).

29. Chou, D. Y. P., "The Literature of Electrochemistry in Japan and China," *J. Chem. Doc.* **4**, 247–251 (1964).

30. Clasquin, F. F., and J. B. Cohen, "Prices of Physics and Chemistry Journals, *Science*, **197**, 432–438 (1977).

31. Crane, E. J., A. M. Patterson, and E. B. Marr, *A Guide to the Literature of Chemistry*, Wiley, New York, 1957.

32. Dirksen, E. F., "Development and Use of Records in the Processing of Technical Papers in an Industrial Organization," *J. Chem. Doc.* **3**, 141–144 (1963).

33. Dyson, G. M., *A Short Guide to Chemical Literature*, Longman, New York, 1958.

34. Elderfield, R. C., "Creativity in Organic Chemistry Based on the Literature," *J. Chem. Doc.* **2**, 64–67 (1962).

35. Ewing, G. J., "Citation of Articles from Vol. 58 of the *Journal of Physical Chemistry*," *J. Chem. Doc.* **6**, 247–250 (1966).

36. Fischer, R. B., "Report for Analytical Chemists," *Anal. Chem.* **37**, 27A (1965).

37. Friedlander, J., "Environmental Chemistry—An Examination of Available Literature," *J. Chem. Doc.* **13**, 189–192 (1973).

38. Friedman, H. J., "The Number of Review Articles in Various Subject Areas of Chemistry," *J. Chem. Doc.* **3**, 139–141 (1963).

39. Garfield, E., and I. H. Sher, "New Factors in the Evaluation of Scientific Literature through Citation Indexing," *Am. Doc.* **14**, 195–201 (1963).

40. Good, M. L., "Primary Publications: Problems, Progress," *Chem. Eng. News*, Aug. 26, p. 30 (1974).

41. Gorin, G., "Contributions to the Periodical Literature of Chemistry from United States Universities in 1955–1960," *J. Chem. Doc.* **3**, 137–138 (1963).

42. Gottschalk, C. M., and W. F. Desmond, "Worldwide Census of Scientific and Technical Serials," *Am. Doc.* **14**, 188 (1963).

43. Gould, R. F., "Reviews of the Chemical Literature," *J. Chem. Doc.* **5**, 143–150 (1965).

44. Grefath, R. W., "A Study of Citations to 308 Journal Articles in Chemistry Published in 1963," *J. Chem. Doc.* **14**, 95–98 (1974).

45. Gross, P. L. K., and E. M. Gross, "College Libraries and Chemical Education," *Science* **66**, 385–389 (1927).

46. Gushee, D. E., "Reading Behavior of Chemists," *J. Chem. Doc.* **8**,191–194 (1968).

47. Gushee, D. E., "Problems of the Primary Journal," *J. Chem. Doc.* **10**, 30–32 (1970).

48. Gushee, D. E., "Factors Affecting Dissemination of Chemical Information," *J. Chem. Doc.* **11**, 201–204 (1971).

49. Gwirtsman, J. J., "Coverage of Russian Chemical Literature in Chemical Abstracts," *J. Chem. doc.* **1** (2), 38–44 (1961).

50. Hall, J., "Science Journals in a Price Jungle," *Nature* **247**, 417–419 (1974).

51. Hancock, J. E. H., "An Introduction to the Literature of Organic Chemistry," *J. Chem. Ed.* **45**, 193–199 (1968).

52. Hawkins, D. T., "Semiconductor Journals," *J. Chem. Info. Comp. Sci.* **16**, 21–23 (1976).

53. Herring, C., "Critical Reviews:The User's Point of View," *J. Chem. Doc.* **8**, 232–236 (1968).

54. Herschman, A., "The Primary Journal: Past, Present, and Future," *J. Chem. Doc.* **10**, 37–42 (1970).

55. Hirayama, K., "Status of Chemical InformationActivities in Japan," *J. Chem. Doc.* **13**, 21–23 (1973).

56. Houghton, B., *Scientific Periodical—Their Historical Development, Characteristics and Control*," Bingley, London, 1975.

57. Kaback, S.M., "User Benefits from Secondary Journals on Microfilm," *J. Chem. Doc.* **10**, 7–9 (1970).

58. Kean, P., and J. Ronayne, "Preliminary Communications in Chemistry," *J. Chem. Doc.* **12**, 218–230 (1972).

59. Kemball, C., and Rees, C., "The New Chemical Journal," *Ind. Res.*, May, p. 95 (1976).

60. Kennard, O., D. G. Watson, and W. G. Town, "Cambridge Crystallographic Data Centre I. Bibliographic File," *J. Chem. Doc.* **12**, 14–19 (1972).

61. Kenyon, R. L., and R. N. Nader, "From Primary Journals to Technical Business Magazines," *J. Chem. Doc.* **5**, 135–139 (1965).

62. Kiehlmann, E., "Journal Coverage by the Major Chemical Title and Abstract Publications," *J. Chem. Doc.* **12**, 157–163 (1972).

63. Kronick, D. A., *A History of Scientific and Technical Periodicals, The Origins and Development of the Scientific and Technological Press*, 1665–1790," Scarecrow Press, New York, 1962.

64. Kuney, J. H., "New Developments in Primary Journal Publication," *J. Chem. Doc.* **10**, 42–46 (1970).

65. Kuney, J. H., and W. H. Weisgerber, "Systems Requirements for Primary Information Systems. Utilization of the *Journal of Organic Chemistry*," *J. Chem. Doc.* **10**, 150–157 (1970).

66. Kuney, J. H., and V. E Dougherty, "The ACS Single Article Service," *J. Chem. Doc.* 11, 9–11 (1971).

67. Kuney, J. H., "The Role of Microforms in Journal Publication," *J. Chem. Doc.* **12**, 78–80 (1972).

68. Leake, C. D., "Primary Journals: Questionable Progress and Present Problems," *J. Chem. Doc.* **10**, 27–29 (1970).

69. Lowry, C. D., and R. Cocroft, "Literature Needs of Food Chemists," *J. Chem. Doc.* **8**, 228–230 (1968).

70. Maddox, J., "Journals and the Literature Explosion," *Nature* **221**, 128–130 (1969).

71. Marschner, R. F., "Concordance Between Divisions and Journals of the American Chemical Society," *J. Chem. Doc.* **3**, 42–44 (1963).

72. Marschner, R. F., "Papers Presented at ACS Meetings," *J. Chem. Doc.* **11**, 294–210 (1971).

73. Martyn, J., and A. Gilchrist, *An Evaluation of British Scientific Journals*, ASLIB Occasional Publications, No. 1, 1968.

74. Matarazzo, J. M., "Scientific Journals - Page or Price Explosion," *Special Libraries* **63**, 38 (1972).

75. McCarthy, G. E., and E. H. Valance, "Photocopying by Libraries of Copyrighted Documents," *J. Chem. Doc.* **2**, 255–256 (1962).

76. Mellon, M. G., *Chemical Publications—Their Nature and Use*, McGraw–Hill, 1958.

77. Michaelson, H. B., "Achieving a More Disciplined R and D Literature," *J. Chem. Doc.* **8**, 198–201 (1968).

78. *MIT Reports on Research*, November, 1971, Massachusetts Institute of Technology, Cambridge, Mass.

79. Moore, F. J., *A History of Chemistry*, McGraw–Hill, New York, 1939.

80. Moore, J. A., "An Inquiry on New Forms of Primary Publications," *J. Chem. Doc.* **12**, 75–78 (1972).

81. Myatt, D. O., "What Authors and Editors Can Do to Provoke the Creative Reaction," *J. Chem. Doc.* **2**, 58–59 (1962).

82. National Academy of Sciences, *Scientific and Technical Communications*, NAS Publication 1707, 1969.

83. National Academy of Sciences, *Scientific, Technical, and Related Societies of the United States*, 9th edition, 1971, Washington, DC.

84. National Science Foundation, *Publication of Basic Research Findings in Industry, 1957–1959*, NSF 61–62, 1961, Washington, DC.

85. National Science Foundation, Characteristics of Scientific Journals, 1949–1959, NSF 64–20, 1964, Washington, DC.

86. Osborn, A. D., *Serial Publications*, American Library Association, New York, 1973.

87. Panton, D., and B. G. Renken, "What Do Chemists Read?", *Chem. Brit.* **7**, 18–22 (1971).

88. Pasternak, S., "Is Journal Publication Obsolete?", *Physics Today* **19** (5), 38 (1966).

89. Pawlikowski, N. J., and R. G. Tucker, "The Untapped Resource—Unpublished Manuscripts," *J. Chem. Doc.* **11**, 215–217 (1971).

90. Pings, C. J., "Publication Delays in the Chemical Engineering Literature," *J. Chem. Doc.* **7**, 179–181 (1967).

91. Pinski, G., "Influence and Interrelationship of Chemical Journals," *J. Chem. Info. Comp. Sci.* **17**, 67–74 (1977).

92. Piskur, M. M., "The Literature of Food Science and Technology," *J. Chem. Doc.* **8**, 93–95 (1968).

93. Porter, J. R., "The Scientific Journal—300th Anniversary," *Bacteriol. Rev.* **28**, 211–30 (1964).

94. Price, D. J. de S., *Science Since Babylon*, Yale University Press, New Haven, Conn., 1961.

95. Price, D. J. de S., *Little Science, Big Science*, Columbia University Press, New York, 1963.

96. Price, D. J. de S., "Ethics of Scientific Publication," *Science* **144**, 655–657 (1964).

97. Price, D. J., de S., "Networks of Scientific Papers," *Science* **153**, 510–515 (1965).

98. Rowles, B. A., and I. B. Wheldon, *A Guide to the Scientific and Technical Literature of Eastern Europe*, prepared by Battelle Memorial Institute for the National Science Foundation, Washington, DC, 1962.

99. Schwartz, E. S. E., and W. H. Powers, "Survey of the Quantity and Distribution of Biochemical Literature," *J. Chem. Doc.* **3**, 37–42 (1963).

100. Seldon, S. W., and L. R. Garson, *Evaluation of a Dual Journal Concept*, NSF Summary Report, 1977, Washington, DC.

101. Skolnik, H., "Why This Journal?" *J. Chem. Doc.* **1** (1) (1961).

102. Skolnik, H., "Problems in Handling Pesticide Information," *J. Chem. Doc.* **4**, 168 (1964).

103. Skolnik, H., "A Sense of History," *J. Chem. Doc.* **7**, 185 (1967).

104. Skolnik, H., "Scientific Journals—Whither or Wither?", *J. Chem. Doc.* **8**, 190 (1968).

105. Skolnik, H., "References Are Not Equal," *J. Chem. Doc.* **10**, 74 (1970).

106. Skolnik, H., "UNESCO Meeting of Editors," *J. Chem. Doc.* **12**, 146 (1962).

107. Skolnik, H., "Copyrights, Photocopying, and Journal Publishers," *J. Chem. Doc* **14**, 56 (1974).

108. Skolnik, H., "The Dilemma Facing Technical Journals," *J. Chem. Info. Comp. Sci.* **18**, 2A (1978).

109. Skolnik, H., and K. M. Reese, "A Century of Chemistry," *American Chemical Society*, Washington, DC, 1976.

110. Smith, H. A., "Creativity in Physical Chemistry Based on the Literature," *J. Chem. Doc.* **2**, 61–64 (1962).

111. Soule, B. A., *Library Guide for the Chemist*, McGraw–Hill, New York, 1938.

112. Starker, L. N., "User Experiences with Primary Journals on 16-mm Microfilm," *J. Chem. Doc.* **10**, 5–6 (1970).

113. Strauss, L. J., I. M. Strieby, and A. L. Brown, *Scientific and Technical Libraries*," Wiley, New York, 1964.

114. Trimble, R. F., "The Journals of Inorganic Chemistry," *J. Chem. Doc.* **3**, 79–80 (1963) and *J. Chem. Ed.* **37**, 419 (1960).

115. Vagianos, L., "Information Patterns of Chemists in a University Environment," *J. Chem. Doc.* **11**, 85–89 (1971).

116. Van Wazar, J. R., "Creativity in Inorganic Chemistry Based on the Literature," *J. Chem. Doc* **2**, 60–61 (1962).

117. Weil, B. H., "Document Access," *J. Chem. lDoc.* **11**, 178–185 (1971).

118. Williams, T. I., "Learned Societies and Their Publications," *Chem. Ind.*, April 5, 288–289 (1975).

119. Williams, T. I., "Communication in Science," *Chem. Ind.*, May 7, 326–332 (1977).

120. Woodburn, H. M., "Retrieval and Use of the Literature of Inorganic Chemistry," *J. Chem. Ed.* **49**, 689–696 (1972).

121. Yagello, V. E., "Early History of the Chemical Periodical," *J. Chem. Ed.* **45**, 426–429 (1968).

122. Yescombe, E. R., *Sources of Information on the Rubber Plastics and Allied Industries*, Pergamon, New York, 1968.

6

SECONDARY PUBLICATION OPERATIONS AND SERVICES

HISTORICAL BACKGROUND

Classifying, indexing, and abstracting of information in documents have a long history. The papyri in Egyptian libraries (see Chapter 1) were packed in labeled jars and shelved chronologically in reigning king order. The 500,000 scrolls in the famous Alexandrian library (see Chapter 1) were classified on 120 scrolls; scholars and scribes copied, abstracted, extracted, and annotated the scrolls to aid their memories and to repackage the information into histories, biographies, and philosophies.

During the Middle Ages (500–1500), the word *abstractus*, meaning "to draw away," was introduced in Medieval latin, the liturgical and literary language then used by monks. A common practice among the monks as they transcribed documents was the writing of marginalia on each page, summarizing the contents. Throughout this period, kings required their generals and ambassadors to write summaries of their reports, and the Vatican abstracted the numerous reports from its envoys; these abstracts have been accumulating in the Vatican since the eleventh century.[24,29]

During the Renaissance (fourteenth to the seventeenth century), scientists communicated with each other throughout the civilized world by letter: full letters to one or two friends and abstracts to others.

Gutenberg's introduction of movable type in the 1450s democratized communication and made possible the scientific journal. The first scientific journal, *Le Journal des scavans*, introduced as a weekly in 1665 by the French Académie des Sciences, listed new books with annotations and abstracted papers reporting new developments. In the same year, the Royal Society of London issued *Philosophical transac-*

tions, which, in addition to publishing papers, abstracted the work in other periodicals.

EARLY ABSTRACT JOURNALS[7,14,15,17]

The first completely abstract journals tended to be universal, covering all subject areas and concentrating mostly on articles and books. The first of these probably was Christian Gottfried Hoffman's *Aufrichtige,* which was issued in two volumes of 12 issues between 1714 and 1717. The first abstract journals in England were the *Universal Magazine of Knowledge and Pleasure* (1747–1815) and the *Monthly Review* (1749–1844). In 1778, the *Monthly Review* carried abstracts of scientific papers from the *Philosophical Transactions,* and from the journals published by the French, Belgian, and other national academies and scientific societies.

The first wholly chemical journal, *Crell's Chemical Journal,* founded in 1778, employed abstracts and extracts to inform readers of what Crell considered to be significant publications. As early as 1817, Leopold Gmelin felt the literature had grown sufficiently to justify the publication of his *Lehrbuch der Chemie* (title changed in 1819 to *Handbuch der anorganischen Chemie*). The rising journal literature prompted Jons Jacob Berzelius to issue in 1821 his *Jahresbericht ueber die Fortschritte der physichen Wissenschaften,* the first review journal in science with emphasis on chemistry. Berzelius produced this yearly review for over 25 years, restricting it after several years to chemistry as reported in books and journals.

In 1830, the number of journals in chemistry had increased to the point where Gustav Theodor Fechner, at the age of 29, introduced *Pharmaceutisches Centralblatt,* the first abstract journal in chemistry. Its name was changed to *Chemisches Zentralblatt* in 1856.

The French Chemical Society introduced abstracts with the 1858 issues of its *Bulletin de la société chimique de France,* and the German Chemical Society with its *Berichte* from 1868 through 1896, when it assumed the responsibility for publishing *Chemisches Zentralblatt.* The Chemical Society and the Society of Chemical Industry in England published their respective abstracts in the *Journal of the Chemical Society* beginning in 1871 and in the *Journal of the Society of Chemical Industry* beginning in 1882, until the two societies founded *British Abstracts.* Japanese chemical literature has been abstracted since 1877; the Japan Information Center for Science and Technology now publishes the *Nippon Kagaku Seran (Complete Chemical Abstracts by*

Japan). The American Chemical Society published abstracts in its *Journal of the American Chemical Society* from 1897 until it introduced *Chemical Abstracts* in 1907.

By 1907, there were over 60 abstract journals. According to the 1969 edition of the International Federation for Documentation's *Abstracting Services*, there are now well over 1500 indexing/abstracting publications[1,7,12,17] Their growth has thus paralleled that of the primary literature.

Originally, abstract journals were very much restricted by geographic and subject coverage. Coverage slowly expanded geographically to include the foreign literature within a given subject area, and broadened into more areas of chemistry and types of documents, such as journal literature, patents, books, and even reports. However, no abstract journal, not even *Chemical Abstracts* with its monitoring of up to 14,000 journals plus patents of most major countries, includes all the literature on the complete spectrum of developments in the chemical industry's laboratories. Chemistry has expanded in terms of both new disciplines and new interdisciplinary interests, such as material science, whose literature embraces that of chemistry, physics, biology, mathematics, and many areas of engineering, for example, mechanical engineering. Consequently, new indexing/abstracting services oriented to both narrow and interdisciplinary interests have been introduced.

INDEXING/ABSTRACTING ORGANIZATIONS[2,6,7,10,11,12,13]

Organizations engaged in indexing/abstracting services are basically of five types:

Governmental Agencies
Scientific and Technical Societies
Commercial
University and Public Libraries
Industrial

Among the fastest growing indexing/abstracting operations are those initiated by many Federal agencies over the past several decades, especially those fostered by World War II, Sputnik, and, most recently, Congressional regulatory acts. By and large, these operations were initiated to serve a well defined subject area, although several, such as the Library of Congress, National Technical Information Service

(NTIS), and the Patent Office have operations based on hundreds of thousands and even millions of documents. Among the Federal agencies with these operations, the following are the more important:

Atomic Energy Commission
Department of Agriculture
Department of Commerce
Department of Defense
Department of Health, Education and Welfare
Library of Congress
National Aeronautics and Space Administration
Smithsonian Institution

Scientific and technical societies and trade associations have been the traditional initiators of indexing/abstracting services, primarily for their members, and thus they have tended to be operated on a nonprofit basis. Since World War II, many depended on governmental support from agencies such as the National Science Foundation.

Some of the more important societies that engage in indexing/abstracting operations relevant to chemistry and chemical technology are the following:

American Ceramic Society
American Chemical Society
American Institute of Aeronautics and Astronautics
American Institute of Physics
American Society of Mechanical Engineers
American Society for Metals
American Society for Testing and Materials
BioSciences Information Service
Chemical Society (London)
Engineering Index, Inc.

Indexing/abstracting operations have attracted the entry of profit-making enterprises and commercial publishers, and numerous high quality and very useful products have resulted. The following list is representative of some of these commercial producers:

American Bibliographic Service
CRC Press
Data Courier, Inc.
Derwent Publications, Ltd.
Foster D. Snell, Inc.
Gaylor Technical Survey Corp.
H. W. Wilson Company
IFI/Plenum Data Company
Institute for Scientific Information
New York Times
Pergamon Press
Preston Publications, Inc.
SRI International
University Microfilms
Wiley-Interscience
Williams and Willkins Company

Representative of the institutional organizations that issue indexing/abstracting products are the following:

Battelle Memorial Institute
John Crerar Library
Johns Hopkins University
Institute of Paper Chemistry
Institute of Textile Technology
North Carolina State College
Ohio College Library Center
Purdue University
Texas Agriculture and Minimg University
University of Tulsa

Chemists and chemical engineers, whether in the academic or industrial sector, need access to documents relevant to their research and development work. From the one-person laboratory to the academic scientific curriculums and to the giant industrial research laboratories, the library of books, patents, journals, trade publications, and indexing/

abstracting products is considered to be a tool of research as much as laboratory apparatus and equipment. Among the latter part of the nineteenth century and well into the twentieth, most serious chemists had personal libraries that contained basic reference works and indexing/abstracting products, such as Beilstein, Gmelin, and *Chemical Abstracts*. Indeed, from the beginning of *Chemical Abstracts* in 1907–1933, every member of the American Chemical Society (there were 17,645 members in 1933) received the publication as part of the membership fee. The subscription price was set at $12; in 1955 it was raised to $20. In the 1960s the cost of the publication was such as to be priced for only institutions and industrial libraries. In 1933 ACS dues were $15, for which members received all ACS publications, including *Chemical Abstracts*.

The period between 1900 and 1945 was one of exceptional growth in the chemical industry; the number of professional chemists and engineers and the chemical literature increased considerably. Although orientation in chemistry first began toward disciplines and subdisciplines in the nineteenth century, it accelerated rapidly in the 1930s and 1940s as a consequence of the rapid growth of industrial research. Thus, what chemists did began to define the disciplines and subdisciplines of chemistry. One of the disciplines of chemistry that emerged in the 1940s was chemical information science; for the most part by industrial chemists.

These chemical information scientists were responsible for designing, establishing, and maintaining indexing/abstracting systems for the community of scientists in the industrial environment. Most important among document classes that involved scientists in this discipline were internal reports for which classification, indexing, abstracting, and current awareness systems were set up. Even though external indexing/abstracting systems were available for the patent and journal literature, the requirements of timeliness and selectivity dictated in-house systems that generally included a weekly or biweekly current awareness bulletin as well as a retrospective retrieval system. The advantages of the in-house system are the following: the reader knows that the references are immediately available in the library, the reader has less to read than in an external system attempting to do all things for all readers, and the indexing and abstracting can be designed to be relevant to the interests of the community of scientists. For maximum effectiveness, these in-house information operations are designed to supplement or complement external information services.[5,8,9,18] With the recent availability of numerous information services online through information brokers, many in-house services have been dropped, especially those for the patent and journal literature. However, timeliness has kept some in-house operations in existence. The average number of days between the receipt of journals in one industrial research and development library and the appearance of the abstract in the in-house current awareness bulletin, in Chemical Abstracts, and online in the Lockheed CA data base were 6, 57, and 71, respectively.[23]

TYPES OF ABSTRACTS[2,3,4,20,22,27,28]

Abstracts in abstract publications can be categorized into three types: indicative, informative, and critical, with the majority being of the first two types. Because of increasing costs of producing abstract publications, the publishers are using author abstracts more and in-house or contract abstractors less. The indicative abstract is designed to provide just enough information to enable the reader to decide whether he is interested in reading the article. The informative abstract provides substantial information, which is sometimes sufficient so that the document itself does not need to be consulted. The critical abstract gives as much information as the other types, plus a personal evaluation that is not necessarily relevant to all readers. Author abstracts may be indicative or informative, but too often they tend to introduce the paper and emphasize one or two conclusions, without always telling the reader what is new.

A number of data bases over the past two decades have opted to eliminate the abstract entirely, depending solely on the document's title to inform readers of the document's potential value or relevance to their interests. The ultimate are those products which list the table of contents of journals issuing within a given period, such as a week or month, as an aid to current awareness.

There are two important aspects in every information system: an indexing and/or classification system that directs the reader to the body of documents of interest and an abstracting system that enables the reader to select reliably only those documents which are relevant.[2,4,17,20] The larger the document collection, the more critical it is that these two aspects be designed to serve the needs of a defined user community. Over the past century, these two aspects were associated closely by indexing/abstracting producers and publishers. With the introduction of the abstracting journals in chemistry, the two aspects became highly differentiated, and each producer evolved its own unique way of abstracting and indexing the contents of articles. Unfortunetely, less attention is being paid currently to the art and science of abstracting.

An abstract, at best, is an abbreviated but accurate representation of a document, a repackaged surrogate of information in a condensed form. Abstracting, however, involves a considerable loss of information and in no way can be the equal of the original document. It is a process of selecting and ignoring information, then generalizing that which is selected so that the potential user can determine the relevance of pertinent documents.

INDEXING CONCEPTS

Indexing and classification systems are the basic retrieval mechanisms for every information operation. A great variety of indexes and classification concepts have been introduced and employed by numerous information organizations. In recent years, classification has been more or less ignored, with very little innovative work reported in the literature.[24] This is unfortunate, in view of the great contributions classification and taxonomic concepts have made in the past to understanding and teaching science and to reducing many facts to a linguistic matrix of knowledge.

Indexing activity, on the other hand, has been relatively high over the past 30 years, and many innovative systems have been introduced and developed. Of the many kinds of indexes in chemistry—author, subject, company or institution, patent number, formula,ring, document identification, etc.—the most important by far has been the subject index.

Up through the 1940s, information processors had directed considerable effort to making indexing into a science and to designing indexes with a purpose, logic, and grammar. This kind of indexing, however, required that indexers know the contents of documents and know how information is used and what constitutes good index terms from the user's viewpoint. Products from such indexers were expensive for the producer or publisher but cost effective for the user. An information system that saves one hour per week of a user's reading time (by directing the user to only relevant documents) increases productivity by 2.5%.[23]

Information producers, not users, determine the method of indexing documents. With the introduction of edge-notched punched and optical coincidence card systems in the 1940s, the uniterm indexing system became the one of choice. As computers entered the scene—the IBM sorter and collator in the 1940s and early 1950s, the IBM 9900 and Bendix G-15 in the late 1950s, the IBM 1401 and 7090 in the early 1960s, the IBM 360 in the late 1960s, and the IBM 370 in the 1970s— the uniterm system was slowly displaced by the keyword concept.

The keyword concept is a distant descendant of the concordance, an alphabetical index of the principal words used in a book (most notably, the Bible). As introduced in the 1950s and used since the 1960s, keyword indexes were based generally on the principal words (with elimination of articles, prepositions, and conjunctions) in titles and, in some cases, in abstracts, and only rarely in the entire text—and then for the computer production of an abstract. The word uniterm, as used by Mortimer Taube[25] represented the single words or terms selected from a document in the following process: Each document is assigned an accession number, a card is made up for each term, and document accession numbers are posted in ascending order on each card that carries the word contained in the document. Thus, the "ethanol" card is posted with the accession numbers of every document concerned with any aspect of ethanol. To retrieve those documents on the oxidation of ethanol, the "ethanol" and "oxidation" cards are pulled, and accession numbers common to both cards represent the desired documents. The matching was called "coordination," the index a "coordinate index," and the cards "uniterm cards." Problems of synonymity soon forced the introduction of "see" and "see also" references on the uniterm cards, and the introduction of other mechanisms for controlling the vocabulary and for decreasing the number of irrelevant documents retrieved.[21]

During the 1960s, the conceptual differences in the two systems were slight—the orientation remained to words with thesaurus control. The major change was at the input and output stages, and the thesaurus was changed from the conventional authority list with definitions to one that listed each word with associated words denoted as narrower, broader, or equivalent with a "see also" or "see" direction. Being oriented to words—those used in the document for uniterms or in the title, abstract, or selected terms for keywords—the indexer as a subject specialist was eliminated or reduced to a bare minimum.

In addition to the uniterm and keyword concepts, others introduced over the past 25 years were the citation index; new formula indexes, fragmentation indexes, reaction indexes, and notation systems.

The major indexing/abstracting operations and services, until relatively recently were associated directly or indirectly with scientific, technical, and trade associations or societies. Not only have these operations and services expanded and new ones introduced, many "for profit" organizations and governmental agencies, universities, libraries, and consulting firms have arisen, and the total today constitute the information industry. Expansion of many of the established information services and the introduction of many new ones have been supported by the federal government, some fully or partially, but some of the "for profit" not at all.[6,11,13,16,19,26]

Only a few years ago, the information industry consisted of two major segments: producers of primary publications, that is, of journals; and producers of secondary publications, such as *Chemical Abstracts*. With the advent of computers, government monies, and computer photocomposition, the data base broker of products from data base processers and producers has entered the picture as the third major segment.

Chapter 7 discusses Chemical Abstracts Service, the major data base processor and producer in chemistry today. Chapter 8 discusses other data base producers important to chemistry and chemical technology currently, and Chapter 9 discusses data base brokers and the data bases they make available online.

REFERENCES

1. Abelson, P., "Custodians of Knowledge", *Science* **159**, 585 (1968).
2. Becker, J., and R. M. Hayes, *Information Storage and Retrieval*, Wiley, New York, 1963.
3. Borko, H., and S. Chatman, "Criteria for Acceptable Abstracts: A Survey of Abstractors' Instructions", *Am. Doc.* **14**, 149–160 (1963).
4. Borko, H., and C. L. Bernier, *Abstracting Concepts and Methods*, Academic Press, New York, 1975.
5. Bowman, C. M., and M. T. Brown, "The Development, Cost, and Impact of a Current Awareness Service in an Industrial Organization," *J. Chem. Doc.* **11**, 72–75 (1971).
6. Chemical Abstracts Service, *Federally Sponsored Information Programs Which Compete with Chemical Abstracts Service*, Columbus, Ohio, 1966.
7. Collison, R., *Abstracts and Abstracting Services*, Clio, Santa Barbara, Calif., 1971.
8. Friedenstein, H., "Alerting with Internal Abstract Bulletins," *J. Chem. Doc.* **5**, 154–157 (1965).
9. Haas, A. K., "Internal Alerting with Keyword-in-Context Indexes," *J. Chem. Doc.* **5**, 160–163 (1965).
10. Herner, S., *A Brief Guide to Sources of Scientific and Technical Information*, Information Resources Press, Washington, DC, 1969
11. Herner, S., and M. J. Vellucci (eds.), *Selected Federal Computer-Based Information Systems*, Information Resources Press, Washington, DC, 1972.
12. Keenan, S., and M. Elliott, "World Inventory of Abstracting and Indexing Services," *Special Libraries* **64**, 145–150 (1973).
13. Klempner, I. M., *Diffusion of Abstracting and Indexing Services for Government-Sponsored Research*, Scarecrow Press, Metuchen, NJ, 1968.

14. Leicester, H. M., The *Historical Background of Chemistry*, Wiley, New York, 1956. 15.

15. Manzer, B. M., *The Abstract Journal, 1790–1920*, Scarecrow Press, Metuchen, N.J., 1977.

16. Martyn, J., "Tests on Abstracts Journals: Coverage, Overlap and Indexing," *J. Doc.* **23**, 45–70 (1967).

17. National Academy of Sciences/National Academy of Engineering, *Scientific and Technical Communication*, National Academy of Sciences, Publication 1707, Washington, DC, 1969.

18. Peterson, J. S., "Replacement of an In-House Current Awareness Bulletin by Chemical Abstracts Section Groupings," *J. Chem. Info. Comput. Sci.* **15**, 169–173 (1975).

19. Schultz, L., "New Developments in Biological Abstracting and Indexing," *Library Trends* **16**, 337–352 (1968).

20. Skolnik, H., "Designing an Index," *The Percolator* **35**, 26–31 (1959).

21. Skolnik, H., "Book Review of NASA Thesaurus," *J. Chem. Doc.* **8**, 53 (1968).

22. Skolnik, H., "The Multiterm Index: A New Concept in Information Storage and Retrieval," *J. Chem. Doc.* **10**, 81–84 (1970).

23. Skolnik, H., "A Computerized Current Awareness System for Journal Literature," *J. Chem. Info, Comput. Sci.* **19**, 76–70 (1977).

24. Skolnik, H., "A Classification System for Polymer Literature in an Industrial Environment," *J. Chem. Info. Comput. Sci.* **19**, 76–79 (1979).

25. Taube, M., et al., "Studies in Coordinate Indexing," Documentation Inc., Washington, DC., 1953–1957.

26. Terrent, S. W., and W. H. Weisgerber, "Evaluation of the ACS Single Article Announcement Service," *J. Chem Doc.* **14**, 23–25 (1974).

27. Weil, B. H., "Some Reader Reactions to Abstract Bulletin Style," *J. Chem. Doc.* **1**, 52–58 (1961).

28. Weil, B. H., "Standards for Writing Abstracts," *J. Am. Soc. Info. Sci.* **21**, 351–357 (1970).

29. Witty, F. J., "The Beginnings of Indexing and Abstacting. Some Notes Toward a History of Indexing in Antiquity and the Middle Ages," *The Indexer* **8**, 193–198 (1973).

7

CHEMICAL ABSTRACTS SERVICE

Since the demise of *British Chemical Abstracts* in 1953 and of *Chemiches Zentralblatt* in 1969, *Chemical Abstracts (CA)* has assumed a dominant role throughout the scientific world for its comprehensive coverage of the chemical literature. The antecedent of *CA* was *Review of American Chemical Research*, founded by Arthur A. Noyes of the Massachusetts Institute of Technology to disseminate abstracts of papers appearing in the journal literature that could be of interest to chemists. Its first two volumes appeared as part of the university's *Technology Quarterly* and, in 1897, as a section in the *Journal of the American Chemical Society*. W. A. Noyes, Sr., who became the editor of the journal in 1902, argued strongly for a separate, and more comprehensive, abstract journal. This became a reality in 1907 with the creation of *Chemical Abstracts* by the American Chemical Society, with W. A. Noyes, Sr., as editor.

Because *Chemiches Zentralblatt* had been covering the literature of chemistry since 1830 and was the primary abstract journal, *Chemical Abstracts* was conceived originally to serve American chemists primarily, and for many of its early years Americans were the main users. With the rapid growth of chemical technology, of the number of chemists, and of the number of journals in the United States, and with the increasing importance of American chemists and chemical engineers in the world of science, *CA* gained worldwide recognition for its comprehensive coverage and outstanding indexing.

In 1907, *CA* monitored approximately 400 journals for the 7994 abstracts of papers selected. By 1912, approximately 600 journals were monitored; in 1922, slightly over 1000; in 1932, over 2000; in 1950, over 5000; in early 1960s, over 10,000; and in the 1970s, up to 14,000. The first millionth abstract (papers, patents, and books) was published in 1939, covering 32 years of *CA* abstracts. The second millionth, covering the next 18 years (1938–1955) was published in 1955; the third millionth, covering the next 8 years (1955–1963) in 1963; the fourth millionth, covering the next five years, in 1968; and the fifth and sixth millionths, covering slightly over 3 years each, in 1971 and 1974; and the seventh and eighth, covering less than 3 years each, in 1977 and 1979. Table 29 shows the yearly and cumulative output of abstracts of journal articles in *CA* from 1907 to 1981.

From its inception, *CA* was unique among the abstracting/indexing services for chemistry in its coverage of applied as well as theoretical chemistry. In 1907, theoretical chemistry was covered by *Chemiches Zentralblatt* and *Journal of the Chemical Society*; and industrial chemistry, by *Journal of the Society of Chemical Industry* and Zeitschrift fuer *angewandte Chemie*. The scope of coverage in *CA* has been all published material containing new information of chemical interest, whether in journal articles, patents, books, or other documents. Books, however, have been announced by title only, with few exceptions. The coverage of patents originaly was good for only U.S. patents, but the coverage soon included patents from the more industrial nations, and in recent years the coverage has included the patents of 26 nations reasonably thoroughly. The vastness of the coverage is evident from the approximately 500,000 documents referenced by *CA* in 1978; some 14,000 different journals from about 150 nations in more than 50 languages were monitored for papers; patents were monitored from 26 nations; and new books, conference proceedings, dissertations, and reports from over the world were abstracted.

When W. A. Noyes, Sr., was editor, the abstracts were distributed over 30 classified sections. There were 33 sections in 1950. Abstracts are now organized in *CA* issues into 80 subject sections; Sections 1–34 (Biochemistry and Organic Chemistry) are issued one week, and Sections 35–80 (Macromolecular Chemistry, Applied Chemistry and Chemical Engineering, Physical Chemistry, and Analytical Chemistry) the following week. Within each of the 80 sections, abstracts of journal articles, proceedings, and dissertations are placed first; these are followed by new book announcements, and then by abstracts of patents. Each *CA* issue includes the following:

Keyword Index.   Listing of words taken from the title, text or context of each abstract, is alphabetical.

Author Index.   Listing of authors of articles, books, etc., and patentees and patent assignees, is alphabetical.

Numerical Patent Index.   Order is numerical within alphabetical listing of nations.

Patent Concordance.   Patents are cross-referenced to the first one abstracted in *CA*.

TABLE 29. **Papers Abstracted in** *Chemical Abstracts,*
1907–1981

Year	Volume	Papers	Cumulative
1907	1	7,975	7,994
1908	2	10,835	19,408
1909	3	11,455	30,863
1910	4	13,006	43,869
1911	5	15,892	59,761
1912	6	15,740	75,501
1913	7	19,025	94,526
1914	8	16,468	110,994
1915	9	12,200	123,194
1916	10	10,519	133,713
1917	11	10,921	144,634
1918	12	9,283	153,917
1919	13	10,957	164,874
1920	14	13,619	178,493
1921	15	15,211	193,704
1922	16	18,070	211,774
1923	17	19,507	231,281
1924	18	20,523	251,804
1925	19	20,951	272,755
1926	20	23,103	295,858
1927	21	25,037	320,895
1928	22	28,153	349,048
1929	23	29,082	378,130
1930	24	32,731	410,861
1931	25	32,278	443,139
1932	26	37,403	480,542
1933	27	36,139	516,681
1934	28	38,371	555,052
1935	29	42,593	597,645
1936	30	41,927	639,572
1937	31	44,032	683,604
1938	32	45,917	729,521
1939	33	45,414	774,935
1940	34	40,624	815,559
1941	35	35,588	851,147
1942	36	30,479	881,626
1943	37	30,523	912,149
1944	38	30,440	942,589
1945	39	22,824	965,413
1946	40	29,943	995,356
1947	41	30,461	1,025,817
1948	42	35,867	1,061,684

TABLE 29. *(Continued)*

Year	Volume	Papers	Cumulative
1950	44	47,496	1,149,792
1951	45	50,657	1,200,449
1952	46	56,419	1,256,868
1953	47	61,273	1,318,141
1954	48	67,606	1,385,747
1955	49	74,664	1,460,411
1956	50	78,009	1,538,420
1957	51	84,205	1,622,625
1958	52	95,736	1,718,361
1959	53	98,680	1,817,041
1960	54	104,484	1,921,525
1961	55	118,337	2,039,862
1962	56	67,730	2,107,592
	57	72,438	2,180,030
1963	58	68,978	2,249,008
	59	72,038	2,321,046
1964	60	78,789	2,399,835
	61	82,700	2,482,535
1965	62	79,911	2,562,446
	63	85,859	2,648,305
1966	64	89,718	2,738,023
	65	91,997	2,830,020
1967	66	99,652	2,929,672
	67	103,032	3,032,704
1968	68	100,545	3,133,249
	69	97,490	3,230,739
1969	70	101,297	3,332,036
	71	109,047	3,441,083
1970	72	115,024	3,556,107
	73	115,878	3,671,985
1971	74	127,514	3,799,499
	75	134,613	3,934,112
1972	76	136,963	4,071,075
	77	143,180	4,214,255
1973	78	141,694	4,355,949
	79	128,017	4,483,966
1974	80	123,191	4,607,157
	81	149,044	4,756,201
1975	82	146,626	4,902,827
	83	170,846	5,073,673
1976	84	150,554	5,224,227
	85	167,431	5,391,658
1977	86	168,915	5,560,573

TABLE 29.   *(Continued)*

	87	179,144	5,739,717
1978	88	172,924	5,912,641
	89	190,271	6,102,912
1979	90 } 91	370,771	6,473,683
1980	92 } 93	400,000	6,873,683 (est.)

Up to 1962, the volume period for *CA* was on an annual basis. Beginning in 1962, because of the expansion of the literature, *CA* was issued in two volumes per year, each volume consisting of 26 issues and a separately published volume index.

Chemical Abstracts is available also in the following five separate publications at $150 (member) and $350 (nonmember) each, issued on a biweekly schedule:

Biochemistry Sections—CA Sections 1–20.

Organic Chemistry Sections—CA Sections 21–34.

Macromolecular Sections—CA Sections 35–46.

Applied Chemistry and Chemical Engineering Sections—CA Sections 47–64.

Physical and Analytical Chemistry Sections—CA Sections 65–80.

Each issue of the Section Groupings includes the complete keyword index from the corresponding *CA* issue.

CA abstracts are informative, brief summaries of the scientific disclosures in the original documents, with special attention given to reactions, chemicals, techniques, procedures, properties, apparatus, and applications. The abstracts are not surrogates of the original documents, but rather guides to the original with sufficient information for the user to know if the original should be consulted.

A typical abstract for a journal article contains the following information:

CA Abstract No. Title of Article. Author (Address of Author). Journal. Year of Publication. Vol. No. (Issue No.). Page No. (Language). Abstract . . .

A typical abstract for a patent contains the following information:

> CA Abstract No. Title of Patent. Inventor. (Patentee). Patent No. (Patent Classification). Date of Patent Grant. Patent Application No. Date of Patent Application. Pages. Abstract . . .

Of the approximately 14,000 journals monitored for CA, less than 300 are devoted entirely to chemistry and chemical engineering, but these yield more than half of the total papers abstracted in CA; about 90% of the abstracts come from slightly more than 2000 journals. Well over 1.5 million papers, patents, and reports are reviewed annually at this time for selecting material for abstracting in CA. About 70% of the documents abstracted originate outside the United States, but 54% of the total documents are published in English, with the remainder in 55 other languages. Whereas considerable abstracting for CA is now done by CAS staff members, CAS still has a worldwide corps of over 1000 part-time volunteers in 50 nations for abstracting assignments. The currency of CA in 1968 was 110 days for journal articles, 100 days for U.S. patents, and 150 days for patents of other countries.

For each volume of 26 issues of abstracts, a separate comprehensive set of indexes is issued by CAS. These indexes are by author, patent, formula, general subject, and chemical substance, and every 5 years (prior to 1957, every 10 years) the volume indexes are merged and published as a *Collective Index*. These indexes provide an average of 19 access points to each reference in CA (2.5 in the *General Subject Index* and 4.1 in the *Chemical Substance Indexes*). The *General Subject Index* and *Chemical Substance Index* are thorough, vocabulary controlled, and in-depth; they use about half the number of pages of the abstracts in a CA volume. These indexes are prepared for the most part directly from the original documents, not from the abstracts. Indexing operations at CAS require the attention of about half of the professional staff at a cost of about 60% of the CA budget. The *Ninth Collective Index*, covering the period 1972–1976, or CA Volumes 76–85, comprises over 60 books of indexes to about two million documents, and sells for $6000. It is estimated that the *Tenth Collective Index*, covering the period 1977–1981, or CA Volumes 86–95, will require over 80 books of indexes to an estimated 2.6 million documents (prepublication price is $7500).

The *CA Issue Indexes* include the following:

Keyword Index. Access to abstract numbers is by words or phrases taken from the abstract, title of the original document, and the text of the original document. The keywords, arranged alphabetically, are those of the author(s) of the document.

Author Index. The first authors (coauthors are cross-referred to the first), inventors, patent assignees, corporations, federal agencies, etc., are listed alphabetically.

Numerical Patent Index. Order is numerical for each country.

Patent Concordance (inaugurated in 1963). Patents are arranged alphabetically by country in ascending numerical order. References to all corresponding patents in other countries are provided, and the abstract number for the one first received and abstracted by CAS is cited.

The *CA Volume Indexes* include the following:

Chemical Substance Index. Up to 1972, each volume index consisted of a single subject index. In 1972, CAS introduced two separate indexes: the *Chemical Substance Index* and *General Subject Index.* Also, in 1972, a new systematic chemical index replaced the former method of indexing chemicals. Entries in the *Chemical Substance Index* are only to completely defined substances with a consistently designed nomenclature. Substances are linked to CA abstract numbers for those cited in the abstracts and for those cited in the original documents on which the abstracts are based. Each entry includes the CAS registry number and a brief statement on the substance's context or relationship in the original document. Synonyms and trivial names are listed as cross-references only in the *Index Guide.*

General Subject Index. Entries in this index are to generic classes of substances; uses and applications, properties, and reactions of substances; apparatus and processes; and biochemical and biological subjects. The terminology is standardized, and the user must consult the *Index Guide* for the correct terminology.

Formula Index. Each compound and element discussed in the papers abstracted is listed by its formula. Formulas are arranged by citing carbons in ascending order, then hydrogens, and finally the remaining elements in alphabetical order. Following each molecular formula are the *CA* names of each compound that has the specific elemental arrangement, its CAS registry number, and the *CA* abstract number of the reference discussing the compound. This index, which is particularly useful for ascertaining the proper name to consult in the *Chemical Substance Index*, was introduced in 1920.

Index of Ring Systems. This index, which CAS introduced in 1916, lists the preferred *CA* name for each cyclic and heterocyclic compound indexed in CA volumes. Once the name is known, the compound can be searched in the *Chemical Substance Index*. This index is an hierarchical arrangement of cyclic compounds by number of rings, sizes of rings, and elemental content of rings. The ring index refers to only the parent ring structure, that is, without any substituent. The *Index Guide* to Volume 76 has a complete list of all the ring systems mentioned in CA for the period 1907–1971.

Hetero Atoms in Context (HAIC) Index.   *HAIC*, introduced in 1967 and discontinued in 1971, contained all the molecular formulas of the *Formula Index* arranged so that each hetero atom—defined as an atom other than carbon or hydrogen—was highlighted in a wraparound of the molecular formula as many times as there were different hetero atoms in the molecule.

Author Index,   Numerical Patent Index, and Patent Concordance. See above under *CA Issue Indexes*.

Since January of 1965, all unique and defined chemical compounds indexed by CA have been assigned a CAS registry number and published in the *Registry Handbook—Number Section*. The first issue covers the period 1965–1971 and includes the registry numbers in ascending numerical order of two million compounds linked to CA *Index* names and to the chemical formulas of the compounds. Beginning in 1972, CAS issued annual supplements to the *Registry Handbook*, each supplement averaging about 360,000 additional registry numbers. The five supplements for the years 1972–1976, inclusive, are now available as *Registry Handbook—Number Section Supplements* (1972–1976) and (1977–1981). A known CAS registry number enables one to ascertain the names of a chemical compound to search for in the CA *Chemical Substance Index* over the period 1965-present *Handbook Update*.

A recent publication of CAS is *Registry Handbook—Common Names* in microfilm or microfiche. Names included in the handbook were selected from the *CAS Registry Nomenclature File* by a computer algorithm that eliminated many complex names. Each name is identified with a CAS registry number and molecular formula. Over four million compounds have been registered in the system. More than 500,000 names are listed in the handbook, with references to over 300,000 specific chemical substances. As many names are ambiguous or are associated with more than one chemical or structural formula, the handbook is particularly useful in describing, through the registry number, the name that should be used in consulting the CA *Chemical Substance Index*. The number section of the handbook collects under one registry number all the synonyms appearing in the alphabetical listing. These synonyms are extremely useful as search terms for online data bases.

The *Chemical Abstracts Service Source Index (CASSI)*, discussed in Chapter 5, identifies 35,000 publications cited by *Chemical Abstracts* from 1907 to 1974, including 25,000 serials and 10,000 nonserials, and specifies which of 398 libraries hold the publication. *CASSI Quarterly Supplements* update *CASSI* 1907–1974, with the last quarterly of each year being cumulative for that year. Coded entries contain information on which journals are monitored by the BioSciences Information Service, the Engineering Index, Inc., and the Original Article Tear Sheet Service of the Institute for Scientific Information. *CASSI* is also available in computer-readable form.

The *Parent Compound Handbook* is issued in two parts: *Parent Compound File* and *Index of Parent Compounds*, which comprise a reference tool to the more than 44,000 ring parents plus 2000 cyclic and acyclic stereoparents, and 100 boron and cage parents referenced in *Chemical Abstracts* from 1907 through 1978 (supplements were issued every two months in 1979 and 1980). The *Parent Compound File* includes the following information: structural diagram and locant numbering, CAS registry number, CA Index name, molecular formula, Wiswesser line notation, and ring analysis data. The *Index of Parent Compounds* is a six-way index (by CA Index name, CAS Registry number, molecular formula, etc.) to the entries in the *Parent Compound File*.

As the price of *Chemical Abstracts* escalated beyond the reach of the individual chemist and chemical engineer, Chemical Abstracts Service introduced in 1963 five CA Section Groupings: Biochemistry, Organic Chemistry, Macromolecular, Applied Chemistry and Chemical Engineering, and Physical and Analytical Chemistry, at a price of $35 (now $150) per Section Grouping to members of the American Chemical Society and $70 (now $350) per Section Grouping to others. Each Section Grouping contains the total abstracts contained in the specific sections of the CA biweekly issues.

The latest publication introduced by Chemical Abstracts Service is CA Selects, a series of current awareness publications, each of which pertains to a special area of interest, such as Gas Chromatography, Mass Spectrometry, Fungicides, Photochemistry, Corrosion, Forensic Chemistry, New Books in Chemistry. In 1981, there were 100 CA Selects topics available, priced at $75. Each issue includes those abstracts and bibliographic citations published in CA related to the special area of interest of each CA Selects.

Chemical Industry Notes, a weekly digest of and index to business and economic news on the chemical industry from over 80 publications, is published by Chemical Abstracts Service and by the ACS Division of Public Affairs and Communication. Coverage is of production, prices, sales, plant expansion, new products and processes, executive changes, etc. Each issue covers 900–1000 items.

Table 30 lists the publications and services of CAS and their prices as of 1981.

TABLE 30.   CAS Publications and Services as of 1981

Publications	Base Price ($)
Abstracts and Indexes	
Chemical Abstracts	
Weekly Issues and Volume Indexes	5500
Weekly Issues Only	5300
Volume Indexes Only	5300
Index Guide, 1977–1981	50
Subject Coverage Manual	5
CAS Printed Access Tools	15
CA Section Groupings	150
CA Chemissues (Microfiche) (No Indexes)	
First Year	5000
Subsequent Years	3500
CA on Microfilm (No Indexes)	
First Year	4300
Subsequent Years	2800
Collective Indexes	
10th, 1977–1981, v80 books	9000
9th, 1972–1976, 57 books	6000
8th, 1967–1971, 35 books	3200
7th, 1962–1966, 24 books	2900
6th, 1957–1961, 15 books	2300
5th, 1947–1956, 19 books	2000
4th, 1937–1946, 6 books	550
3rd, 1927–1936, 5 books	400
2nd, 1917–1926, 5 books	300
1st, 1907–1916, 4 books	200
27-Year, 1920–1946, Collective Formula	200
10-Year, 1937–1946, Numerical Patent	50
Collective Indexes on Microfilm or Microfiche[a]	
7th, 8th, and 9th	
First Year	2245
Subsequent Years	920

TABLE 30. *(Continued)*

Publications	Base Price ($)
1st–6th[a]	
First Year	1000
Subsequent Years	425
Handbooks and Directories	
CASSI (Source Index)	
1907–1979 and	
Quarterly Supplements (1980–1984)	1218
*Registry Handbook—*Number Section	1018
1965–1971	
1972–1976	116
1977–1981 (Free with 10th Collective)	136
Registry Handbook—Common Names	546
(Microfilm or Microfiche)	₁500
Parent Compound Handbook	
1979 Edition and Supplements	500
1981–1983 Supplements and Indexes	350
International CODEN Directory (1980–1983)	1150
CA Selects	
At the time of this writing (June, 1981) there were 110 special topics available in areas such as analytical, biochemistry, physical, environmental, and general, priced at $75.	
Chemistry Industry Notes and Index	700
Chemical Titles	
ACS Members	90
Others	180

[a]For the 1st–6th, there are 44 microfilm rolls or 791 microfiche; for the 7th–9th, there are 103 microfilm rolls or 2050 microfiche.

From 1907 until a few years ago, CAS abstracts were prepared by an international cadre of about 3600 abstractors. Most recently, abstracting combined with indexing is now performed by CAS staff at Columbus, Ohio. In 1979, approximately 85% of the abstracts were prepared in-house. There were good reasons for this change, the most important being that it was compatible with the high degree of computerization in practically all CAS operations, and the computerization provided on-line assistance for interactive editing and analysis. Volunteer abstractors, about 1200, are still an essential component of the CAS operation, and the majority of them, who reside in Japan, Czechoslovakia, Poland, and other nations, is needed for their linguistic skills and scientific knowledge. There is, of course, considerable linguistic skill and scientific expertise throughout the CAS staff, who come from many of the 135 countries from which CAS receives documents in 55 languages.

Between 12 and 15 years ago, the American Chemical Society and the Organization for Economic Cooperation and Development (OECD) initiated discussions on the feasibility for international sharing of the production and distribution of chemical information services based on the CAS data base. Following these discussions, 12 chemical information scientists from six OECD countries plus several from Japan worked as full-time employees in Columbus. On returning to their native countries, these so-called interns established national information services with CAS computer-readable files.

In addition, CAS had working relationships with organizations in several nations, such as England, Germany, Japan, Switzerland, and France. The Chemical Society (London) set up one of the first centers using CAS computer-readable data bases. BASF, Bayer, and Hoechst in Germany, through the Internationale Dokumentations gesellschaft fuer Chemie (IDC), an organization of 11 German companies, use the CAS chemical substance identification data base as input to their substructure search and retrieval system. Likewise, the French Association for Research and Development in Chemical Information (ARDIC) cooperated with CAS in developing a structure handling system and integrating it with a text search system. The Basel Information Center for Chemistry (BASIC), a cooperative organization whose members are Ciba-Geigy, Hoffman-LaRoche, and Sandoz in Switzerland, uses CAS files for substructure search services. The Japan Information Center of Science and Technology (JICST) has been extremely active in utilizing CAS data bases for disseminating information services.

Under a bilateral agreement with The Chemical Society (London), the United Kingdom Chemical Information Service (UKCIS) provides abstracts and index entries for journal articles and patents published in the United Kingdom. UKCIS also markets CAS publications and services. A similar agreement exists with the Gesellschaft Deutscher Chemiker (GDCh) and (in 1975) with IDC (did not include abstract and index input), with JAICI (for developing CAS Services to the Japanese chemical community), and with France's Centre National de l'Information Chimique (CNIC). CNIC is a nonprofit association of academic, industrial, governmental, and scientific societies to coordinate French information activities. One of the members of CNIC is the Centre National de la Recherche Scientifique (CNRS) which, among other operations, publishes the *Bulletin Signaletique* series of abstract journals.

The participating organizations in England, Germany, and France assume a share of the production costs of CAS data bases, in return for which they have marketing rights for CAS publications and services. Their representatives serve CAS in an advisory capacity on various committees.

CAS COMPUTERIZED OPERATIONS AND DATA BASES

Many evolutionary changes took place at CAS during the 1960s. With financial support from the National Science Foundation, planning was begun for building a highly automated processing system and creating a computer-readable data base. Early results were realized in the person–machine interactions for handling bibliographic data, abstracts, and index entries with a minimum of intellectual input. Computerization allowed data to pass through many editorial stages with only the initial human input and allowed the production of a variety of publications and services as repackaged outputs from the single input. In the computer photocomposition process, complexities of chemical nomenclature required over 1500 different character sets and symbols. Because different outputs were produced in a variety of fonts and formats, it was necessary for CAS to develop its own software for computer processing. By the end of 1970, CAS was well on the way to producing its major products via computer. It is now photocomposing most of the ACS primary journals and using this input also in processing CAS publications and services. Each character input at CAS appears between two and three times in CAS products, and most proofing is handled by computer checking and error recording. One of the major accomplishments of computerization at CAS has been the Chemical Registry System, which became an integral part of indexing operations for *CA* by providing controls for structure diagrams and index names.

Chemical Titles (CT), introduced in 1961, was the first product to come out of CAS's computer-based methods. This biweekly lists titles of papers appearing in 700 journals wrapped around each significant word (key word in context) in the title and arranged in alphabetical sequence in the center of the page, with parts of the title on either side. It is available in hard copy and as a computer-readable file.

In addition to CT, the following computer-readable files are available:

Chemical-Biological Activities (CBAC). Introduced in 1965 as an abstract/index publication, *CBAC* now contains on computer-readable tape about 60,000 abstracts from sections 1–5 and 62–64 of CA. CBAC covers interactions of chemical substances with biological systems, and pharmacological and pharmaceutical techniques.

Polymer Science and Technology (POST).   Introduced in 1967 as an abstract/index publication, POST now contains on computer-readable tape about 40,000 abstracts from Sections 35–46 on various aspects of macromolecular chemistry.

Ecology and Environment.   It covers about 60,000 abstracts from Sections 4, 17, 19, 53, 59, 60, and 61.

Energy.   Some 44,000 abstracts from Sections 50–52, 69, and 70–72 are covered.

Food and Agricultural Chemistry.   About 42,600 abstracts from Sections 4, 5, and 16–19 are covered.

Materials.   About 80,000 abstracts from Sections 35–39, 41–43, and 53–58 are covered.

CA Condensates.   Introduced in 1968, CA Condensates was the first data base covering all documents abstracted in CA weekly issues. The file is searched by key words found in the titles or selected from the abstracts, with output by abstract numbers and bibliographic information.

REG/CAN.   A useful companion to CA Condensates, REG/CAN provided CA abstract numbers for documents containing information on specific chemicals identifiable by CAS registry numbers. the CA abstract number was used to access CA Condensates for bibliographic information, that is, titles, authors, and references. CA Condensates, however, was replaced with CA BIBLO File at the end of 1979; the new computer-readable service links bibliographic information with CA abstract numbers.

CASIA (CA Subject Index Alert).   CASIA allows the retrieval of CA abstract numbers for documents by terms used in the Chemical Substance Index, General Subject Index, and Formula Index, and by CAS registry numbers.

CA SEARCH.   The product of the merger of CASIA and CA Condensates, CA SEARCH has the advantages of both files for computer searching.

CA Index Guide.   In computer-readable form, CA Index Guide is particularly useful with CASIA and CA SEARCH for the development of profiles. This file contains cross-references that link common chemical names and general subjects to valid CA index headings.

CASSI (Chemical Abstracts Service Source Index).   CASSI allows retrieval by identification of any of 50,000 titles of serials and nonserials and informs users which libraries hold specific documents of interest.

Patent Concordance. Approximately 80,000 patents were processed in 1979 by the Patent Concordance, which links equivalent patents and patent applications to the CA abstract number of the patent or patent application first received and processed for the specific invention. Beginning in 1980, CAS has drawn patent information for its publications and services from computer files compiled by the International Patent Documentation Center (INPADOC) in Vienna, Austria. INPADOC receives and standardizes information from 46 national patent offices and two international organizations, INPADOC's data base contains information on over 8 million patents going back to 1968, and links patent documents issued by various nations on the same invention. Approximately 18,000 newly issued patents are input to the data base each week. CAS now prepares the CA Patent Concordance from the weekly updates and backfile for its weekly, semiannual, and five-year collective indexes to CA. The computer-readable form ceased publication in 1980.

CIN (Chemistry Industry Notes). With its information on the business aspects of the chemical industry, CIN allows retrieval of extracts from articles published in trade and industrial journals relating to production, pricing, sales, plants, products, and processes, to government and industrial activities, and to people. Keyword and corporate name indexes are provided.

Table 31 lists the CAS computer-readable files and their prices as of 1981.

Subscribers to CAS computer-readable files may choose either 800 or 1600 bpi. All are in Standard Distribution Format (SDF), by which information entered is recorded by defining the content and format of each type of information (such as the title of a document) as a particular data element and, once a search technique has been developed for a given data element, by applying the same technique to other CAS files for that data element.

CAS provides a variety of publications and aids in the use of its computer-readable files (see Table 32).

Document Delivery Service, the latest service introduced by CAS, provides copies of papers and patents cited in its publications and computer files. Copies of most documents cited since 1972 and of most Russian documents cited since 1960 are available at $10 per document under 51 pages and $20 per document of 51 pages or more. CAS, which pays copy fees to publishers loans the original documents whenever the copyright status is not clear.

TABLE 31.   CAS Computer-Readable Files and Prices as of 1981 for Annual License Fee

File	Base fee + postage ($)
CA SEARCH	10,520
CA BIBLIO FILE	5,520
REG/CAN	4,120
CA Index Guide	
10th Collective Index	2,420
9th Collective Index	2,420
8th Collective Index	2,420
CASSI	
First Year	3,060
Subsequent Years	1,540
CT	1,860
CIN	4,020

TABLE 32.   CAS Aid Packages for Their Computer Files

Aid	Price ($)
Evaluation Aids	
CA Condensates	50
CA Index Guide	50
CA SEARCH	50
CASIA	30
CASSI	50
CBAC	30
CIN	30
CT	30
Ecology and Environment	30
Energy	30
Food and Agriculture	30
Materials	30
Patent Concordance	30
POST	30
REG/CAN	50
SDF Specifications Manual	30

8

OTHER INDEXING/ABSTRACTING SERVICES

Although *Chemical Abstracts* is an invaluable tool for chemists and chemical engineers, it cannot serve all their information needs. For many aspects of the literature matrix of chemistry and chemical technology, other indexing/abstracting services are highly relevant and useful and play an important role as current awareness and retrieval mechanisms. Some of these services were developed to handle broad disciplines, such as chemistry, physics, and biology, and some to handle subdisciplines, such as analytical chemistry, ceramics, and corrosion. One result of computerization of indexing/abstracting services has been by products that are essentially hand-tailored, such as *CA Selects*, or that are directed to use by small groups or even individual scientists, such as ASCATOPICS or SDI (selective desemination of information) services.

The more important indexing/abstracting services are described below. Additional services are listed in the appendix of this chapter.

AGRICULTURAL SERVICES AND TECHNOLOGY INFORMATION SYSTEM (AGRIS)

AGRIS is an international development of the Food and Agriculture Organization (FAO) of the United Nations under the leadership of the National Agricultural Library. The data base, initiated in 1971, consists of about 100,000 references accumulated annually on magnetic tape to provide current awareness printouts and an in-depth retrieval system. AGRINDEX is the monthly index publication of AGRIS.

AMERICAN PETROLEUM INSTITUTE (API) INFORMATION SERVICES

The American Petroleum Institute (API) produces three data bases which consist of over 200,000 journal literature citations and 98,000 patents from over the world. They may be searched online via SDC's ORBIT system. The three bases are APILIT (journal literature), APIPAT (patents), and P/E News. APILIT and APIPAT are available only to subscribers. P/E News, which is available to anyone, contains over 50,000 items taken from a core of business oriented magazines. Items in the journal and patent data bases go back to 1964.

BIOSCIENCES INFORMATION SERVICE OF BIOLOGICAL ABSTRACTS (BIOSIS)

Founded in 1927 as *Biological Abstracts* (BA) in the zoology department of the University of Pennsylvania, BIOSIS is today the major alerting and retrospective information service (BA is now one of the products from BIOSIS) for those in the life sciences. Whereas Volume 1 of *Biological Abstracts* contained about 15,000 abstracts, recent volumes now average about 250,000 abstracts, which come from approximately 8000 primary publications and from some 90 countries, and which cover the entire spectrum of life sciences. *BA* is issued twice each month, with four computer-generated indexes: author, biosystematic, subjects in context, and subject specialities. *BioResearch Index*, published monthly, provides citations to references related to but not appearing in *Biological Abstracts*, such as symposia, letters, and government reports. *Microfilmed BA* comprises the complete *Biological Abstracts*, from 1927, on 16-mm microfilm. *BA Previews* is the magnetic tape version of *Biological Abstracts* and *BioResearch Index*. Other publications and services are the following:

Abstracts of Mycology, published monthly with abstracts and references reported in *Biological Abstracts* and *BioResearch Index*.

Current Literature Alerting Search Service (CLASS), a selective dissemination and current awareness service based on customized profiles.

Custom Search Service, retrospective searches of *BIOSIS* tapes on a contract basis.

Abstracts on Health Effects of Environmental Pollutants (HEEP), a printed and tape version of abstracts and citations dealing with drug toxicity produced for the National Library of Medicine for inclusion in the *TOXLINE* data base. Approximately 10% (about 23,000) of the articles reviewed by *BIOSIS* are in this category.

BRITISH ABSTRACTS

A section of *Journal of the Chemical Society* (1871–1925) was relegated to abstracts of pure chemistry articles published in the more important journals throughout the world, as was a section of *Journal of the Society of Chemical Industry* (1882–1925) to applied chemistry. In 1926, the abstract sections of these two journals merged to become *British Chemical Abstracts. Physiological Abstracts* merged with it in 1938 under the name *British Chemical and Physiological Abstracts,* which was changed to *British Abstracts* in 1946. Increasing costs combined with a greatly expanding literature forced the operation to cease in 1953. The *Journal of Applied Chemistry* assumed the responsibility for abstracting the applied literature. Other areas were assumed by the *Journal of the Sciences of Food and Agriculture, Analytical Abstracts,* and *International Abstracts of the Biological Sciences.*

Although the quality of abstracts was very high, indexing and coverage of the literature were somewhat below the American and German standards. *British Abstracts* is still extremely valuable for its list of British patents over its period of existence and for its excellent coverage of Allied Intelligence Mission Reports, such as *FIAT* (Field Information Agency—Technical) and *BIOS* (British Intelligence Objectives Subcommittee). Annual indexes of subject, author, and patent were issued annually, and collective indexes were issued for the periods 1923–1932 and 1933–1937.

BULLETIN SIGNALÉTIQUE

This French abstract journal, introduced in 1940, is issued by Centre National de la Recherche Scientifique in Paris as 22 monthly, separately available publications, such as *Informatique, Chimie, Polymeres,* and others. It is a particularly useful source of French university theses and dissertations and of European conference proceedings. Original articles abstracted in the *Bulletin* are available as microforms. Author and subject indexes are issued annually.

CAIN NATIONAL AGRICULTURAL LIBRARY AGRICULTURAL SCIENCE DATABASE

CAIN is the acronym for Cataloging-Indexing, a document locator and bibliographic system for the National Agricultural Library (NAL) collection. NAL is responsible for collecting and disseminating agricultural information on an international basis. This literature comprises chiefly books and journals. Since 1970, newly acquired publications, including articles selected from over 6500 journals, have been input for the data base in economics, rural sociology, animal husbandry, engineering, entomology, nutrition, forestry, pesticides, soils, fertilizers, etc. This data base is accessible by purchase of magnetic tapes or by online terminals with Lockheed, SDC, University of Florida, University of Georgia, and others.

Printed products produced from CAIN tapes include book catalogs, bibliographies, journal title listings, etc. Each issue of *Bibliography of Agriculture*, a monthly author/subject index to the literature of agriculture, contains an average of about 10,000 entries.

CHEMISCHES ZENTRALBLATT

Originally introduced in 1830 under the name *Pharmaceutisches Centralbatt* (1830–1849), it was later published under the title *Chemisches-Pharmaceutisches Centralblatt* (1850–1856), then *Chemisches Centralblatt* (1856–1896) as the emphasis was changed to chemistry, and finally *Chemisches Zentralblatt* from 1897 to 1969, the year it ceased publication. This was the outstanding abstracting/ indexing service in chemistry until the outbreak of World War II. Publication stopped in 1945, then resumed with a West and East German edition. In 1952, it was published again as one edition with special efforts to cover the 1945–1951 period with its usual high quality abstracts and indexes.

Issues appeared weekly with abstracts arranged under nine major classes, which were further subdivided within a well defined classification system. The original intent was to cover only papers concerned with pure chemistry, particularly those produced in Germany. In 1919, this intent was broadened considerably by the incorporation of the abstract section of *Angewandte Chemie* to cover the world's literature for both pure and applied chemistry. Beginning in 1919, it also broadened its coverage to patents from almost wholly German ones to those issuing from the major industrial nations, although the coverage of patents continued to be comphrehensive for German patents only. Announcements of new books began in 1926, and again the coverage of those issuing in Germany was best.

Indexes were issued every three or four years; then, beginning in 1925, indexes were issued cumulatively every five years, for the periods 1925–1929, 1930–1934, and 1935–1939. Formula indexes, arranged by the Richter system, were introduced in 1922. Although the abstracts were excellent, they were designed to be extremely concise, with heavy use of abbreviations. This made them difficult to read even for those fluent in German, but expertise came with experience.

CURRENT RESEARCH INFORMATION SYSTEM (CRIS)

CRIS is produced by the U.S. Department of Agriculture as a service to researchers in agricultural areas to inform them of ongoing research. The system collects and disseminates information on some 20,000 projects of nearly 100 federal and state agricultural agencies.

CURRENT CONTENTS

The Institute for Scientific Information (ISI) publishes a series of Current Contents, a pocket size, weekly publication in which tables of contents of selected journals are reproduced. Examples are *Current Contents, Physical and Chemical Sciences (CCP & CS)*, *Current Contents, Life Sciences (CCLS)*, and *Current Contents, Engineering and Technology (CCE & T)*. CCLS covers about 1000 journals, announcing 3000 articles per week, in biochemistry, medicine, botany, zoology, pharmacology, etc. CCP & CS covers about 1700 journals, announcing some 3000 articles per week, in chemistry, chemical engineering, and other physical sciences.

CURRENT INDEX TO CONFERENCE PAPERS

Current Index to Conference Papers (CICP), published monthly by CCM Information Corporation, is an alerting publication to papers which are to be delivered or which have been presented at over 1000 scientific and technical meetings throughout the world in three areas: chemistry, life sciences, and engineering. CICP in chemistry covers about 25,000 papers presented annually at some 250 meetings or conferences. The subject index includes the title of the paper, author's name and address, and the meeting.

CURRENT ABSTRACTS OF CHEMISTRY AND INDEX CHEMICUS

Index Chemicus (IC) was introduced in 1960 by ISI as a comprehensive and concise publication to report information on new chemical compounds and new synthetic methods published in a core of important journals. The format was designed for easy scanning by use of structural diagrams and equations, a graphic abstract summarizing analytical methods, and a use profile of the chemicals and of the activities of compounds, supported by data. Indexes are included monthly, semi-annually, and annually by subject, author, journal, and molecular formula.

In 1970, *IC* split into two publications: one was called *Current Abstracts of Chemistry (CAC)*, while the other retained the name *Index Chemicus (IC)*. *CAC* abstracts all articles from the core journals and is published weekly in two parts: one on new compounds and reactions, and one on all other areas. *IC* is the index to *CAC* and is included in the weekly CAC and issued separately as quarterly and annual cumulations.

CURRENT PHYSICS INDEX AND INFORMATION NOTICES

The American Institute of Physics (AIP), founded in 1931, is a federation of seven leading American societies in the fields of physics and astronomy which operates within one agency those functions essential for all seven societies. The institute publishes scientific journals, provides abstracting and indexing services, serves as the communication channel to the public, carries on manpower studies, participates in the documentation and study of the history and philosophy of physics and related disciplines, and interacts with other scientific societies. AIP membership is slightly over 60,000.

In addition to publishing 18 scientific journals, three member-society bulletins, and 19 translation journals (which are also available in 16-mm microfilm cartridges or reels), AIP produces the following two abstracting/indexing services:

Current Physics Index. With quarterly and annual cumulative indexes, CPI provides author and subject indexes to the AIP and member-society primary research journals. Each quarterly index contains abstracts and bibliographic information from articles published the preceding quarter; the annual index (without abstracts) includes information from the articles published during the year. Subscription rate is $95 ($30 to members).

Searchable Physics Information Notices (SPIN).   This is a computer readable magnetic tape with titles, authors, abstracts, primary journal references, cited journal articles, key words, and reel and frame numbers of the microfilm edition of the journals. An average of about 1500 articles from AIP and member-society journals are covered each month. This coverage represents about 25% of the world's physics literature.

THE ENGINEERING INDEX

Volume 1 of *The Engineering Index Annual* was issued in 1884 with 924 items. It now averages over 85,000 abstracts from over 2000 publications on research and applications relevant to engineering. Journal articles, conferences, and patents are abstracted and indexed. Copies and translations of most of the articles appearing in *Engineering Index* are available from the Engineering Societies Library. The index is in three parts: subject, author, and author affiliation. A microfilm edition is available. The *Engineering Index Monthly* was introduced in 1962. Other services available are:

CARD-A-LERT—abstracts on 5-in. × 3-in. cards as entered in *Engineering Index Monthly*.

COMPENDEX—a monthly computer tape service of the *Engineering Index Monthly*.

PIE—publications indexed for *Engineering Index*.

SHE—subject headings used for *Engineering Index*.

Plastics Monthly—a selection coverage, in printed form, of the plastics field going back to 1965.

Energy Abstracts—a monthly publication of abstracts and references covering the world's literature of energy as a subset of the *Engineering Index* plus items from the Energy Research and Development Administration (ERDA) and National Technical Information Service (NTIS), with indexing terms based on the ERDA's thesaurus.

FEDERAL ENERGY DATA INDEX (FED)

The Energy Information Administration (EIA) of the U.S. Department of Energy (DOE) is developing an online data base of statistics on energy reserves, production, demand, and technology. The tabular data in Volumes II and III of EIA's *Annual Report to Congress* are searchable input in the data base.

FOOD SCIENCE AND TECHNOLOGY ABSTRACTS (FSTA)

FSTA, produced by the Institute of Food Technologists (IFT) beginning in 1968, is a monthly abstract journal covering the world's literature relating to food research and development. It also has been available since 1972 on computer-readable magnetic tapes, and is online from the Illinois Institute of Technology, North Carolina Science and Technology Research Center, Lockheed, and Systems Development Corp. *FSTA* is a cooperative venture of IFT, the Commonwealth Agricultural Bureaux in England, and the Institut fuer Documentationswesen in West Germany. More than 1200 journals from about 50 countries, patents from 20 countries, and all books are scanned regularly to produce about 1500 abstracts per month, which are indexed by author and subject. A one-year subscription costs $480, and the magnetic tapes are available at $2500 per year. The abstracts are arranged under 19 major classes.

INDEX TO SCIENTIFIC REVIEWS

This publication, introduced by ISI in 1975, lists and indexes 20,000 review papers from over 2700 journals in the physical, chemical, medical, and life sciences, and in engineering, agricultural, biological, and environmental areas. Items can be retrieved by author, key words in the title, organizations, and citation.

INDEX TO SCIENTIFIC AND TECHNICAL PROCEEDINGS

This publication, introduced by ISI in 1978, covers annually more than 80,000 papers from some 3000 proceedings, with indexes to those appearing in books and in journals. The publication is issued monthly with semiannual cumulations. The indexes include editor, author, topic of conference, key words in title, conference sponsor, meeting location, author's organization, and address of first author of each paper.

INTERNATIONAL PATENT DOCUMENTATION CENTER (INPADOC)

INPADOC was founded in 1972 to gather and store in a central data base the bibliographic data of patent documents on a worldwide basis. This centralization was a consequence of the 1970 Patent Cooperation Treaty with the support of the World Intellectual Property Organization. In its Vienna office, INPADOC currently has in machine-readable form patent information office from 46 countries (in 14 languages).

As a central data exchange agency for patent offices of the 46 participating countries, INPADOC has computerized the bibliographic information from over eight million patents it has so far received with computer output on microfilm (COM) for those wishing microfilm or with computer printouts. The data base currently consists of a back file (to 1968) and a current one for updating. These files are searchable by priority date, country, and number; IPC; applicant; inventor; and publication date, country, and number of equivalent patents. The services are available to anyone for a charge. Among the services is the *INPADOC Patent Gazette (IPG)*, a weekly microfiche publication in three parts: IPC, a selected classification service, and selected patent numerical service. IPG, a COM byproduct, covers the patents of 46 countries added to the data base the preceding week, and lists all equivalents or patent family numbers stored in the INPADOC data base. The three parts are complemented with a corresponding cumulative index service. INPADOC services, including copies of complete patents from 23 countries and microfilm copies from 19 countries, are available in the United States from IFI Plenum Data Company, Arlington, Va. INPADOC is now in the process of making the data bases available via an online network.[1]

INTERNATIONAL REGISTER OF POTENTIALLY TOXIC CHEMICALS (IRPTC)

In 1976, the United Nations Environment Program established in Geneva the IRPTC to collect and store in a computer all data relating to environmental hazards associated with chemicals. The data are available to U.N. member countries through a network of cooperating data bases and institutions. The file has been built along the lines of the one compiled by the National Institute for Occupational Safety and Health (NIOSH) for its own register of the toxic effects of 21,000 chemical substances and will include the NIOSH file along with others. IRPTC includes data on mammalian, marine organism, and vegetation toxicology, and deals with products such as food additives, pesticides, oil spills, and general ecological effects. The major products are printed books, quarterly bulletins, and workshops.

JAPAN INFORMATION CENTER OF SCIENCE AND TECHNOLOGY (JICST)

JICST was founded in 1957 as the Japanese government's information center to publish current bibliographies and to establish a bibliographic data base. In 1972 JICST initiated SDI (selective dissemination of information) services using its own data base, CACon, and MEDLARS. Online retrieval services were initiated in 1976.

References are put into the data base by UDC (universal decimal classification) and JICST classification codes; journal abbreviations, CODEN (five-letter code name for journals), and ISSN (International Standard Serial Number); descriptors assigned by indexers; and author, company or university, type of publication, language, etc. There were 270 terminals online as of may 1979.[2]

NATIONAL TECHNICAL INFORMATION SERVICE (NTIS)

NTIS was created by the U.S. Congress in 1950 within the U.S. Department of Commerce, as the central source for the sale and distribution of reports resulting from government-sponsored research and development. In 1978, NTIS distributed about 23,000 documents daily or about six million throughout the year. Its collection now exceeds one million separate documents, of which about 150,000 are of foreign origin. All costs of operating NTIS are covered by its sales.

Its online computer covers the holdings from 1964 on—some 680,000 reports—and 70,000 new reports are added annually. Copies of the documents are available as photocopies or microforms. NTIS issues the biweekly journal Government Reports Announcements & Index (GRA & I), which summarizes current reports under various subject categories, and the biweekly Tech Notes, which contains one-page summaries of new applications of technology developed by nine Federal agencies, including NASA, Army, and Air Force, and their contractors. *Tech Notes* also includes *Selected Technology for Licensing*, one-page summaries of government inventions.

Research summaries from originating agencies in 33 categories, such as chemistry, energy, and library and information science, are issued by NTIS on a subscription basis. Its custom searches, an online search in a specified area of the entire collection, is called NTISearch. Summaries in the printout average about 250 words and cost $50 for up to 100 summaries. NTIS now has available in printed form many computer searches that it sells at $28.

Translations for the federal government are processed by the National Science Foundation under the Special Foreign Currency Science Information Program (SFCSIP). About 50,000 pages per year of foreign documents result from this program, and, since 1959, over 750,000 pages of translations have been completed. Newly completed translations are announced in NTIS's GRAI.

SRIM (Selected Research in Microfiche) is a new NTIS service which provides full texts in microfiche of selected topics or from selected agencies. SRIM reports are provided biweekly at a cost of $0.45 per title.

NTIS is the national marketing coordinator for the following Information Analysis Center Services sponsored and partially financed by governmental agencies: CPIA (Chemical Propulsion Information Agency), CDC (Cryogenic Data Center), Infrared Information and Analysis Center, NSI (Nuclear Safety Information Center), PTEC (Plastics Technical Evaluation Center), Thermophysical Properties Research Center, and Toxicology Information Response Center.

Despite the pervasive coverage of NTIS, each federal agency also has the privilege of determining the dissemination of its own technical reports. This policy affects the Government Printing Office (GPO) and the Depository Library Program particularly. GPO is responsible for printing and distributing government publications for the 1230 libraries in the Depository Library Program, and NTIS is presumably responsible for distributing reports not otherwise available. Furthermore, certain agencies, such as NCLIS (National Commission on Libraries and Information Science), NSF (National Science Foundation), and NIH (National Institutes of Health), issue publications at no charge or at a subsidized charge, whereas NTIS reports are rather costly, usually two to three times that of GPO for the same number of pages, and NTIS products often are of low photocopy quality. Moreover, NTIS advertises reports that are available in the journal literature without noting the fact, and fails to distinguish between interim and final reports.

NIH/EPA SUBSTRUCTURE DATA BASE

Work towards designing a substructure online searching system at the National Institutes of Health (NIH) and the Environmental Protection Agency (EPA) has resulted in its application to over 20 data bases through Fein-Marguart Associates, Baltimore, Md. or through Tymshare. Some of the data bases integrated into the overall system and the number of chemicals each contains are the following:

TSCA Candidate List (30,000)
Mass Spectrometry (25,000)
Cambridge X-Ray Crystallography (10,000)
Merck Index (9,000)
NCI PHS-149 (5,500)
Carbon-13 NMR (3,700)

Chemical compounds can be retrieved on the basis of their structural characteristics, with output such as the following:

CAS Registry Number
Molecular Formula
Systematic Chemical Name
Synonyms
Structural Image

The structural image is derived from the CAS connection table, which is stored in the data base for each compound. A search may be made for all substances having certain substructure features in common.

NATIONAL LIBRARY OF MEDICINE (NLM)
INFORMATION SERVICES

Beginning in 1879, the National Library of Medicine introduced its *Index Medicus*, an abstract service of the medical and biomedical literature. The citations to monographs, theses, reports, and journal articles are indexed on the basis of NLM's *Medical Subject Headings* (*MeSH*), with a controlled but open-ended vocabulary of two types: an alphabetic list of subjects with cross-references, and a categorized list of

14 major classes and 65 subclasses arranged hierarchically with alphanumeric designations. *MeSH* is revised and printed annually.

In 1962, NLM began to investigate the possibility of computerizing *Index Medicus*, and succeeded in establishing the system in 1964. The computerized system was assigned the acronym MEDLARS (Medical Literature Analysis and Retrieval System), and was used for the production of *Index Medicus*. Individualized bibliographies, an immediate by-product, were made available to health scientists on request.

NLM began its experiments with online search services in 1967 using the ORBIT programs of Systems Development Corporation, and the MEDLINE prototype became operational in 1970. TOXLINE was demonstrated and made operational in 1972, and was transferred to the NLM system in 1974.

TOXLINE consists of six data files or subfiles of the CAS *Chemical-Biological Activities (CBAC)*, NLM *Toxicity Bibliography*, BIOS *Abstracts on Health Effects of Environmental Pollutants (HEEP)*, American Society of *Hospital Pharmacists International Pharmaceutical Abstracts*, EPA Health Aspects of Pesticides Abstract Bulletin, and the W. J. Hayes, Jr., file *Pesticides, 1940–1966*. TOXLINE contains over 500,000 bibliographic citations, the majority with abstracts and about one-fifth with MeSH terms. More recently CAS registry members were assigned to the TOXLINE chemicals. This file, called *CHEMLINE*, was created for NLM by CAS. *TOXLINE* and *CHEMLINE* were heavily used by information scientists in the chemical industry for registering manufactured chemicals for EPA under the Toxic Substance Control Act.

Other data base systems online at NLM are the following:

SDILINE *(Selective Dissemination of Information Online).* Citations from forthcoming issues of *Index Medicus* are selected on the basis of a profile of interest.

Current Catalog. Over 200,000 monographs cataloged at NLM since 1965 and their locations at various libraries are listed.

CANCERLINE. The National Cancer Institute's (NCI's) CANCER-LINE, available through the MEDLINE system, consists of three data bases: CANCERLIT, containing over 80,000 abstracts of published cancer literature, updated monthly, and growing at about 25,000 abstracts per year; CANCERPROJ, containing 16,000 descriptions of ongoing cancer research projects, updated quarterly; and CLINPROT, containing about 1000 summaries of clinical protocols for treating specific types of cancer, with anticancer agents and modalities employed. Instructions for using CANCERLINE, which are very much similar to those for using TOXLINE, have been included in the Initial and Advanced Online Services Training Classes periodically scheduled at NLM.

NUCLEAR SCIENCE ABSTRACTS (NSA)

Nuclear Science Abstracts (NSA) was introduced in 1948. Its semi-monthly issues contain abstracts of technical reports of the U.S. Atomic Energy Commission and of other government agencies and publications (journal articles, patents, conference proceedings, and translations) relating to nuclear science and technology. The abstracts are categorized in ten major fields, such as general physics, high energy physics, nuclear physics, life sciences, chemistry, reactor technology, metals, and ceramics. The scientific and technical report collection contains well over 400,000 items of interest to the nuclear energy program, and 20,000 items are added annually. Input to NSA also comes from the scanning of over 1600 scientific and technical journals.

Input to the computer for each record is by bibliographic data, subject headings with modifiers, keywords, classification, and an indicative abstract of less than 200 words. Each record is assigned an accession number, which is used for retrieval and for duplicating references as requested. NSA is produced by the AEC's Division of Technical Information, Oak Ridge, Tenn.

OHIO COLLEGE LIBRARY CENTER (OCLC)

Among the early developers of online systems during the 1960s were the Columbia–Harvard–Yale medical libraries, which shared a catalog project that was a precursor to OCLC. Many people were involved in the creation of MARC (Machine-Readable Cataloging Formats) by the Library of Congress[4-6] which led to the introduction of the LC MARC tape service in 1968.

In 1965, F. G. Kilgour and R. Parker (3) proposed the Ohio College Library Center which went online in 1971. The file grew from 100,000 records to the present approximately five million. Recently the OCLC network has been implemented with a nationwide interlibrary loan subsystem. In 1979 OCLC was online to about 1800 libraries, whose users add 3000 new shared-cataloging records and 40,000 additional holdings symbols each day. Users are charged per title cataloged; unlimited searching generally is included in the cataloging charge.

SCIENCE CITATION INDEX (SCI)

Science Citation Index, published quarterly by the Institute for Scientific Information since 1964, is one of the newer reference search tools. SCI is arranged alphabetically by cited author. Each cited author entry, listed by the author's name and initials, gives the year the cited item was published and the publication containing the cited item with volume and pages. Cited items by the same author are listed chronologically. The citing reference is listed under the cited author, giving first the citing author's name, the publication and year, followed by volume and page of the citing reference. A code indicates whether the citing item is an article, abstract, editorial, or book. Source item authors are arranged alphabetically in a separate section called the "Source Index" which gives the full title of the citing (source) item, journal, volume, issue, pages, year, type of publication, and number of references cited. The "Source Index" also includes a "Corporate Index," arranged alphabetically by author under each corporate entry. Also included as a separate index is the "Permuterm Subject Index," in which all significant words in each title and subtitle alone or paired with other words are listed alphabetically as an index entry.

The citation index concept, first used in 1873 to relate legal cases with precedents, is known among lawyers as "Shepard's Citations." As a structured list of all cited references in a core collection of documents, SCI does indeed add a new dimension to the retrieval of documents. If we know the name of an author who has worked on a given topic, under this author's name in SCI we may identify all references in which the author has been cited. SCI has been used rather extensively as the basis for studies on the productivity of scientists and on the relative value of journals.

SMITHSONIAN SCIENCE INFORMATION EXCHANGE (SSIE)

The Smithsonian Science Information Exchange (SSIE) was founded in 1949 to develop and maintain a current, comprehensive inventory of ongoing, unclassified research projects sponsored or supported by federal agencies. The inventory is compiled on Notices of Research Project forms, a one-page summary of the project giving the supporting agency, contract number, title of the project, names of the investigators, address of where the work is being done, and period of the contract. Although the primary function of the data base is to inform the federal agencies of potential duplication of work, it is available to the public.

The exchange has been registering about 100,000 projects per year, not only from the federal agencies but also from nonfederal organizations, such as the Petroleum Research Fund, the Robert Welch Foundation, universities, and state agencies, and even from a few private companies. Since SSIE came into existence, over a million projects have been registered and are now available online or by SDI (selective dissemination of information) subscription with the Smithsonian Science Information Exchange, Inc., Washington, DC.

TEXTILE INFORMATION TREATMENT USERS' SERVICE (TITUS)

TITUS was introduced in 1970 by Institut Textile de France in cooperation with research institutes in Belgium, Germany, Italy, Spain, and the United Kingdom. The computer data base contains over 100,000 abstracts added since 1970 and currently being added at over 20,000 per year. The articles abstracted come from over 800 scientific and technical periodicals on textiles and textile-related subjects. TITUS is online in Europe and also in the United States through the SDC ORBIT system and NC/STRC (North Carolina Science and Technology Research Center, Research Triangle Park, N.C.). Monthly printout listings of abstracted literature references as well as bimonthly summaries in a specified field (SDI service) are available.

APPENDIX: ADDITIONAL INDEXING/ABSTRACTING SERVICES

ACS Single Article Announcement—monthly (1969), $24. American Chemical Society, Washington, DC 20036.

Abstract Review—monthly (1928), $15. National Paint and Coating Association, Washington, D.C.

Abstracts of Petroleum Substitutes Literature—monthly (1969), $400. American Petroleum Institute, New York.

Abstracts of Refining Literature and Petrochemicals Literature—weekly (1954), $8000. American Petroleum Institute, New York.

Abstracts on Health Effects of Environmental Pollution—monthly (1972), $115. BIOSIS, Phildelphia.

Agricultural Engineering Abstracts—monthly (also mag. tape), $85, Commonwealth Agricultural Bureaux, Farnham, England.

Analytical Abstracts—monthly (1954), £85. Chemical Society (London), London.

Applied Science and Technology Index—monthly (1958). H. W. Wilson Company, New York. A cumulative subject index to English language periodicals in aeronautics and space science, automation, chemistry, construction, earth sciences, electricity, and electronics.

Bibliography of Rubber Literature—annual (1942), $30. University of Akron, Akron, Ohio.

Bibliography on High Pressure Research—bimonthly (1968), $8. U.S. National Bureau of Standards, Washington, D.C.

Biological and Agricultural Index—monthly (1916). H.W. Wilson Company, New York.

BioResearch Index—monthly (1967), $600. BIOSIS, Philadelphia.

British Ceramics Index—monthly (1958), £20. British Ceramics Research Association, Penkhull, England.

Ceramic–Metal Systems Bibliography and Abstracts—loose-leaf (1929), $3. American Ceramic Society, Columbus, Ohio.

Chemical Substructure Index—monthly (1968), $1000. ISI, Philadelphia.

Computer and Information Systems, Riverdale, Md.—semimonthly (1962), $350.

Concrete Abstracts—bimonthly (1972), $70. American Concrete Institute, Detroit.

Corrosion Abstracts—bimonthly (1962), $95. Association of Corrosion Engineers, Houston, Tex.

Current Papers in Physics—biweekly (1966), £12. Institution of Electrical Engineers, London.

Dairy Science Abstracts—monthly (1939), $130. Commonwealth Agricultural Bureaux, England.

Dissertation Abstracts—monthly (1938), $125. University Microfilms, Ann Arbor, Mich.

Ecological Abstracts—bimonthly (1974), $40. Corpus Publ., Service, Toronto.

Energy Abstracts—monthly (1974), $265. Engineering Index, Inc., New York.

Energy Research Abstracts—simimonthly (1976), $184. U.S. Energy Resource and Development Administration, Oak Ridge, Tenn.

Environment Abstracts—monthly (1971), $225. Environment Information Center, New York.

Fertilizer Abstracts—monthly (1968), $25. Tennessee Valley authority, Muscle Shoals, Ala.

Gas and Liquid Chromatography Abstracts—quarterly (1958), $36. Applied Science Publishers, Ltd., London.

Gas Chromatography Literature Abstracts and Index—monthly (1952), $324. Preston Publications, Inc., Nilas, Ill.

Index of Reviews in Organic Chemistry—annual (1971). Chemical Society (London), London.

Index to Forthcoming Russian Books—monthly (1970), $106. Scientific Information Consultants, London.

Information Science Abstracts—bimonthly (1966), $60. Documentation Abstracts, Inc., Philadelphia.

Institute of Paper Chemistry Abstract Bulletin—monthly (1930), $550. Institute of Paper Chemistry, Appleton, Wis.

Institute of Paper Chemistry, Keyword Index to Abstract Bulletin—monthly and semi-annual (1966), $360. Institute of Paper Chemistry, Appleton, Wis.

International Aerospace Abstracts—semimonthly (1961), $400. American Institute of Aeronautics and Astronautics, New York.

International Polymer Science and Technology—monthly (1974), $240. Rubber and Plastics Research Association (RAPRA), Shrewsbury, England.

Lead Abstracts—bimonthly (1958), free. Lead Development Association, London.

Liquid Chromatography Literature—bimonthly (1972), $180. Preston Publications, Inc., Niles, Ill.

Mathematical Reviews—monthly (1940), $850. American Mathematical Society, Providence, R.I.

Metalert—monthly (1974), $60. American Society for Metals, Metals Park, Ohio.

Metals Abstracts—monthly (1968). American Society for Metals, Metals Park, Ohio.

Nuclear Magnetic Resonance Literature—monthly (1964), $324. Preston Publications, Inc., Niles, Ill.

Nucleic Acids Literature—bimonthly (1973). Calatomic, Los Angeles.

Pesticides Abstracts—monthly, $18.75. U.S. Environmental Protection Agency, Washington, D.C.

Physical Review Abstracts—semimonthly (1970), $12. American Physical Society, New York.

Physics Abstracts—biweekly (1898), $380. Institution of Electrical Engineers, London.

Polarography Abstracts—quarterly (1976), $90. Science and Technology Agency, London.

Pollution Abstracts—bimonthly (1970), $99. Data Courier, Inc., Louisville, Ky.

Rheology Abstracts—quarterly (1958), $54. British Society of Rheology, Oxford, England.

Science Books and Films—quarterly (1965), $16. American Association for the Advancement of Science (AAAS), Washington, DC.

Solid State Abstracts—10/year (1957), $265. Cambridge Scientific Abstracts, Inc., Riverdale, Md.

STAR (Scientific and Technical Aerospace Reports)—semimonthly. (1963), $95. Superintendent of Documents, Washington, D.C.

Technical Book Review Index—10/year (1935), $20. JAAD Publishing Company, Pittsburgh.

Textile Technology Digest—monthly (1944), $100. Institute of Textile Technology, Charlottesville, Va.

Translations Register–Index—semimonthly (1959). The John Crerar Library, Chicago.

Weed Abstracts—monthly (1953), $85. Commonwealth Agricultural Bureaux, England.

World Textile Abstracts—semimonthly (1969), $120. Shirley Institute, Manchester, England.

World TransIndex—monthly (1967), $240. International Translation Centre, Delft, The Netherlands.

Zinc Abstracts—bimonthly (1943), free. Zinc Development Association, London.

REFERENCES

1. Pilch, W., and W. Wratschko, "INPADOC: A Computerized Patent Documentation System," *J. Chem. Info. Comput. Sci.*, **18**, 69–75 (1978).
2. Uchida, H., *Information System, Data Bases, and Online Services of JICST*, presented at ACS/CSS Chemical Congress, Honolulu, April 5, 1979.
3. Kilgour, F. G., and R. F. Smith, "Regional Plans for Medical Library Services—

Regional Library Services of the Yale Medical Library," *Bull. Med. library Assoc.* **52**, 501–502 (1964).

4. King. G. W., *Automation and the Library of Congress: A Survey Sponsored by the Council on Library Resources, Inc.,* Library of Congress, Washington, DC, 1963.

5. Markuson, B.E., "A Systems Development Study for the Library of Congress," *Library Quart. 36,* 197–273 (1966).

6. Avram, H. D., "Machine-Readable Cataloging (MARC) Program," in Vol. 16 of *Encyclopedia of Library and Information Science,* Dekker, New York, 1976.

9

COMPUTER-BASED INFORMATION SERVICES

Over the past 20 years the information complex entered into a new phase, one in which communications and interfacing with computers have arisen from a metamorphosis very much like that which occurred after the invention of the telephone on March 10, 1876. With the current rapid expansion of computerized data bases, we tend to think of their development as being of very recent vintage. It was in 1945, however, that Vannever Bush in his famous *Atlantic Monthly* article, "As We May Think," stated: "the instruments are at hand which, if properly developed, will give man access to, and command over, the inherited knowledge of the world." We still await the realization of online access to the world of chemistry.

Computers and telecommunications have been a major factor in the changing trends of chemical information science over the past 20 years. Both are magnificent tools for processing and communicating chemical information. However, they have not reached the point of displacing the library or of being common tools of laboratory scientists—or even of the majority of chemical information scientists.

Chemical information is a resource, and online data bases can be a major tool in facilitating the utilization of information. We are fairly successful at producing information—so successful that our journal, book, and patent literature overwhelms us daily, weekly, monthly, and yearly. The emerging information industry, the data base processor and the broker of products from data base processors for online users, has focused attention on input (in terms of the processor's convenience) and communications (in terms of the broker's convenience) very much in isolation from the ultimate user. It is people, not computers, who process information and communicate it meaningfully, but relatively little is being done to design systems that fit ultimate users; this awaits future development. In a broad sense, the communications revolution is beginning, and online data bases are part of it.

Before 1965, the products of journal publishers were documents to be processed by human hands and minds within indexing/abstracting services. These services handled the documents as many times as there were variables in their products, that is, for author, company, subject, classification, formula indexes, and abstracts, in addition to what was required for checking and proofing. In short, the operations were highly people-intensive, expensive, and prone to human errors and delays.

Chemical Abstracts, for example, would have encountered enormous difficulties had it continued to process and publish its products by the traditional methods for producing abstracts and indexes. With the advent of the third generation computer and massive storage devices and the employment of computerized photocomposition, Chemical Abstracts Service was able to build a highly automated processing system for producing abstracts and indexes efficiently, economically, and within rigid time constraints, and also to create a computer-readable information base that made possible a stable of new products. The computer-readable base, furthermore, was made available to brokers for online accessing by many users.

What Chemical Abstracts Service accomplished was the elimination of a great amount of redundant work and document handling, such as document analysis, information extraction by many people, and sorting, organizing, and arranging information for each product separately. Approximately 14 professional and 21 clerical operations were required between the selection of a document for the system and final publication of the abstract and index entries. With computerization, most data are handled only once, or with a minimum of professional or clerical intervention, even though the input may be used in several different outputs and in different formats.[43]

Chemical Abstracts Service developed its chemical registry system[17] in the 1960s based on a system described by Gluck[26] as a computer-based identification of molecular structures.[42] In this system a number, assigned to each unique substance, comprises a machine address that allows linkage of files containing structural information, nomenclature, index terms, and bibliographic information. Registry I was operational in 1964. The scope expanded in 1968 (registry II), and further increased in 1974 (registry III). The foundation of the system is an algorithm that generates a unique and unambiguous computer language description of each molecular structure in terms of atoms, bonds, spatial arrangements, etc. Over five million unique structures have been assigned numbers over the past 16 years, and new structures are entered at the rate of about 350,000 per year.

The registry is now used to identify about 6000 substances (about 1500 are new compounds) each working day in support of indexing and nomenclature operations at CAS. Index terms for approximately 75% of the substances in the current literature can be retrieved automatically by matching the names from the literature with those in the registry files or by matching the structured diagrams with those in the registry. Of the five million substances so far registered, 97% have a full molecular identification and 3% are identified by only molecular formula, name, or definition; about 12% of the file contains substances identified by their components, namely, alloys, polymers, mixtures, addition compounds, and complex salts. More than 75% of the registered substances contain at least one ring. Stereochemistry is specified for about 22% of the compounds. Statistically, an average compound in the system contains 43 atoms, of which 22 are hydrogen; 96% of the compounds contain carbon. There are 7.7 million names for the five million substances; polyethylene has 945 names. About 75% of the five million substances registered since 1965 were mentioned only once; about 1% of the registered substances account for 45% of those mentioned in the literature.

CAS registry numbers are now widely used in publications and computer files. They are also used by many information operations, such as those established in the Environmental Protection Agency, National Institute of Occupational Safety and Health, National Cancer Institute, International Occupational Safety and Health Center, and European Community's Environmental Chemicals Data and Information Network. CAS provides registry numbers at a charge of $3.75 for each number requested.

The distribution of CAS computer-readable files was initiated in 1965 with *Chemical Titles* on magnetic tape[23,24] Many more have become available since then through online services, such as Bibliographic Retrieval Services, Lockheed Information Systems, and SDC Search Service. The most basic CAS computer-readable files are CA BIBLIO FILE, CA SEARCH, CASSI, Chemical Industry Notes, Chemical Titles, and REG/CAN.

CACon (*CA Condensates*), introduced in 1969, corresponded to the documents abstracted in the *CA* printed issues from 1969 to 1980, inclusive, and included authors' names and affiliations; patentees and assignees; titles of papers, books, patents, and conference proceedings; and source document bibliographic data, *CA* section and subsection numbers, *CA* reference numbers, and keywords (author terminology). These were searchable items online.

CASIA (*CA* Subject Index Alert), introduced in the late 1970s, was issued every two weeks. This file contained the index entries for the *CA* *Chemical Substance* and *General Subject Indexes* sorted by *CA* publication citations since 1967. This file also contained molecular formulas and CAS registry numbers. On June 30, 1979, CASIA was replaced with CA SEARCH, and like CACon and CASIA is available only on a yearly license basis.

In November, 1980, CAS introduced CAS ONLINE for online searching of its file containing structure records for about two million substances cited in the literature since 1977. Substances registered in the chemical registry system prior to 1977 will be added to the file by the end of 1981. Newly registered substances will be added weekly at the rate of about 6000 per week. Access to the system is through Telenet via a compatible graphics terminal, although offline printouts are available to users without a graphics terminal. Search questions currently (1980 and early 1981) are phrased in terms of seven numbers assigned to some 5000 specific structural features and fragments for the identification of substances sharing the several screens of importance to the searcher—retrieved answers are displayed as two-dimensional structure diagrams with molecular formulas, CAS registry number, and stereochemical data on the graphics terminal or offline printouts. A search takes about five minutes. The system is available only after at least one member of an organization has completed a CAS workshop, the cost of which is included in the $250 start-up fee for the service.

THE DEVELOPMENT OF ONLINE INFORMATION SYSTEMS

The introduction and widespread use of edge-notched and optical coincidence cards during the 1940s and 1950s, and the design of information systems for these cards, established a good foundation for the design of information systems employing computers. Chemical information scientists who had played an important role in the design and develpment of systems for these cards particularly were receptive to conversion of card systems to computerized systems. Other positive factors were the National Science Foundation's support of systems developments for computers in the 1960s and 1970s, the information processors' recognition that computerization was an economic neces-sity, and the metamorphosis of computers through three generations from accounting machines to highly sophisticated, relatively low-cost, fast machines.[8,10,20,28,58,59]

The uniterm concept of indexing became popular in the 1940s and 1950s. Dissatisfaction with library classification and indexing systems and with the way documents were filed on library shelves motivated the adoption of the uniterm system as described by Taube[63]; the assignment of single words or concepts to represent the contents of a document, the assignment of an accession number to documents as received, and the posting of the accession numbers on each uniterm card characterizing the subjects of the document. It was not unusual for as many as 20–40 uniterms to be used for a single document. Whereas traditional subject indexing, when done properly, required the indexers to have knowledge of the contents of documents being indexed, the uniterm system generally was premised on the author's vocabulary. Although the uniterm system required fewer cards than that of the traditional subject index, users encountered a new experience: false drops, that is, the obtaining of unwanted references in the retrieval stage. To counteract the high probability of obtaining false drops, the system was modified with thesaurus control, or what used to be called subject authority list, and with links and rolls. Thus two new terms were introduced: *relevance* or *precision*, the ratio of the number of relevant references retrieved to the total references retrieved; and *recall*, the ratio of the number of relevant references retrieved to the number of relevant references in the system.

As chemical information scientists began to use accounting machines, namely, the sorter and collator, in the 1950s, then the computers through the 1950s and 1960s, the uniterm system was the indexing method of choice. However, as the use of computers increased for the processing of information systems, the uniterm system concept was displaced by the key word concept. At the beginning of the displacement, the conceptual differences were slight. The orientation to words remained; the major difference was at the input and output stages. Whereas the uniterm system appreciably reduced the need for the indexer to be a subject specialist, keyword indexing eliminated the indexer completely by the introduction of computerized KWIC (keywords in context) indexes.[22,37,38]

Titles of scientific papers, in general, are fairly representative of authors' objectives and sometimes of the contents of the papers. With the advent of second generation computers in the 1950s, and specifically with the availability of the IBM 7090 in the late 1950s, it was logical to explore the use of the computer in automatic indexing. One of the earliest publications on this concept was that by H. P. Luhn[37] in 1958. Luhn had titles of papers keypunched on tab cards, which were then processed in the IBM 7090 to shift each significnt word in the title to a fixed position for printing in an alphabetical array (the rest of the title surrounded each keyword). Within two years, over 30 applications of this technique were introduced, including the production of *Chemical Titles* by CAS under a National Science Foundation grant. Many variations of KWIC appeared in the early 1969s, for example, combining authors with keywords, using formats that conformed to the traditional ones, and placing the keywords in front of the titles. Studies on the validity of keywords versus subject indexes followed. It was generally agreed that titles needed to be improved if KWIC keywords were to specify the contents of a journal article. Many authors compose titles to attract the reader's attention, such as "Thinking Small" for a paper on microforms. These titles are useless in a keyword index.

Keyword indexes as produced in *Chemical Titles* have one advantage over uniterm indexes: the keywords are displayed with as much of the full title as permitted by the line limitation. In the 1960s, when print chains were highly limited by the number of characters that could be printed (many chains allowed only printouts by capital letters), lower case letters, superscripts, subscripts, chemical symbols, and many conventions had to be marked and altered editorially. Generally, the keyword index reference was a numerical or alphameric notation, and recourse was made to the bibliographic printout. As a subject index, keywords had many limitations. Document titles fall short of conveying the contents of documents, and the words in the title are too often variants of a subject and result in an alphabetical scattering of terms meaning the same thing. The literature erroneously characterized these indexes as permuted keywords in title — they are really wrapped around from the first to last keyword in each title, with the word order maintained intact.[31] Input until well into the 1960s was via tab cards, with up to 10 or more tab cards per document. The tab cards were then translated via computer onto magnetic tape and finally onto disk for storage, accessing, and processing.

A 1961 study, reported in 1964 by Freeman et al.,[24] with the CAS *Chemical Titles* magnetic tape for selective dissemination (SDI) based on keyword searching, resulted in retrieval of titles of interest that varied from 1.6% to 32%. Using a single keyword as against multiple keywords (with exclusion, that is, NOT, terms) resulted in 2015 references versus 910, with 18 and 17, respectively, being relevant. In evaluating the value of the tapes in producing an annual bibliography, it was found that valuable references were absent, especially those in journals such as *Journal of Chromatography*, in which 74 out of 301 titles did not use the word chromatography or any of its fragments, which would be redundant in this specialized journal.

Bond et al[7] set up an SDI system for Dow personnel using the CAS magnetic tape Chemical–Biological Activities (CBAC) system. The system set up in 1965 included 40 profiles based on keywords (title and abstract), authors, and journal CODEN (name of journal in a 5-letter code), with terms assigned positive and negative weights. Profiles established with the users generally took 15 minutes to one hour; the average profile consisted of 48 words. Articles of interest averaged about 20%, marginal interest 15%, and no interest 65%. The poor results were attributed to lack of vocabulary control in free-text searching. Another conclusion from this study was that inverting the entire file of words in titles and abstracts is very expensive, because each reference had an average of 93 different words; file inversion required between 200 and 300 users to be economically acceptable.

In developing a profile, we are restricted by the data base input, that is, we must subordinate what we consider to be good retrieval terms to the idosyncrasies of each data base we wish to use. Some data bases are helpful in providing aids, such as a word frequency listing, a manual describing how to use the system, or a thesaurus. It is important to test the profile and to adjust or refine the terms to make them as relevant as possible to both the data base and the user.[13,32,34,45,52,67]

NASA was an early exponent of SDI (selective dissemination of information). Its abstract journals, *STAR (Scientific and Technical Aerospace Reports)* and *IAA (International Aerospace Abstracts)* provided a large volume of abstracts in each issue, too large to satisfy the current awareness needs of many scientists and engineers working in specialized areas. In 1963, NASA began to operate a program that combined the promptness of its abstract announcement products with selectivity of individual or group interests as specified by an interest profile, that is, a list of subjects chosen from NASA's thesaurus. This profile list was matched via computer with the terms assigned to the documents in current issues of *STAR* and *IAA*, and a bibliographic listing of the matched documents was sent to the user.

ASCA (Automatic Subject Citation Alert, a product of the Institute for Scientific Information) was the first commercially available SDI product for the journal literature.[25] Introduced in 1965, ASCA covered the approximately 1600 journals ISI input to its *Science Citation Index (SCI)*. The ASCA output or printout is an individual weekly report of references selected by matching profile terms with those in the current issue of SCI. In the ASCA system, a profile consisting of keywords in titles, authors of papers, an author's organization, papers published in a given journal, a cited reference, or any combination of these parameters. A paper by Garfield and Sher[25] in 1967 stated that in an average week the production of ASCA required the computer to examine about 6000 items having some 180,000 index terms (60,000 cited references, 68,000 cited and publishing authors, 37,000 title keywords).

Current awareness searches of *Chemical Titles*, using the University of Pittsburgh's time-sharing computer (IBM 760/50) system over the period 1967–1969 encountered a variety of difficulties, leading to the conclusion that it was unsuitable and inefficient for handling automatic dissemination.[6] The program provided by CAS had to be rewritten, there were system hardware and software failures, and the terminal time was excessive. Average relevant items of those retrieved was 44% per issue of *Chemical Titles*; terms per profile averaged between 14 and 24, yielding from 28 to 55 references per profile.

In the late 1960s, the Computer Search Center of the Illinois Institute of Technology Research Institute (IITRI) became a center for handling a variety of machine-readable data bases. Because none of the available computer search programs met the center's criteria and because of the need to handle a variety of data bases, IITRI wrote a new general purpose computer program and developed a new tape format to provide current awareness (SDI) and retrospective search services based on such elements as source information, title, author, keyword, registry number, molecular formula, and abstract or text. The service was initiated with *CA Condensates* tapes in the batch mode, and expanded to include CBAC, POST-J, BA Previews, COMPENDEX, and ISI Source Tapes. The basic problem was the lack of standardization among the data bases.[75] Profile users could have up to 100 terms with truncation options.

The Information Science Unit of the University of Georgia Computer Center initiated search services in 1968 on data bases from several producers in the fields of chemistry, biology, and nuclear science. To determine the cost of the service, Park, Carmon, and Stearns[46] analyzed operations with *CA Condensates* tapes. The entries on the tape averaged 25 words per document, with 6.6–7.0 characters per word. The costs were found to be directly related to the number of documents in the file and the number of profile terms. The number of terms per profile ranged from 5 to 26, with an average of 19.

Indiana University's Aerospace Research Applications Center (ARAC) developed a chemical information system in 1968 based on *CA Condensates* tapes, reformatting it to the RAC Standard File Format then being used for NASA and COMPENDEX. Profile term tapes were matched against the *CA* tape in a batch mode and hits printed out and sent to the users.[52]

Online searching became commercially available in the early 1970s from several data base brokers, such as BRS, ESRIN/IRS, LEADER-MART, SDC (ORBIT), Lockheed (DIALOG), Chemical Data Center, and NLM (MEDLARS) with online acess to *CA Condensates*, MEDLINE, CAIN, NTIS, INSPEC, COMPENDEX, INFORM, and Chemical Market Abstracts. For example, CA SEARCH is accessed with Lockheed's

DIALOG on files 2, 3, and 4 and CHEMNAME and CHEMSEARCH; with SDC's ORBIT on CAS files and CHEMDEX; with BRS on CHEM and CHEX; with ESRIN/IRS on CHEMABS; with INFOLINE and CISTI on CAS; and with AUSINET on CHEM and CHEU. By 1977, well over 350,000 terminals were online to data base brokers with about 1.5 million search questions. In the early 1970s most data base brokers provided batch searching with delays of about two weeks for printouts that were mailed to the requesters. Having experienced the ease of batch searching, the demand grew rapidly for online systems, which had the advantage of fast response time (minutes versus weeks) and interactive facilities for posing questions and changing keywords or profiles. Concomitant with the expressed demand and increasing use, online systems refined their data bases, new and better terminals became available, and computer hardware and storage became better and cheaper.[10,13,14,20,27,32,35,48,51,65,71,77]

An online system consists of three parts: the data base, the search system, and the user at a terminal. Searching, for example, *CA SEARCH* requires the formulation of a search strategy composed of keywords which, to be effective, must be chosen with knowledge of the contents of the data base. The searcher needs to know that to search on the preparation of a given chemical, keywords, other than preparation, that should be entered are prepn, prepd, prepg, production, prodn, synthesis, manufacture, manuf, manufg, and manufd, or else employ a truncation convention with prep, prod, and manuf. For the given chemical, an entry must be made for every potentially possible name, synonym, and trade name the searcher can think of. These keywords are entered on the terminal singly and in combinations of preparation and chemical with the operators AND, OR and AND NOT. The computer responds with the number of citations in the data base file for each single and combined entry, reflecting the keywords in the title plus the additional ones added from the abstract.

Online searching is challenging, even for the experienced specialist.[9,12,27,34,48,50,64,65,69,70,72,73] Failure to obtain desired documents results because we misuse, misunderstand, or overlook abbreviations, punctuate abbreviations when the data base does not, use prefixes and numerical notations not allowed by the file, or fail to use a specific search technique the file requires. Knowing how to search a given file with one broker, such as ORBIT, does not make us knowledgeable with another, such as DIALOG. Online commands are not uniform among the brokers, and data bases are more dissimilar than similar in terms of record lengths, formats, abbreviations, bibliographic citations, and conventions. Consequently, some data base producers, such as the

National Library of Medicine, insist that potential users take their training course, and data base brokers issue detailed manuals on how to use their various data bases. It is important for the user to realize that the connect time per online search is dependent on the search question, the contents of the data base, the software used to access it, and the total time is from sign-on to sign-off, or log-on to log-off. Thus, everything being equal, it costs more for a poor typist than for an expert typist, and a 30-character-per-second terminal is more cost effective than a 10-character-per-second terminal (a good typist's rate, 60 words per minute, is five characters per second). As far as output goes, the most cost effective is a 120-character-per-second CRT, but then recourse must be had to a high speed printer or a 30-character-per-second typewriter terminal if a printout is required by the user.

Other things being equal, a user who knows the data base thoroughly is considerably more cost effective than one who does not. One data base may cost less than another in terms of connect time, but require several times the input for defining the parameters of a problem[1,2]

Cost effective comparisons on online searches of different data bases usually are based on relevance and recall, at a given cost or number of relevant references per dollar or dollars per 100% of relevant references. Unfortunately, it is almost impossible to conduct completely fair comparisons because of the limitations imposed by each data base.

Consider, for example, the retrieval of information in U.S. patents by three data bases: CLAIMS, WPI, and CA Condensates.[54,60]

The coverage varies from 1950 to the present for CLAIMS, 1963 to the present for WPI, and 1967 to the present (Lockheed) or 1970 to the present (SDC) for Condensates.

Online access terms vary from 5 for CLAIMS to 11 for WPI, with CA being 7 (SDC) or 8 (Lockheed). Only CA, however, has the CAS registry number as an access term.

The three data bases differ in designating patent assignees. Assignees are spelled out completely in Condensates, requiring the online user to expand or neighbor to be sure that a subsidiary would not be missed. Assignees have a five-digit code in CLAIMS and a four-letter code in WPI, which makes retrieval fast and low cost.

The U.S. patent classification system is an access term in CLAIMS to all U.S. patents. Inasmuch as about 50% of U.S. patents are retrievable in CA only as equivalents (to the first in the family of equivalents received and abstracted in CA), they are not retrievable by the patent class. The U.S. patent class is assigned to all patents in CLAIMS. WPI assigns the international patent class (IPC) to both basic and equivalent patents, although an abbreviated code is assigned to equivalents.

Free language searching is possible with each of the three data bases. Patent titles are expanded in WPI and CLAIMS and are the only free language keywords that can be accessed, although, since 1978, CLAIMS has provided an abstract from which keywords are searchable. Both keywords and index terms are provided in *CA SEARCH*.

Patent equivalents are retrievable by different methods in the three data bases. Using Lockheed's DIALOG, CA Patent Concordance is used as a separate data base. Equivalents are retrievable directly in CLAIMS and WPI.

Another variable that online users need to be aware of is software incorporated by venders such as for stringsearching, in which a string of characters can be searched serially (such as a fragment of a chemical name, for example, *poly* in *polystyrene*, *poly*merization, or co*poly*merization), or for the use of linking operators,by which two or more terms occur within a specified number of words.

Data base vendors and data base producers of interest to American Chemists are listed in Table 33 and Table 34, respectively.[33, 36, 40a, 47, 51, 53, 57, 62, 64, 65, 71, 74–76]

EUROPEAN DATA BASE VENDORS AND SERVICES

The European Association of Scientific Information Dissemination Centres (EUSIDIC), which was organized to promote the use of machine-readable data bases, is composed of over 100 organizations that produce and process data bases. Most of these organizations process *CA SEARCH*, MEDLARS, MARC, INSPEC, BIOSIS, CLAIMS, NTIS, TITUS, COMPENDEX, etc.

Access to many external online data bases is by networks, namely TYMNET and TELENET. The SCANNET is the network used among the Scandinavian countries. EURONET, the European online network, has over 100 data bases available. The more important data base vendors in Europe are the following:

BLAISE (British Library Automated Information Service), which began operations in 1977, makes available MEDLINE, SDILINE, TOXLINE, and MARC.

CNDST/NCWTD (Centre National de Documentation Scientifique et Technique or National Centrum voor Wetenschappelijke en Technische Documentatie of Belgium) provides the more important data

TABLE 33. Data Base Vendors

Abbreviation	Name and Address
Basis	Battelle Automated Search Information System 505 King Ave., Columbus, OH 43201
BRS	Bibliographic Retrieval Services Corporation Park, Scotia, NY 12302
CAN/OLE	Council of Ontario Universities Office of Library Coordination 130 St. George St., Toronto, Canada
CIC	Chemical Information Center Indiana University, Bloomington, IN 47401
CISTI	Canada Institute for Scientific and Technical Information National Research Council of Canada Ottawa, Ontario, Canada
GIDC	Georgia Information Dissemination Center University of Georgia Athens, GA 30602
IITRI	Illinois Institute of Technology Research Institute 10 W. 35th St., Chicago, IL 60616
I	Informatics, Inc. 6011 Executive Blvd., Rockville, MD 20852
IPC	Institute of Paper Chemistry 1083 ES River St., Appleton, WI 54911
ISC	Interactive Sciences Corp 918 16th St., N.W., Washington, DC 20006
KASC	Knowledge Availability Systems Center University of Pittsburgh, Pittsburgh, PA 15260
LC	Library of Congress Information Systems Office Washington, DC 10017
LIS	Lockheed Information Systems 3251 Hanover St., Palo Alto, CA 94304
MDC	Mead Data Central 200 Park Ave., New York, NY 10017
NASA/RECON	National Aeronautics and Space Administration S & T Information Office Washington, DC 20546
NLM	National Library of Medicine 8600 Rockville Pike, Bethesda, MD 20014
NERAC	New England Research Application Center University of Connectcut, Storrs, CT 06268
NC/STRC	North Carolina S & T Research Center P.O. Box 12235, Research Triangle Park, NC 27709

TABLE 33 (Continued)

NYT	New York Times Information Bank
	1719 Route 10, Parsippany, NJ 07054
OCLC	OCLC, Inc.
	1125 Kinnear Rd., Columbus, OH 43212
SDC	Systems Development Corp., Search Service
	2500 Colorado Ave., Santa Monica, CA 90406

bases in medicine, physics, chemistry, engineering, agriculture, and information science, and uses Lockheed, SDC, and ESA.

EMDDOK (the Eidgenossichen Militardepartments Zentraler Dokumentationsdienst) coordinates information services for the various departments of the Swiss Department of Defense.

ESA (European Space Agency), based in Rome but available via the ESANET or EURONET network, provides search service on *CA SEARCH, COMPENDEX, INSPEC, and other data bases.*

INFOLINE (INFOLINE, Ltd., a British company formed in 1976 by the British Library, Chemical Society, Department of Industry, Derwent Publications, Ltd., and the Institution of Electrical Engineers) operates a United Kingdom online service for CA SEARCH, INSPEC, and Derwent's patent products.

INPADOC (International Patent Documentation Center) is owned by the Austrian Ministry of Finance, Vienna, Austria, and operated by agreement of the World Intellectual Property Organization.[47] Input is received from 46 national patent offices and two international organizations. The computer data base covers 7.5 million patents issued since 1968, with links to corresponding patents. Currently, 18,000 newly issued patents are added each week. In 1980, Chemical Abstracts Service ceased publication of its *CA Patent Concordance* in computer-readable form and used INPADOC in the automation of chemical patent coverage by CAS for publication in the weekly, semianual, and five-year collective indexes to *Chemical Abstracts.*

ITF (Institut Textile de France) in cooperation with the Shirley Institute (England), Zentralstelle fuer Textildokumentation und Information (West Germany), and Stazione Sperimentale per la Cellulosa (Italy) developed and produced TITUS (Traitement de l'Information Textile Universelle et Selective). A multilingual (German, French, and English) system, TITUS is available online from SDC. Input consists of a controlled vocabulary (7000 descripters and 2000 instrumental terms) and a highly structured abstract.

TABLE 34.   Data Base Producers

Acronym	Supplier and Subject Scope	Vendor
AGRICOLA	U.S. Department of Agriculture Covers all literature (one million references) in agriculture from 1970 to present with monthly updatings.	BRS, LIS, SDC
APILIT and APIPAT	American Petroleum Institute Covers 260,000 citations to journal literature and 122,000 citations to patents (updated monthly) relevant to petroleum from 1964 to date.	SDC
APTIC	U.S. Environmental Protection Agency 90,000 air pollution citations and abstracts of air pollution literature from 1966 to date, updated monthly.	LIS
BIOSIS	BioSciences Information Services *Biological Abstracts*, world coverage of life sciences with over two million citations from 1969 to present, updated monthly.	BRS, LIS, SDC
BOOKSINFO	Brodart Current cumulation of *Books in Print*.	BRS
CAPC	Chemical Abstracts Service *CA Patent Concordance* from 1972 to present of about 400,000 citations to over 120,000 basic patents. Discontinued in 1980 and replaced with INPADOC, Vienna.	LIS
CAB Abs.	Commonwealth Agricultural Bureaux 450,000 citations with abstracts to the journals published by CAB from 1973 to present.	LIS
CANCERLIT	National Cancer Institute, NIH 125,000 citations with	NLM

TABLE 34. *(Continued)*

	abstracts from *Carcinogenesis Abstracts* and *Cancer Therapy Abstracts* from 1963 to present.	
CATLINE	National Library of Medicine 175,000 citations and abstracts to books and journals cataloged in NLM from 1965 to present.	NLM
CDA	University Microfilms International 550,000 citations to doctoral dissertations from U.S. and Canadian universities from 1861 to present.	BRS, LIS, SDC
CHEMCON	Chemical Abstracts Service Coverage corresponds to the printed abstracts from 1970 to present, updated biweekly, with over three million citations. Since 1972, CASIA (Chemical Abstracts Subject Index Alert) has provided additional index entries plus CAS registry numbers. The combination is called CA SEARCH.	BRS, LIS, SDC
CHEMDEX	Chemical Abstracts Service Compound dictionary file with CAS registry number, CA nomenclature, and molecular formula for 350,000 records from 1972 to present.	SDC
CHEMLINE	National Library of Medicine and CAS Same as CHEMDEX plus synonyms.	NLM
CHEMNAME	Chemical Abstracts Service Same as CHEMLINE.	LIS
CIN	Chemical Abstracts Service 200,000 citations with abstracts from 1974 to date of *Chemistry Industry Notes*, business literature of the chemical industry.	LIS, SDC
CLAIMS	IFI/Plenum Data Company 360,000 citations to U.S.	LIS

TABLE 34. *(Continued)*

Acronym	Supplier and Subject Scope	Vendor
	chemical patents from 1950 to present and 15,000 records from 1977 to present based on classification codes of all classes and selected subclasses of U.S. patents.	
COMPENDEX	Engineering Index, Inc. 672,000 citations with abstracts from 1970 to present (monthly updating) of the EI data base of engineering literature.	LIS, SDC
ENERGYLINE ⎫ ENVIROLINE ⎭	Environment Information Center, Inc. 36,000 citations (since 1971) with abstracts (since 1975) of environmental economics literature and 75,000 citations, with abstracts, from 1971 to present on environmental literature.	LIS, SDC
EPB	Environmental Studies Institute About 100,000 records from 1973 to present from over 300 journals in all environmental areas, updated bimonthly.	LIS
EXCERPTA MEDICA	Excerpta Medica Foundation 500,000 citations, with abstracts, from 1975 to present of medical science literature.	LIS
FSTA	International Food Information Service 153,000 citations, with abstracts, since 1969, corresponding to the printed *Food Science and Technology Abstracts*.	LIS, SDC
GPO Monthly Catalog	*Monthly Catalog of U.S. Publications* List of publications issued by U.S. federal agencies since 1976.	BRS, LIS

TABLE 34. *(Continued)*

GRA	National Technical Information Service Computerization of *Government Reports Announcements*; about 400,000 citations since 1970 and over 600,000 since 1964 (LIS).	BRS, LIS, SDC
NYT IB	*New York Times* Information Bank Over one million citations with abstracts on items from the *New York Times* and other news sources from 1969 to present (connect charge is $90/hr).	IB
INSPEC	Institution of Electrical Engineers One million citations with abstracts from 1969 to present, with monthly update, of the literature of physics, electrical engineering, computer science, etc.	BRS, LIS, SDC
IPA	American Society of Hospital Pharmacists 45,000 citations with abstracts on use of drugs from 1970 to present; corresponding to *International Pharmaceutical Abstracts.*	LIS
LISA	Library Association of England 36,000 citations with abstracts from 1969 to present; corresponds to the printed *Library and Information Science Abstracts.*	SDC
MEDLARS	National Library of Medicine Over three million citations with abstracts from 1966 to present, with MEDLINE being the basic system.	BRS, NLM
METADEX	American Society for Metals 300,000 citations from 1966 to present, corresponds to *Metals Abstracts Index* and *Alloys Index.*	LIS

TABLE 34.   *(Continued)*

NTIS	National Technical Information About 500,000 citations with abstracts from 1964 (LIS) and 1970 (BRS, SDC) to U.S. sponsored research reports.	BRS, LIS, SDC
PAPERCHEM	Institute of Paper Chemistry 125,000 citations with abstracts of journal and patent literature in pulp and paper from 1968 to present.	SDC
PNI	Data Courier, Inc. About 25,000 citations to food, drug, and cosmetic literature from 1974 to present. Called *Pharmaceutical News Index.*	BRS, LIS, SDC
Pollution Abstracts	Data Courier, Inc. 50,000 citations from *Pollution Abstracts* of literature since 1970; updated bimonthly.	BRS, LIS, SDC
Predicasts	Predicasts, Inc. Citations from 1971 to present of statistics on industries and products; various data bases.	LIS
RAPRA Abstracts	Rubber and Plastics Research Association, England Index to rubber and plastics literature from 1972 to present.	LIS
RINGDOC	Derwent Publications, Inc. 700,000 citations to world's pharmaceutical literature from 1964 to present.	SDC
RTECS	National Institute for Occupational Safety and Health Registry of toxic effects of 26,500 chemical substances from the literature of the past six years; updated quarterly.	NLM
SCISEARCH	Institute for Scientific Information Over two million records from *Science Citation Index* from 1974 to present, updated biweekly.	LIS
SPIN	American Institute of Physics Over 100,000 citations with abstracts from 1975 to present	LIS

TABLE 34. *(Continued)*

	of American physics journal literature and conference proceedings; updated monthly.	
SSIE	Smithsonian Science Information Exchange Over 100,000 citations with summaries from 1974 to present of research in progress.	LIS, SDC
TITUS	Institut Textile de France 140,000 citations and abstracts from 1970 to present of textile literature.	SDC
TOXLINE	National Library of Medicine About 500,000 records from 1971 to present of toxicity literature.	NLM
WAB	American Society for Metals 50,000 records from World Aluminum Abstracts, 1968 to present.	LIS
WPI	Derwent Publications, Ltd. Over one million patents, from 1963 to present, corresponding to *Central Patents Index* and *World Patent Index.*	SDC

INSPEC (International Information Services for the Physics and Engineering Communities) is produced by the British Institution of Electrical Engineers from *Physics Abstracts, Electrical and Electronics Abstracts*, and *Computer and Control Abstracts*. It is available online from ESA, Lockheed, and SDC.

Lockheed data bases (over 70) are accessible to European users through TYMNET or TELENET.

New York Times data base is accessible through TYMNET or TELENET.

NOCI (Netherlands Organization for Chemical Information) was established in 1969 within the Royal Netherland's Chemical Society and in 1977 became a part of the Netherland's Organization for Applied Scientific Research. NOCI provides services on BIOSIS, CA SEARCH, CLAIMS, WPI, INSPEC, MEDLARS, METADEX, NASA, NTIS, and SCISEARCH, and uses Lockheed and SDC.

NSI (Norwegian Center for Informatics) is the main source in Norway for services such as ESA, Lockheed, SDC, and SCANNET.

SDC (Systems Development Corp.) data bases are available through TYMNET or TELENET.

UKCIS (United Kingdom Chemical Information Service) was set up by the Chemical Society (London) to provide machine-readable data bases in chemistry, biology, and related fields. It has cooperated with Chemical Abstracts Service in data base developments and initiated CA Selects. It has exclusive rights for marketing CAS products in the United Kingdom and Ireland.

PRESENT STATUS OF ONLINE SEARCHING

Over the past 20 years, computer technology has undergone three major changes:

1. Operational speeds have increased from seconds to nanoseconds.
2. Storage capacity has increased phenomenally and concomitantly with decreased space requirements. The progression has been from tab cards to magnetic tape, to magnetic drum and disk, and to storage on a chip the size of a fingernail, with the number of characters increasing from 80 (card) to several million (chip).
3. Online interaction with computers via terminals has been introduced.

As the previous sections have pointed out, we have experienced the evolution from the use of computers for the production of indexes and abstracts. Once the indexes and abstracts were in machine-readable form, the next step was to make them available for SDI services and for the batch processing of printouts to meet specified information needs. With increasing storage capacity and increasing computer processability, online data bases became an interactive reality. Telex network has made possible worldwide accessibility to a variety of data bases.

All that is needed to establish access to a computer network is a telephone-coupled terminal and the knowledge of how to use the data bases. These terminals are available from many manufacturers at purchase prices of $800 to over $10,000. Most operate at 100–300 baud (10–30 characters per second), and those with CRT's (cathode ray tube) can receive at 1200 baud (120 characters per second).

We are now at the point where online searching is fairly routine in many organizations. There are over 500 data bases available world-wide, and during 1979 over 50 new ones were introduced. It was estimated in 1978 that about a half million terminals were online with these data bases, making over two million search runs.

There are several costs connected with online searching:

1. Connect time with the computer. This can vary from $15 to $150 per hour, depending on the data base and the broker's system. Some brokers also charge a subscription fee before access is granted.
2. Terminal cost or rental plus telephone charges. (Telephone charges through a network average about $10 per hour of connect time.)
3. Offline prints. These may vary from $0.08 to $0.15 per citation, up to $0.50 per page, plus mailing costs.

In addition, some data base processors and brokers require that users attend a training course of several days at a cost of several hundred dollars plus travel and living expenses.

With the increasing introduction of new online data bases, we now have more information services and products than ever before. This does not mean that access to desired information is better or easier. Unfortunately, information processors and data base brokers have expended their energies and talents on the reduction of clerical and processing operations, and on the development of key word indexes and registry systems. In short, they have ignored the basic problems of information storage and retrieval and the user's need for interacting productively in a time-sharing environment. As now constituted, the user of an online data base must bring to the terminal a great amount of background knowledge of the data base characteristics. However, familiarity with one data base is not generally useful with another. The user has little freedom at the terminal; and there is no possibility for browsing as it is with hard copy information sources. Learning command languages is time consuming. Consequently we tend to use online systems through an intermediary, the specialist who devotes full time to online searching.

Computers and telecommunications have been a major factor in the changing trends over the past 20 years of chemical information science, and the chemical information specialist has played an important role during this evolutionary period. We have not reached the stage where online interaction with data bases contributes very much to the fundamental logical nature of chemical information. Chemistry is not concerned with references per se but with the relationship between facts, the dependence of facts with other facts, the systematic analysis and arrangement of information, and the underlying principles that govern the relationship between facts.

We still have these goals to achieve: retrieval systems that yield only desired references or data, information systems that allow us to browse as we now do in a chemistry library, and online data bases that allow us to interact with the computer as we do now with other chemists.

REFERENCES

1. Almond, J. R., and C. H. Nelson, "Improvements in Cost Effectiveness in Online Searching," *J. Chem. Info. Comput. Sci.* **18**, 13–15 (1978).
2. Almond, J. R., and C. H. Nelson, *Improvements in Cost Effectiveness in Online Searching*, ACS National Meeting, Miami, Florida, September 1978.
3. Artandi, S., "Online Information Systems in Perspective," *J. Chem. Info. Comput. Sci.* **16**, 80–81 (1976).
4. Bayard, T., and J. Persoz, "Comparison Between CACon and CASIA Files for Development of New SDI Service in 1977," *J. Chem. Info. Comput. Sci.* **17**, 89–94 (1977).
5. Beauchamp, Jr., R. O., M. A. Dougherty, J. L. Garber, and D. D. Myers, "Comparative Searching of Computer Data Bases," *J. Chem. Doc.* **13**, 32–35 (1973).
6. Bloemeke, M. J., and S. Treu, "Searching *Chemical Titles* in the Pittsburgh Time-Sharing System," *J. Chem. Doc.* **9**, 155–157 (1969).
7. Bond, L., C. M. Bowman, and M. T. Brown, "A Computerized Current Awareness Service Using Chemical–Biological Activities (CBAC)," *J. Chem. Doc.* **9**, 158–161 (1969).
8. Bowman, C. M., and P. F. Roush, "Status of Computers and the Information Industry and Potential Future Trends," *J. Chem. Info. Comput. Sci.* **16**, 210–212 (1976).
9. Buckley, J. S., "Planning for Effective Use of Online Systems," *J. Chem. Info. Comput. Sci.* **15**, 161–164 (1975).
10. Bourne, C. P., "Online Systems: History, Technology, and Economics," *J. Am. Soc. Info. Sci.* **31**, 155–160 (1980).
11. Buntrock, R. E., "Searching Chemical Abstracts vs. CA Condensates," *J. Chem. Info. Comput. Sci.* **15**, 174–176 (1975).
12. Calkins, M. L., "Online Services and Operational Costs," *Spec. Libr.* **67**, 559–567 (1976).
13. Carmon, J. L., and M. K. Park, "User Assessment of Computer-Based Bibliographic Retrieval Services," *J. Chem. Doc.* **13**, 24–27 (1973).
14. Caudra, C A., "SDC Experiences with Large Databases," *J. Chem. Info. Comput. Sci.* **15**, 48–51 (1975); "Directory of Online Data Bases," Caudra Associates, Santa Monica, Cal., Vol. 1, 1979.
15. Dayton, D. L., M. J. Fletcher, C. W. Moulton, J. J. Pollack, and A. Zamora "Comparison of the Retrieval Effectiveness of CA Condensates (CA Con) and CA Subject Index Alert (CASIA)," *J. Chem. Info. Comput. Sci.* **17**, 20–28 (1977).

16. Devon, T. K., J. S. Buckley, Jr., E. D. Taylor, and M. E. D. Koenig, "Comparative Evaluation of Ringdoc and CBAC," *J. Chem. Doc.* **13**, 30–32 91973).

17. Dittmar, P. G., R. E. Stobaugh, and C. E. Watson, "The Chemical Abstracts Service Chemical Registry System. I. General Design," *J. Chem. Info. Comput. Sci* **16**, 111, 121 (1976)

18. Donovan, K. M., and B. B. Wilhide, "A User's Experience with Searching the IFI comprehensive Database to U.S. Chemical Patents," *J. Chem. Info. Comput. Sci.* **17**, 139–143 (1977).

19. Doszkocs, T. E., R. J. Schaultheisz, and B.M. Vasta, "Analysis of Term Distribution in the Toxline Inverted File," *J. Chem. Info. Comp. Sci.* **16** 131–135 (1976).

20. Darrow, J. W., and J. R. Belilov, "The Growth of Databank Sharing," *Harvard Bus. REV.* **56** (6), 180–188 (1978).

21. Elman, S. A., "Cost Comparison of Manual and Online Computerized Literature Searching," *Spec. Libr.* **66**, 121–18 (1975).

22. Fischer, M., "The KWIC Index Concept: A Retrospective View," **Am. Doc. 17**, April, 57–70 (1966).

23. Freeman, R. R., and G. M. Dyson, "Development and Production of *Chemical Titles*, a Current Awareness Index Publication Prepared with the Aid of a Computer," *J. Chem. Doc.* **3**, 16–20 (1963).

24. Freeman, R. R., J. T. Godfrey, R. E. Maizell, C. N. Rice, and W. H. Shepherd "Automatic Preparation of Selected Title Lists for Current Awareness Services and as Annual Summaries," *J. Chem. Doc.* **4**, 107–112 (1974).

25. Garfield, E., and I. H. Sher, "ISI's Experiences with ASCA—A Selective Dissemination System," *J. Chem. Doc.* **7**, 147–153 (1967).

26. Gluck, D. J., "A Chemical Structure and Search System Developed at Du Pont," *J. Chem. Doc.* **5**, 43–51 (1965).

27. Hawkins, D. T., "Impact of Online Systems on a Literature Searching Service," *Spec. Libr.* **67**, 559–567 (1976), "Online Information Retrieval Bibliography," *Online Review*, **3**, 37–73 (1979).

28. Holm, B. E., M. G. Howell, H. E. Kennedy, J. H. Kuney, and J. E. Rush, "The Status of Chemical Information," *J. Chem. Doc.* **13**, 171–183 (1973).

29. Hummel, D. J., "A Comparative Report on an Online Retrieval Service Employing Two Distinct Software Systems," *J. Chem. Info. Comput. Sci.* **15**, 24–27 (1975).

30. Kaback, S. M., "A User's Experience with the Derwent Patent Files," *J. Chem. Info. Comput. Sci.* **17**, 143–148 (1977).

31. Kennedy, R. A., "Library Applications of Permutation Indexing," *J. Chem. Doc.* **2**, 181–185 (1962).

32. Kent, A., and T. Galvin, "The On-line Revolution in Libraries. Proceedings of the 1977 Conference in Pittsburgh," Dekker, N.Y., 1978.

33. Kissman, H. M., "The Toxicology Data Bank (TDB)," *NLM Techn. Bull.* **113**, 5–6 (1978).

34. Krentz, D. M., "Online Searching—Specialist Required," *J. Chem. Info. Comput. Sci.* **18**, 4–9 (1978).

35. Lancaster, F. W., and L. C. Smith, "On-line Systems in the Communication Process: Projections," *J. Am. Soc. Info. Sci.* **31**, 193–200 (1980).

36. Landau, R. N., J. Wanger, and M. C. Berger, *Directory of Online Data Bases*, Vol. 1, Caudra Associates, Santa Monica, Cal., 1979.

37. Luhn, H. P., "Keyword-in-Context Index for Technical Literature (KWIK Index)," *IBM Report RC-127*, August 1959.

38. Luhn, H. P., "Selective Dissemination of New Scientific Information with the Aid of Electronic Processing Equipment," *Am. Doc.* **12**, 131–138 (1961).

39. McCarn, D. B., "MEDLINE: An Introduction to On-line Searching," *J. Am. Soc. Info. Sci.* **31**, 181–192 (1980).

40. Michaela, C. J., "Searching CA Condensates Online vs. the CA Keyword Indexes," *J. Chem. Info. Comp. Sci.* **15**, 172–173 (1975).

40a. Milne, G. W. A., S. R. Heller, A. E. Fein, E. F. Frees, R. G. Marquart, J. A. McGill, J. A. Miller, and D. S. Spiers, "The NIH-EPA Structure and Nomenclature Search System," *J. Chem. Info. Comput. Sci.* **18**, 181–186 (1978).

41. Marcus, R. S., and J. F. Reintjes, "A Translating Computer Interface for End-User Operation of Heterogeneous Retrieval Systems," *J. Am. Soc. Inf. Sci.* **32**, 287–303 and 304–317 (1981).

42. Morgan, H. L., "The Generation of a Unique Machine Description for Chemical Structures—A Technique Developed at Chemical Abstracts Service," *J. Chem. Doc.* **5**, 107–113 (1965).

43. O'Dette, R. E., "The CAS Data Base Concept," *J. Chem. Info. Comput. Sci.* **15**, 165–169 (1975).

44. O'Donohue, C. H., "Comparison of Service Centers and Document Data Bases—A User's View," *J. Chem. Doc.* **13**, 27–29 (1973).

45. O'Donohue, C. H., "Profiling, the Key to Successful Information Retrieval," *J. Chem. Doc.* **14**, 29–31 (1974).

46. Park, M. K., J. L. Carmon, and R. E. Stearns, "The Development of a General Model for Estimating Computer Search Time for CA Condensates," *J. Chem. Doc.* **10**, 282–284 (1970).

47. Pilch, W., and W. Wratschko, "INPADOC: A Computerized Patent Documentation System," *J. Chem. Info. Comput. Sci.* **18**, 69–75 (1978).

48. Prewitt, B. G., "Online Searching of Computer Data Bases," *J. Chem. Doc.* **14**, 115–117 (1974).

49. Prewitt, B. G., "Searching the Chemical Abstracts Condensates Data Base via Two Online Systems," *J. Chem. Info. Comput. Sci.* **15**, 177–183 (1975).

50. Radwin, M. S., "The New Era of Online Information Retrieval—Evaluation of Its Costs and Benefits—A Professional Imperative," *Proc. Am. Soc. Inf. Sci.* **10**, 191–192 (1973).

51. Regazzi, J. J., B. Bennion, and S. Roberts, "On-line Systems of Disciplines and Specialty Areas in Science and Technology," *J. Am. Soc. Info. Sci.* **31**, 161–170 (1980).

52. Roberts, A. B., I. O. Hartwell, R. W. Counts, and R. A. Davila, "Development of a Computerized Current Awareness Service Using CA Condensates," *J. Chem. Doc.* **12**, 221–223 (1972).

53. Rogalski, L., "Online Searching of the American Petroleum Institute's Databases," *J. Chem. Inf. Comput. Sci.* **18**, 9–12 (1978).

54. Ross, J. C., "Searching the Chemical Literature via Three Online Vendors: A Comparison," *J. Am. Soc. Info. Sci.*, March, 103–106 (1979).

55. Ruhl, M. J., and E. J. Yeates, "Introducing and Implementing Online Bibliographic Retrieval Services in a Scientific Research and Development Organization," *J. Chem. Info. Comput. Sci.* **16**, 147–150 (1976).

56. Santodonato, J., "A Comparison of Online and Manual Modes in Searching Chemical Abstracts for Specific Compounds," *J. Chem. Info. Comput. Sci.* **16**, 135–137 (1976).

57. Schick, R., and B. Huybrechts, *Directory of Online Information Resources*, March 1979, Capital Systems Group, Inc., Rockville, Md.

58. Skolnik, H., "The What and How of Computers for Chemical Information Systems," *J. Chem. Doc.* **11**, 185–189 (1971).

59. Skolnik, H., "Milestones in Chemical Information Science," *J. Chem. Info. Comput. Sci.* **16**, 187–193 (1976).

60. Smith, R. G., L. P. Anderson, and S. K. Jackson, "Online Retrieval of Chemical Patent Information. An Overview and a Brief Comparison of Three Major Files," *J. Chem. Info. Comput. Sci.* **17**, 148–157 (1977).

61. Summit, R. K., "Lockheed Experience in Processing Large Databases for its Commercial Information Retrieval Service," *J. Chem. Info. Comput. Sci.* **15**, 40–42 (1975).

62. Tancredi, S. A., R. H. Amacher, J. H. Schneider, and B. M. Vasta, "Cancerline: A New NLM/NCI Data Base," *J. Chem. Info. Comput. Sci.* **16**, 128–130 (1976).

63. Taube, M., et al., *Studies in Coordinate Indexing (1953–1957)*, Documentation Inc., Washington, DC.

64. Tedd, L. A., *Case Studies in Computer-Based Bibliographic Information Services*, Report No. 5483, June 1979, The British Library, London.

65. Trenchard, B., *"New Data Bases for Management"*, *Administrative Management*, pp. 59–61, February (1979).

66. Wanger, J., M. Fishburn, and C. A. Cuadra, *Online Impact Study. Survey Report of Online Users, 1974–1975*, Systems Development Corp., Decembver 1975.

67. Wente, V. A., and G. A. Young, "Selective Information Announcement Systems for a Large Community of Users," *J. Chem. Doc.* **7**, 142–147 (1967).

68. Wilde, D. U., "Computerized Chemical Information Retrieval Techniques," *J. Chem. Info. Comput. Sci.* **15**, 183–185 (1975).

69. Williams, M. E., "Criteria for Evaluation and Selection of Databases and Database Services," *Spec. Libr.* **66**, 561–569 (1975).

70. Williams, M. E., "Progress and Problems of the Data Base Community," *J. Am. Soc. Info. Sci.*, Sept.–Oct., 305–306 91975).

71. Wanger, J., and R. N. Landau, "Nonbibliographic On-line Data Base Services," *J. Am. Soc. Info. Sci.* **31**, 171–180 (1980).

72. Williams, M. E., "Analysis of Terminology in Various CAS Data Files as Access Points for Retrieval," *J. Chem. Info. Comput. Sci.* **17**, 16–20 (1977).

73. Williams, M. E., "Education and Training for Online Use of Data Bases", *J. Libr. Automation* **10**, 320–334 (1977).

74. Williams, M. E., and T. Brandhorst, "Data Bases Online in 1978," *Bull. Am. Soc. Info. Sci.* **4** (6), 20–26 (1978).

75. Williams, M. E., and S. H. Rouse, "Computer-Readable Bibliographic Data Bases. A Directory and Data Sourcebook," *Am. Soc. Info. Sci.*, Washington, D.C., 1979.

76. Williams, M. E., and P. B. Schipma, "Design and Operation of a Computer Search Center for Chemical Information," *J. Chem. Doc.* **10**, 158–162 (1970).

77. Wolpert, S. A., "Use and Implication of Online Information Retrieval for Management," *J. Chem. Info. Comput. Sci.* **16**, 150–151 (1976).

10

EVOLUTION OF THE LITERATURE FROM ANTIQUITY TO THE EARLY TWENTIETH CENTURY

Science and technology cannot exist without a viable literature—the accumulation of information and knowledge of those who have shaped our past and of those who are shaping our present.

Relative to the total literature, the literature of science and technology was slow in starting. Although many today think technology evolved from science, history tells us the reverse. In the begininings of history, there was no science, and there continued to be no science as humanity progressed through the Paleolithic (Old Stone Age), Mesolithic (Transitional Stone Age), Neolithic (New Stone Age), Bronze, and Iron ages, spanning, respectively, the periods 1,000,000–16,000, 16,000–10,000, 7000, 5000, and 4500 B.C. Over this period of time humanity emerged from the cave to become hunter, farmer, navigator, and artisan.

During this evolutionary process, man discovered fire; learned to shape tools for his foraging, hunting, and fishing; learned to domesticate animals; discovered agriculture; and, along the way, learned to write.

Although we do not know how these innovations occurred, it is quite apparent that they had a marked influence on evolving civilizations. Fire supplied early man with heat and protected him against predatory animals. Once he learned to apply fire to the preparation of food, he was able to augment his diet of fruits and roots with cooked meat and to preserve food. In short, he began to control his environment. Just as fire led to cooking and preservation of foods, so cooking led to the invention of cooking utensils and eventually to pottery and metallurgy.

243

The innovation of agriculture marked the emergence of community life and civilization. It motivated early man to learn to cooperate with nature in what to plant, when to plant, and when to harvest. It forced him to cooperate with his neighbor to protect the community from conflicts with animals and with other human beings. It forced him to learn about his environment, to begin to solve the riddles of nature, and to begin to think in terms of energy.

Related to the agriculture for food, early civilizations learned to cultivate plants such as flax and hemp for use as fibers for textile and rope, papyrus for paper, and other plants for extracts of oils and for dyestuffs. Linen was woven on handlooms 4000 years ago in Egypt, cotton was spun and woven in ancient India before 2500 B.C., and the silk industry was flourishing in China before 2000 B.C. Fermentation to alcoholic beverages, such as beer from barley and wines from fruits, was known in the Egyptian and Mesopotamian civilizations.

Agriculture was the primary impetus to technology throughout man's history, and in many ways shaped this history. Until relatively modern times, agriculture dominated the economy of succeeding civilizations, and thus motivated the introduction of new technologies. Not until the end of the nineteenth century and well into the twentieth century did agricuture change, with the introduction of the power revolution, from a one-man or one-family operation into a whole new industry.

Until recently, technology had little relation to science. For the most of history, man used natural products and made machines and devices without knowing how or why they worked. Anthropologically, man differed from the rest of the animal kingdom by his employment of tools. Indeed, it is doubtful if mankind could have survived without this differentiation, and it is not without significance that the evolving civilizations—Stone Age, Bronze Age, Iron Age, Atomic Age—relate to mankind's technological mastery of his environment, beginning some millions of years ago.

Antiquity is without records, except for what archeologists and anthropologists have been able to piece together from discoveries of fossil skeletons and of products of early civilizations. The written record came into existence in the sixth and fifth centuries B.C. in Greece and somewhat earlier in India and China. Analyses of articles of metal, pottery, glass, mortars, and dyed textiles from excavations tell us, for example, that copper as a product of mining and metallurgy is at least 5000 years old. Bronze (copper and tin) was used in statues at least 3000 years ago. Iron and iron products were known as early as 2500–2900 B.C. in Egypt and probably much earlier in Babylon. By about 1300 B.C., the Egyptians were using steel. Gold ornaments probably date from prehistoric times. Mercury was known to the Egyptians (1500–1600 B.C.), and ancient Hindu and Chinese literature refers to it by various names.

Salt was also known to prehistoric man. Because man learned early that salt preserved many foods and was essential to his diet, salt became a prime item of trade between communities from early civilizations well into recent history.

In the grand perspective of the history and evolution of technology, most of the interplays of knowledge and its applications have been largely affairs of chance. Technology was mostly a matter of art, handed down from generation to generation and transferred from one civilization to another. Technological advances arose slowly, almost imperceptibly, yet technological developments over the ages were well developed and evolved progressively.

Writing, the outstanding invention of our prehistoric ancestors, began around 3500 B.C. The earliest documents extant are cuneiform clay tablets from Mesopotamia or Sumeria. This early language was based on pictographs in which related concepts (words) were agglutinated, that is, new words were formed from a base or root word with prefixes and suffixes. Paper was known in various civilizations; the Egyptians used papyrus and the Chinese made paper from the rice plant. The alphabet was probably invented in Egypt and then spread throughout the Mediterranean area by the Phoenicians. Writing was essentially an outgrowth of and a convenience to commerce; it did not evolve from the needs of education or culture in these early civilizations. Without the event of writing, it is questionable how far civilization would have progressed. Science and technology, as we know it today, certainly would not have come about.

Though the Egyptians were skilled in metallurgy, enameling, glass tinting, dyeing, and extraction of plant oils, they left essentially no record of these accomplishments. Yet early Greek and Roman sources, and many alchemists up to the fifteenth century alluded to Egyptian recipes. According to Plutarch (A.D. 100), Egypt was known as *Khem* (the land of the black soil) and Arabs referred to it as *Al Khem*, from which the word alchemy arose. Many of the early references are to the writings of Hermes Trismegistus, a legendary ruler of Egypt (ca. 3400 B.C.), who was reputed to have authored about 3600 writings, for which he became known as the founder of alchemy. It is also possible that alchemy had its first roots in China, as the first known document on alchemy is a Chinese treatise (A.D. 142); Ko Hung (A.D. 281–361) described the three goals of alchemy as being conversion of base metals to gold, preparation of edible gold (to impart immortality), and preparation of other medicines.

Where alchemy originated—Egypt, Asia Minor, Persia, India, or China—is less important than the impetus it received by those in Alexandria in the first and second centuries A.D. These Alexandrians, skilled in the metallurgical arts of earlier civilizations and knowledgeable in the teachings of Aristotle, were essentially the first practicing chemists whose experimental work was based on an apparently sound hypothesis best expressed by the syllogism

1. All things tend to grow to perfection.
2. Gold is the most perfect metal.
3. Therefore, gold occurs in nature as the result of the perfection of baser metals.

What nature can do, they reasoned, could be duplicated more rapidly in their laboratories.

Unfortunately, another hypothesis, that the alchemists' wealth (assuming success in the quest for gold) would enable them to finance a revolt against the empire, prompted Emperor Diocletian in A.D. 290 to decree the destruction of all works concerned with alchemistry. The few documents that survived the fire still puzzle chemistry historians by the strange symbolism the Alexandrian chemists used in recording their observations and results.

The Greek civilization was not only the bridge over which came prior civilizations such as Sumeria, Babylonia, Egypt, Assyria, Persia, and India, it was in its own right the greatest civilizing force in Europe from the rise of the Roman empire to the present day. It appeared slowly and matured over the period 1000–480 B.C.

Among the early Greek scientists, Thales (640–546 B.C.) advanced the thesis that water is the origin of all things; Anaximenes (560–500 B.C.) believed that air is the fundamental substance; Heraclitus (536–470 B.C.) held that fire is the primordial substance; Empedocles (490–430 B.C.), the eclectic, is credited with being the first to speak of four elements— earth, air, fire, and water; Democritus (460–370) advanced the hypothesis of atoms with form, size, and weight, invisible and indivisible, in constant motion; but we are indebted to Aristotle (384–322 B.C.) for recording the thoughts of these men as well as Plato's (428–348 B.C.) teachings. Aristotle's lyceum emphasized natural science, and he had his pupils gather and coordinate knowledge in every field. From their records he drew data, although sometimes with too much faith, for the writing of his many treatises by which he became the best known of the Greek scholars.

Although war was used by the Greek states to impose their power and rule over the Mediterranean world and beyond, Greek culture pervaded and dominated the then known world by commerce. Consequently, long after the Peloponnesian War, which vitiated the Greek states, especially Athens, and marked the beginning of the decline of their dominance, Greek civilization was dispersed, disseminated, and enhanced throughout the conquered world. This period (322–146 B.C.), now known as the Hellenistic dispersion, took roots predominantly in Macedon, Epirus, Asia, and Egypt. Thus, as the power of the Greek states declined and disappeared, Greek letters, science, and art won a wide victory.

Two factors, in particular—Greek as a common language, and the ascendency of writers, books, and libraries—immortalized the Greek philosophers, scientists, and dramatists. For nearly a thousand years, the Greek language was the primary medium of diplomacy, commerce, literature, and science, and what was written in Greek could be read by all educated people from Greece to the Near East, throughout the Middle East to Egypt, and along the Mediterranean lands as far as the Greek states had ventured and conquered. This immense audience created a great demand for books, and thousands of writers in every field of Hellenistic life obliged with hundreds of thousands of books written in a cursive script, mostly on paper (Egyptian papyrus) or parchment rolls.

The written word was held in high esteem, and libraries, such as the Alexandrian library, were considered a measure of power. The importance of this library can be appreciated by the order of Ptolemy III that every book entering Alexandria had to be deposited in the library; copies were then made (the library retained the original). Furthermore, the office of librarian was considered to be one of the highest that the king conferred. However, this great monument to mankind's intellectual progress suffered at the hands of history: In 47 Ceasar burned his fleet harbored at Alexandria, and the fire consumed part of the library (which was rebuilt and refurnished in succeeding years); in 392 Christians under the Patriach Theophilus burned a large number of works; and disuse, abuse, and neglect had their affect, so that most of the library had disappeared by 642. Nevertheless, through the period of the decline of Greece and the ascendancy of the Roman empire, the Alexandrian library played an essential role in transferring the heritage of the Greek civilization throughout the Roman world. Although Rome conquered Greece, the Greek civilization conquered Rome, and the intellectual spirit of Greece seeped into the stream of history.

As the Greek civilization began to evolve slowly about 900 B.C., technology was reaching a high level. Fire had been discovered and put to many uses. The preceding civilizations' agriculture, animal husbandry, mining, metallurgy, spinning, weaving, and construction with wood, brick, and stone would prevail until the industrial revolution, with only relatively minor advances. Much of what we know about the technology of antiquity is from the writings of the Greek philosophers and classicists, such as Democritus, Plato, Aristotle, and Archimedes.

Among the literature of this period, one of the most scientifically prolific was Hippocrates (460–359 B.C.), whose textbooks for physicians and clinical records were dominant for many centuries.

Because the Greek civilization placed a high value on scholarship, writing became a profession, not only copying works in a library, but also writing of the past. Some of the writing was eclectic, but much was plagiaristic, and most was unscientific.

Among the more important early writers was Pliny the Elder (23–79 A.D.), whose *Historia Naturalis*, although hardly good science, was an encyclopedic attempt to summarize all that was known. He covered 20,000 topics, with references to about 500 authors and their many works. The topics covered astronomy, geography, mining and metallurgy, medicine, botany, animals, and alchemy.

Galen (129–199 A.D.), who has been regarded as one of the first experimentalists in medicine, wrote about 500 treatises. Another important writer was Celsus, a Roman aristocrat, whose *de Medicina*, written in Latin, played an important role in the nomenclature of medicine for many centuries.

The period ranging from about 900 B.C. to about 500 A.D., the Greco–Roman period, was one of great advances from which our own science and technology evolved. The evolution was excruciatingly slow, for the Greco–Roman period was followed by a cultural and scientific decline that lasted from the fifth to the middle of the fifteenth century throughout Europe. This is not to say that the world was without science or scientists, for much of the Greco–Roman civilization continued in Byzantium. From 800 to 1200 A.D., scientists flourished in Islam, particularly in the university centers at Alexandria, Beirut, Antioch, and Nisibis, where Greek science and philosophy were preserved in Arabic translation. It is through these translations that much of the works from the Golden Age of Greece are known today, by scholars from Greece and Byzantium to Eastern and Spanish Islam, and then to Europe.

Chemistry and alchemy were the same in Alexandria. However, the Alexandrian alchemists, being experimentalists (in contrast to the Greeks), made many advances in the chemistry of metals and alloys. Zosimos was among the earliest authors of alchemy in Egypt, and those who followed him based their writings on his work, of which only a little survived. The style of writing, although permeated with mysticism, was primarily one of recipes, with directions for mixing, heating, coloring, and separating. One of the early developments was the alembic for distillation of mixtures. These alchemists believed that all metals could be transmuted into any other metal. Their aim, of course, was to transmute the base metals, especially lead, into gold. One of the more famous of these alchemists was Jabir ibn-Haijan (702–765) (known as Geger or Giaber, as the name was transliterated into Latin by European alchemists). He wrote many books that became widely read in the Middle Ages throughout Europe.

Alchemy or chemistry, except for its occult and mystical content, had relatively little effect from the tenth into the thirteenth century, that is, until near the end of the Middle Ages. Through his many writings, Roger Bacon (1214–1292), who studied medicine at Oxford, was the major influence in the awakening of chemical experimentation. According to Bacon, experiment is the only proof in natural science. Chemistry to him, however, was alchemy. Despite his exaltation of experiments, he made essentially no contribution of an experimental nature to chemistry, although his studies on explosives had merit.

Although the Renaissance brought forth an intellectual reawakening in poetry, art, and scholarship, science was slow in making significant advances, even though the explorations of Columbus, Vasco de Gama, Magellan, and others presaged an expanding world. There were at least two reasons for the low position of science in the Renaissance, especially in Italy, where it began: Patrons favored the poets, artists, and scholars; and the Church, which was dominant, did not look with favor on those whose work might be in conflict with its views on the nature of things, from Creation to the movements of heavenly bodies relative to earth.

Whereas science was scarcely pursued, except for certain areas of physics and medicine, technology gained new momentum during the Renaissance. Three important factors contributed to this momentum: the fall of Constantinople in 1453, with the consequent dispersion of scholars from the fallen empire through Europe; the development of gunpowder, which eliminated the medieval castle as a fortress and center of power, and consequently feudalism as a way of political control; and Gutenberg's introduction of movable type in the 1450s and the democratization of communication by the printed word.

With the development of printing, a flood of pamphlets and books became readily available to the general public. With the flood of printed matter within a century of Gutenberg's movable type, there arose problems of widespread plagiarism and the passing off of fiction for fact. There was no copyright, and what one publisher printed was copied by others as fast as type could be set. Authors became well known, but received little monetary reward for their efforts. Many publications for a century or so after Gutenberg were works of art in terms of typography, illustrations, and bindings. Most importantly, the private, city, and state library took root, and these began to number in the thousands by the end of the fifteenth century. Only a few of the more than 30,000 books printed in the fifteenth century, however, were in science or technology.

With the rise in technology and the increasing use of machines in the manufacture of metals, bricks, glass, pewter, and cannon, wood as a fuel became scarce. Fortunately, coal from northern Europe and England became the energy source that made the industrial revolution possible. Iron and steel enjoyed an increasing demand for use in weapons, nails, anchors, and tools. Iron displaced copper and its alloys, and became the metal in greatest demand. With the greatly rising demand for iron and the increasing need for bronze (copper and tin alloy) for guns, statues, and home appliances, brass (copper and zinc alloy) for instruments, and other alloys, metallurgy became of prime importance. Vannuccio (also spelled Vanoccio) Biringuccio (1480–1539), of Siena, Italy, acquired an extensive knowledge of mining and metallurgy as practiced in Italy and in Germany and was well read in the existing literature. His single publication, De la Pirotechnia, a 10-volume work printed in Venice in 1540, was the first systematic text on mining and metallurgy. Books I and II describe the recovery of silver, gold, copper, lead, tin, iron, mercury, sulfur, antimony, aluminum, arsenic, etc., from their ores. Book III covers testing, roasting, and cupellating methods. Book IV describes the preparation of aqua fortis and its use in parting. Alloys of gold, silver, copper, lead, and tin are the subject of Book V. Casting, molds, and furnaces are covered in Books VI, VII, and VIII. Books IX and X describe the arts of distillation, sublimation, extraction, amalgamation, and the manufacture of gunpowder, saltpeter, and projectiles.

Because De la Pirotechnica was written in vernacular Italian, rather than in scholarly Latin, it did not enjoy widespread use beyond Italy. It appeared in six Italian and three French editions; its first English edition, translated by Cyril S. Smith and Martha T. Gnudi, was published by the American Institute of Mining and Metallurgical Engineers in 1942.

Georg Bauer (1494–1555) (whose name was Latinized to Georgius Agricola) of Saxony was educated at the University of Leipzig and in Italy as a physician. Practicing medicine in Joachimstahl, a mining town, he became intensively interested in mining, mineralogy, and metallurgy. Agricola's first major work relative to chemistry was his *De Natura Fossilium*, published in 1546, in which he classified minerals into *earths* (clays and chalks), *stones* (gems), *solidified juices* (salt and alum), *rocks* (marble), *metals* (mercury), and *compounds* (other ores). Despite the lack of knowledge of the chemical composition of ores, minerals, and salts, Agricola's classification had a reasonably logical basis.

Agricola's major work was *De Re Metallica*, published posthumously in 1556 in Basel, first in Latin as a folio of about 600 pages, then in German (1557) and in Italian (1563). It was translated first in English from the original by Herbert C. Hoover and his wife (L.H.) in 1912 with biographical information on Agricola and with annotations on the development of mining, metallurgy, geology, and mineralogy from antiquity to the sixteenth century. *De Re Metallica* consisted of 12 books, covering the review of the existing literature, a discussion of mines and of mining operations, assaying, the preparation of ores for smelting, the obtaining of metals from ores, the preparation of soluble salts, and the manufacture of alum, vitriol, sulfur, and glass, among others. This folio remained the standard reference work for over a century and accounted for Agricola being named the father of mineralogy.

Lazarus Ercker (1530–1593), like Agricola, was a resident of the mining area of Central Europe, and also wrote a treatise (288 folio pages) on mineral ores, mining, and smelting operations. It was published in 1556 with the title *Beschreibung allerfürnemstem Mineralischen Ertzt und Berckwercksarten*, and enjoyed the popularity of Agricola's treatise.

Of particular significance is that with Gutenberg's introduction of printing in the 1450s, over 30,000 books were issued by the end of the fifteenth century. Science and technology were not well represented. Chemistry was not, because it was still in the alchemy period of secrecy. Technology, especially that which was based on art and craftmanship, began to appear slowly in the sixteenth century. The works of Biringuccio, Agricola, and Ercker were among the first of these technological treatises to be produced by printing. Agricola's and Ercker's benefited from the production of excellent printed illustrations.

Paracelsus (1493–1541), also known as Philip Theophrastus Bombast von Hohenheim, is credited with the introduction of iatrochemistry, chemistry applied to medicine, which initiated a new interest in chemistry other than alchemy, and maintained dominance through the seventeenth century. Actually, Paracelsus contributed little to the advancement of chemistry. His main interest was in correcting the medical errors of Galen and in encouraging others to question the writings of the Greeks and to think for themselves from observations and experiments.

Alchemia, written by Andreas Libavius (1540–1616) and published in 1597, was probably the first textbook of chemistry. Libavius (also known as Libau), a physician and teacher and a follower of iatrochemistry, disagreed with many of the doctrines of Paracelsus. His book, among the most used for many decades, surveyed completely the chemistry of the sixteenth century, including laboratory equipment and procedures. He classified *alchemia* (chemistry as used today) into *encheria* (chemical methods) and *chymia* (the combining of chemical substances), introduced the term *magisterium* to denote a chemical substance as it occurs in nature but with removal of external impurities, and distinguished between *magisteria* of substance (kind) and of quality (properties).

There was little progress in science well into the seventeenth century. Yet there were significant advances, motivated primarily by the expanding industries and commerce and by the new plants and ores brought into Europe from the Americas. Some of the scientific advances included the invention of the logarithm, calculus, the compound microscope (1590), telescope (1608), barometer (1643), and scientific instruments. Terrestrial magnetism was becoming known, and one of the great books of English science, *On the Magnet, and the Great Magnet the Earth*, was written in 1600 by William Gilbert, who by means of the compass was able to calculate latitudes. Sir William Harvey, who explained the circulation of blood via the heart through the arteries in his 1628 book, *Circulation of the Blood*, was one of the greatest English scientist in this period.

Francis Bacon (1561–1621), one of the greatest intellects of his period, wrote that science is the theoretical road to technology and that knowledge is a virtue for its own sake. He viewed science as an aspect of man's dignity. In *The Advancement of Learning*, Bacon argued for the support and expansion of universities, libraries, museums, and scientific laboratories. In *Novum Organum*, Bacon proposed induction as the proper way to study nature through observation and experimentation without preconceptions, assumptions, or prejudices. He espoused the accumulation of all observable facts and their analysis, comparison, classification, and correlation into an underlying law of nature. Rather than considering Bacon a scientist, we should consider him a philosopher of science. His induction theory might have been relevant to the astronomers of his day; it could not be applied, however, to physics and chemistry as they evolved to the present. Nevertheless, what he wrote is quite relevant to the social responsibility that scientists and engineers are beginning to feel vis-à-vis the consequences of their work, that is, as Bacon put it, to study ends as well as means. It was Francis Bacon's work that inspired the founding in 1660 of the Royal Society of London for Improving Natural Knowledge.

Jan Baptist Van Helmont (1577–1644), a disciple of Paracelsus, was educated as a physician but devoted his life to chemistry. He coined the word *chemistry*, deriving it from the Greek *chaos*, and was the first one to use the word *gas*. Contrary to the Greeks, he argued that air and water were the only two elements. He was the first to use quantitative measurements in chemical experiments and to emphasize the value of using a balance. Through his pioneering work on gases he became known as the founder of pneumatic chemistry. His work in chemistry was collected and published in 1648 (the English edition appeared in 1662 under the title *Oriatricke or Physick Refined*).

Through his 30 odd publications, Johann Rudolf Glauber (1604–1670) became one of the best known iatrochemists. His book, *Furni novi philosophici*, published in 1648 in Amsterdam, is considered one of the most outstanding works of chemistry of the seventeenth century. It covers exensively plant equipment, such as furnaces; distillation apparatus; and sources, processing, and uses of oils and spirits. Glauber may be considered one of the first chemical engineers, as he developed processes for the manufacture of sulfuric, nitric, acetic, and hydrochloric acids (he used the name *muriatic acid*, from *muria*, the brine he used). Many of his ideas on chemical engineering were expounded in his book *Teutschlands Wohlfahrt* (1656). He was the first to describe the preparation of sodium sulfate, which he called *sal mirible*, but which became known as Glauber's salt; it is still used as an aperient.

Not to be overlooked in the seventeenth century evolvement of chemistry is the work of Galileo (1564–1642), more properly known as a physicist and mathematician. His work, especially on falling bodies, was outstanding in overturning Aristotlean science. Of particular importance are Galileo's experiments, which he reported near the end of his life in *Dialogues Concerning Two New Sciences* (statics and dynamics), in which he discussed the indestructibility of matter; the principles of the lever and pulley, free falling bodies, the inclined plane, and the law of inertia; and the application of mathematics to science. Besides being the father of modern physics, he was an astronomer of note. Many of his observations were made with telescopes he had provided himself, which were improved versions of those reported by others.

Although Robert Boyle (1627–1691), discoverer of Boyle's law, was primarily a physicist, he has been called the father of modern chemistry because of his work on gases and because his scientific contributions helped to initiate the foundation of analytical chemistry. His book *The Sceptical Chymist*, published in 1661, was one of 20 that made him a major contributor to scientific advances of the seventeenth century. Robert Hooke (1635–1703), who was closely associated with Boyle, advanced the first rational explanation of combustion, but, unfortunately, his theory made essentially no impact on his contemporaries, who became entangled with the phlogiston theory. He is best known through his work (Hooke's law) on the elasticity of solid bodies. His book *Micrographia*, published in 1665, which included his theory of combustion, made him a scientist of high importance.

Undoubtedly, the greatest scientific impact of the seventeenth century was the introduction of the pholgiston doctrine by Johann Joachim Becker (1635–1682) in Germany. Becker's concepts of combustion were promulgated in his book, *Acta Laboratorii chymici Monacensis, Seu Physical Subterraneae*, published in 1669. It remained for Becker's student, Georg Ernst Stahl (1660–1734), however, to formulate the phlogiston doctrine and to introduce the word *phlogiston*, which he derived from the Greek word, meaning to inflame. Stahl's phlogiston doctrine was published in 1697 in his book *Zymotechnia Fundamentalis.*

Despite the fact that the phlogiston construct was erroneous and that it probably inhibited the discovery of oxygen and the understanding of the function of air in combustion, it was an important generalization in chemistry. As a generalization, the phlogiston theory allowed chemists for almost a century to correlate a large number of experiments in chemistry and to relate a variety of results. Possibly most important, the theory served to encourage and to motivate chemical experimentation.

Not all of Stahl's contemporaries were adherents of the phlogiston theory. Notable among his critics were Hermann Boerhaave (1668–1738) and Friedrich Hoffmann (1660–1742). Boerhaave's fame was as a teacher of chemistry, and his book *Elementa Chemiae*, published in 1724, was widely used throughout Europe for half a century, as it gave an excellent account of chemical knowledge up to that time. The book does not mention Stahl or the phlogiston theory. Although Hoffmann, a professor of medicine at Halle, Germany, was responsible for Stahl's appointment, he differed with Stahl's interpretation of combustion. Hoffman is remembered for introducing the mixture of alcohol and ether (equal volumes) for reducing pain, that is, as an anodyne, and for his highly popular books, *Chymia rationalis et experimentalis* and *Opera amnia physico-medica.*

Starting in Germany and finding wide support among German chemists, the phlogiston theory was widely accepted throughout Europe: by Pierre Joseph Macquer (1718–1784), Guyton de Morveau (1737–1816), and Etienne Francois Geoffroy (1672–1731) in France; Tobern Olaf Bergman (1735–1784) and Karl Wilhelm Scheele in Sweden; and Joseph Black (1728–1799), Henry Cavendish (1731–1810), Joseph Priestley (1728–1804), and Richard Kirwan (1733–1812) in England.

Geoffroy (1672–1731) is best known for his memoir, *Table des differents rapports observés en chimie entre differentes substances*, which he presented before the Academy of Sciences, Paris, in 1718, and in which he compared and summarized a large number of chemical data in his table of affinities. This work was used heavily during most of the eighteenth century for elucidating the reactivities of chemicals relative to each other. His table of affinities is replete with the chemical symbolism of his day.

Macquer (1718–1784), who contributed many memoirs to the Paris Academy, wrote several widely used texts: *Elements de Chymie théoretique* (1709), *Elements de Chymie pratique* (1751), and *Elements de la Théorie et de la Pratique de la Chymie* (1775). He is best known, however, for his monumental four volume *Dictionnaire de la Chymie* (1778), the first great encyclopedia of chemistry.

Mikhail Vasilevich Lomonosov (1711–1765) is an important figure of eighteenth century chemistry. He created the scientific language of Russia and made chemistry an integral subject in the University of Moscow, which he headed from 1755 to his death. Beyond this, he was instrumental in developing physical chemistry through his marriage of chemistry with physics and mathematics.

Curiously, the downfall of the phlogiston doctrine began with the experimental results on the chemistry of gases by believers in the doctrine. These experimenters were Joseph Black (1728–1799), Henry Cavendish (1731–1810), and Joseph Priestley (1733–1804), who worked on the preparation, properties, and reactions on gases: Black on carbon dioxide, Preistley on oxygen and nitrogen dioxide, and Cavendish on hydrogen and carbon dioxide. From a knowledge of the work of these chemists and others, and from his own experiments on calcination, Antoine Laurent Lavoisier (1743–1794) deduced the role of oxygen in combustion and thus initiated the foundations of modern chemistry. Lavoisier's interpretations of combustion were published in Rozier's *Observations sur la physique* and as memoirs of the Paris Academy. His most important book, *Traité élémentaire de chemie*, was published in 1789. An important landmark work during this period was the combined effort of Lavoisier, Guyton de Morveau (1737–1816), Antoine Francois de Fourcroy (1755–1809), and Claude Louis Berthollet (1748–1822), which resulted in 1787 in the publication of *Methode d'une Nomenclature Chimique*, which eliminated many arbitrary names of that period and attempted to introduce a systematic nomenclature based on chemical composition, the emphasis being on the base or acid from which a compound was derived.

Both the *Methode* and the *Traite* enjoyed a wide circulation well into the early part of the nineteenth century, with translations into English, German, Italian, Dutch, and Spanish. Louis Bernard Guyton de Morveau (1737–1816), as one of the editors of *Annales de Chimie*, carefully examined French publications for adherence to the nomenclature of the *Methode*, and carried on a crusade for such adherence throughout the scientific world. Most importantly, the *Methode* engendered a new interest in chemical nomenclature and resulted in a spate of publications on alternative nomenclatures, critical as well as supportive publications in Great Britain by James St. John, George Pearson, Robert Kerr, William Nicholson, Henry Cavendish, Joseph Black, Joseph Priestley, James Keir, Stephen Dickson, and Charles Webster, and in Germany by J.F. Goettling, C. Girtanner, J. F. von Jacquin, J. B. Richter, L. W. Gilbert, and F. A. C. Gren. In 1794, Samuel Mitchell of Columbia College, the first American supporter of the new nomenclature, published his *Nomenclature of the New Chemistry* based on Girtanner's book, *Neue chemische Nomenklatur fuer die deutsche Sprache*, which was published in Berlin in 1791.

Nomenclature in the *Methode* was primarily qualitative, as only a relatively few compounds were known quantitatively. In the process of preparing a pharmacopoeia in 1811, the Swedish chemist Jons Jacob Berzelius (1779–1848) proposed a new nomenclature, based on Latin, that expressed the quantitative nature of chemical compounds. Many chemists in the early part of the nineteenth century, and especially Berzelius, devoted considerable effort to the quantitative analysis of chemicals and made the quantitative nomenclature of Berzelius [*J. Physique* **73**, 262, 266 (1811)] a timely achievement, particularly when extended and improved by others. Thus, by the midnineteenth century, inorganic nomenclature had evolved to what is generally accepted today, with some exceptions.

One of the great achievements of the early nineteenth century chemists was the development of chemical symbols, which, with progress in chemical nomenclature, resulted in a highly communicable language of chemistry. Although the atomic construct could be said to have originated in Greece with Empedocles (490–435 B.C.), who postulated four elements—air, earth, fire, and water—or with Democritus (460–370

B.C.), who introduced the concept of elemental particles that were qualitatively the same, differing only in size, shape, and mass, the atomic theory played no role until John Dalton (1766–1844) introduced the concept that chemical elements are composed of atoms and that they maintain their unique individuality in chemical reactions; that the atoms of each element are the same, but the atoms of different elements differ in weight (Thomas Thomson, *System of Chemistry*, 1807, Edinburgh; John Dalton, *New System of Chemical Philosophy*, 1808).

In conjunction with the atomic concept, Dalton introduced a system of symbols in 1803 in a lecture [*Memoirs of the Literary and Philosophical Society of Manchester* (1), (2) 271–287 (1805)]. Dalton represented each element with a circle, such as ⊙ for hydrogen, O for oxygen, ⓛ for azote (nitrogen), and ● for carbon, each with a definite weight. The 36 elements known in the first decade of the nineteenth century soon exhausted the circle symbolism, so Dalton introduced the use of letters in the circles, such as Ⓖ for gold. Dalton used his symbols in his publications for well over 30 years, even though he was aware of the Berzelian system.

Jöns Jakob Berzelius (1779–1848), born in Sweden, studied medicine at the University of Upsala, practiced in Stockholm, but spent his spare hours working on chemical problems. This attracted the attention of the University of Stockholm, which appointed him professor of chemistry. Berzelius achieved a wide reputation for his work and publications on analytical procedures that made possible the determination of the composition of a large number of compounds, the verification of the laws of constant and multiple proportions, and the determination of atomic weights pretty much as accepted today. Possibly his greatest contribution was the system of chemical symbols that he introduced in 1813 in England [*Annals of Philosophy* **2**, 359 (1813) and **3**, 51 (1814)] and that was based on the initial letter of the Latin name of each element. By 1814, Berzelius had assigned symbols for the approximately 50 elements then known (*Forsok*, Stockholm, 1814). The Berzelius symbols were accepted readily in France and in Germany, but somewhat tardily in England. The initial difficulty was the reluctance to adopt Latin over French, German, or English usage. By the 1830s the symbols of Berzelius began to achieve international acceptance, with a few exceptions.

A prolific writer, Berzelius wrote an annual report on chemical progress, which was published in Germany under the title *Jahresbericht über die Fortschritte der physischen Wissenschaften*.

Until the 1820s, chemistry was dominated by work on inorganic chemicals. Yet many organic chemicals, such as acetic acid (vinegar), ethyl alcohol (from wine; therefore called spirit of wine), dyes of plant and vegetable origin, and perfumes from plants were known in the pre-Christian era. Glacial acetic acid, benzoic acid (called salt of benzoin, as it was obtained by distilling gum benzoin), acetone (by distillation of verdigris and of wood), methyl alcohol (by distillation of wood), formic acid (by distillation of red ants), lactic acid (from milk), citric acid (from lemons), malic acid (from apples), and tartaric acid (from tartar) were known by the nineteenth century.

One of the earliest workers in organic chemistry, considered by some to be the father of organic chemistry, was Michel Eugene Chevreul (1786–1889), whose major contribution was on the composition of oils and fats and on the derived fatty acids, such as butyric acid (from butter), stearic and oleic acids (from many oils), and capric and caproic acids (from goat milk—*capra* in Latin is a female goat [*Ann. chim* **88**, 231 (1813)].

In the early part of the nineteenth century, organic compounds were considered to be formed in nature through a "vital force," and thus differed radically from inorganic compounds. What there was of organic chemistry as described in the books of Thomson and of Berzelius (see above) was dichotomized into vegetable and animal chemistry. The "vital force" concept was negated by Friedrich Wöhler (1800–1882), who obtained urea on evaporating an aqueous solution of ammonium cyanate [Poggendorff's *Ann. der Physik und Chemie* **12**, 253–256 (1828)].

A particularly influential chemist in the second and third quarters of the nineteenth century was Justus von Liebig (1803–1873). A student of Kastner, von Humboldt, and Gay-Lussac, he was appointed professor of chemistry at the University of Giessen, where he set up a model laboratory for training students from over the world in quantitative and qualitative analysis and in preparative organic chemistry. Among his many contributions were hippuric acid (1820), chlorform and chloral (1832), uric acid and derivatives (1834–1837), alkaloids (1839), amino acids and amides (1846–1852), creatine and creatinine (1847), and methods of organic analysis (over many years). Beginning in 1831, Liebig was a founder and a coeditor (with Wöhler) of *Annalen der Chemie und Pharmacie*. Liebig was also a leader in the development of agricultural chemistry, and his *Die organische Chemie in ihrer Anwendung auf Agricultur und Physiologie* was the definitive book on the subject for many years.

Jean Baptiste Andre Dumas (1800–1884) was best known for his methods for the determination of nitrogen and oxygen/hydrogen ratios in organic compounds and of vapor densities, for his work on esters, which advanced the theory and nomenclature of organic chemistry, and for his excellently written *Traité de chimie*, which was published in eight volumes over the period 1828–1848.

Although colloidal phenomena were known even among the alchemists, they were not studied scientifically until well into the nineteenth century. The name "colloid" (from the Greek word *kolla*, meaning glue) was introduced by Thomas Graham (1805–1869) in 1861. Graham is regarded as the father of colloidal chemistry. His contributions included adsorption of salts by charcoal (1830), polybasicity of phosphoric acid (1833), diffusion of gases (1833), and heats of reactions (1845). His *Elements of Chemistry*, published in 1841, was one of the outstanding texts even in the twentieth century, and the text translated by Otto was the basis for the popular Graham–Otto text. He was the first president of the Chemical Society of London, which was formed in 1841, and which A. W. Hofmann used as the prototype on forming Die Deutsche Chemische Gesellschaft in 1867.

Electrochemistry had its beginning with the work of Michael Faraday (1791–1867) and his notable book *Experimental Researches in Electricity*, which was published in three volumes over the period 1839–1855, and which was a collection of Faraday's papers published in the *Philosophical Transactions*, 1831–1852. It was in these publications that Faraday introduced the terms electrode, anode, cathode, ion, anion, and cation. In addition, Faraday also did considerable work in chemistry: he isolated benzene, butene, hexachloroethane, tetrachloroethylene, and two isomers of naphthalenesulfonic acid. His work in chemistry was published as articles in the *Philosophical Transactions* and other journals over the period 1821–1857 and as a collection under the title *Experimental Researches in Chemistry and Physics* in 1859.

Organic chemistry began to be transformed into the concepts as we know them today by Auguste Laurent (1808–1853) and Charles Frederic Gerhardt (1816–1856), who worked together as a team in the elucidation of organic chemical reactions, particularly those involving substitution and metathesis. Laurent's book *Methode de chimie*, published in 1854 and translated into English the following year with the title *Chemical Method, Notation, Classification, & Nomenclature*, played an important role in advancing organic chemistry, as did Gerhardt's fourth volume of his *Traité de chimie organique* (1853–1856), in which organic formulas were written for the first time much as we think of them today.

The work of Laurent and Gerhardt was extended by Alexander William Williamson (1824–1904), Charles Adolph Wurtz (1817–1884), and August Wilhelm von Hofmann (1818–1892). Williamson's important work on etherification was done in the 1850s and published in the *Alembic Club Reprints, No. 16, Papers on Etherification and on the*

Constitution of Salts by Alexander W. Williamson (1850–1856) in Edinburgh in 1902. Wurtz was a prolific synthetic organic chemist, who made notable contributions in the fields of glycols, amines, hydrocarbons, metallic hydrides, hydroxy acids, and organophosphorus compounds. Among the books he wrote were a translation of Gerhardt's *Précis de chimi organique* into German, his massive *Dictionnaire de chimie pure et appliqué*, and his *Traite de chimie biologique*. His *Histoire des doctrines chimiques*, with its opening statement "Chemistry is a French science . . . founded by Lavoisier," was subjected to an understandable degree of chauvinistic criticism by other nationalities. Hofmann, as mentioned earlier, founded the German Chemical Society, yet spent many productive years in England as professor of chemistry at the Royal College of Chemistry in London (among his students were Crookes, Abel, and Perkin). Much of Hofmann's work dealt with fundamental principles of organic chemistry, such as the nature of amines (published in the *Philosophical Transactions* in 1850 and 1851), aniline, fuchsine, and other chemicals, that eventually led to the creation of the coal tar and dye industries. In 1900 the German Chemical Society published a memorial, *August Wilhelm von Hofmann, ein Lebensbild.*

Modern structural chemistry realistically was initiated by the works of Herman Kolbe (1818–1884), Edward Frankland (1825–1899), Stanislao Cannizzaro (1826–1910), Friedrich August Kekulé (1829–1896), Wilhelm Körner (1839–1925), Jacobus Henricus van't Hoff (1852–1911), and Joseph Achille Le Bel (1847–1930).

Kolbe's electrolysis of potassium acetate, which yielded ethane (1849), and Frankland's reaction of ethyl iodide with zinc to yield butane (1849) led to the beginning of the valence theory. (Kolbe's work was summarized in Ostwald's *Klassiker, No. 92* in 1897 and Frankland's work in his collected papers under the title *Experimental Researches in Pure, Applied and Physical Chemistry* published in London, 1877).

Until the publications of Stanislao Cannizzaro (1826–1910), the literature failed to distinguish between atoms and molecules and between equivalent or combining weights and atomic weights. Cannizzaro's theoretical concepts, which he taught at the Royal University of Genoa, were published in *Il Nuovo Cimento* **7**, 321–366 (1858) and other papers in the same journal. Cannizzaro's concepts elucidated the terms atoms and molecules, resurrected and made meaningful the Avogadro hypothesis (Cannizzaro's teacher) for the determination of molecular weights, and made hydrogen the reference for the atomic weights of the other elements. It was not until 1860, however, at the international congress of chemists in Karlsruhe, that Cannizzaro's concepts had an

audience through the paper he presented and disseminated. It is significant that the Avogadro hypothesis of 1811 was ignored for half a
century and then, through Cannizzaro's paper, became a paradigm in
chemistry and physics. Cannizzaro's collected papers were published as
Alembic Club Reprints, No. 18 in Edinburgh, 1910, and as *Ostwald's
Klassiker, No. 30*, in Leipzig, 1891.

That carbon is tetravalent and that carbon can be connected to
another carbon were established by Friedrich August Kekulé (1829–
1896 [(*Annalen der Chemie 106*, 129–159 (1858)]. These two concepts
yielded the key to the understanding of the structural constitution of
organic compounds, that is, the writing of formulas as we do today. It
was not until 1865 that Kekulé conceived the hexagonal structure for
benzene [*Annalen der Chemie* **137**, 129–196 (1865)]. Although this
opened the door to the understanding of aromatic structures, the work
of Wilhelm Körner (1839–1925), a student of Kekulé, elucidated the
isomeric structures of benzene derivatives, such as the dibromo-,
tribromo-, dibromo-nitrobenzenes [*Gazzetta chimica italiana* **4**, 305–446
(1874)].

The final chapter in structural chemistry was written by Jacobus
Henricus van't Hoff (1852–1911) and Joseph Achille Le Bel (1847–1930),
who, independently and within months of each other, proved the
existence of three-dimensional molecules by the optical properties of
compounds containing an asymmetric carbon atom. Van't Hoff's theory
first appeared as a pamphlet, then was published in *Archives néerlan-
daises des sciences exactes et naturelles* **9**, 445–454 (1874) (in French). In
addition to his stereochemical work, van't Hoff also elucidated geome-
cal isomerism, such as for maleic and fumaric acids. Le Bel's theory
appeared in *Bull. soc. chim.* **22**, 337–347 (1874), about two months after
van't Hoff's. Together, these two established stereochemistry, which
was extended by Johannes Wislicenus (1835–1902), Victor Meyer (1848–
1897), and Adolph Baeyer (1835–1917) for organic molecules and by
Alfred Werner (1866–1919) for inorganic molecules. The work of Louis
Pasteur (1822–1895) on the optical isomers of sodium ammonium
tartrate [*Compt. rend.* **26**, 535 (1848)] was interpreted in terms of
constitution by van't Hoff and Le Bel.

Throughout the nineteenth century, many chemists directed attention to Dalton's atomic theory as described in his 1808 publication *New
System of Chemical Philosophy*. As chemistry became more quantitative through the work of Berzelius, Gay-Lussac, von Humboldt, Avogadro, Prout, Dumas, Stas, Pettenkofer, and others, atomic weights of the
known elements were being determined more accurately. Thus, Prout
noted in 1815 that the atomic weights approximated whole numbers,

although he had difficulty in explaining the atomic weight of chlorine, 35.5. Prout postulated that the chemical resemblance of iron, cobalt, and nickel was due to their having the same combining weight, 28. That groups of elements, such as the halogens and the alkali metals, had characteristically similar chemical and physical properties was attributed to definite relationships among the atomic weights of the elements in each group, as, for example, the Triads of Johan Wolfgang Dobereiner (1780–1849), which resulted from his observation [Poggendorf's *Annalen der Physik und Chemie* **15**, 301–307 (1829)] that the atomic weight of the second element (for example, bromine) in a group of three was the average of the first (chlorine) and third (iodine).

The periodicity of chemical elements was noted by many nineteenth century chemists, such as Max Joseph von Pettenkofer (1818–1901), John Hall Gladstone (1827–1902), Josiah Parsons Cooke (1827–1894) (professor of chemistry at Harvard), William Odling (1829–1921), A. E. Béguyer Chancourtois (1819–1886), and John Alexander Reina Newlands (1838–1898) (Law of Octaves). But the major breakthrough was that of Julius Lother Meyer (1830–1895) and of Dmitrii Ivanovich Mendeleev (1834–1907). Although Mendeleev's publication was first [*J. Russian Chem. Soc.* **1**, 60–77 (1869)], Meyer's table was prepared in 1868 but not published until 1870 [*Ann. der Chemie*, Supplement band **7**, 354–364 (1870)]. Meyer's table influenced Mendeleev to make several revisions in his subsequent publications. The Royal Society conferred the Davy medal in 1882 with equal recognition to both for the periodic table. The first account of Mendeleev's periodic table in English appeared as 18 installments in 1879–1880 in the weekly *Chemical News*.

Well over 700 formal arrangements of the chemical elements in periodic tables have been published since the nineteenth century chemists initiated an interest in the periodicity of the elements. This history has been well documented in books by Francis P. Venable (*The Development of the Periodic Law*, Chemical Publ., Easton, Pa., 1896) and by Edward G. Mazurs *Graphic Representations of the Periodic System During One Hundred Years*, Alabama Univ. Press, 1974) and in the pages of the *Journal of Chemical Education*.

The second half of the nineteenth century marked the beginning of the Golden Age of organic chemistry, and by the twentieth century organic chemistry, inorganic chemistry, analytical chemistry, and physical chemistry were recognized disciplines of chemistry in which many chemists specialized. Some of the outstanding contributors to the advancement of organic chemistry included the following:

Emil Erlenmeyer (1825–1909). Author of about 150 published research papers, in 1859 Erlenmeyer founded the *Zeitscrift fuer Chemie* *und Pharmazie*, on which he served as editor until 1869. He was appointed one of the editors of Liebig's *Annalen der Chemie und Pharmazie* in 1871.

Carl Schorlemmer (1834–1892).   Professor of organic chemistry at Manchester, Schorlemmer authored *Chemistry of Common Life* (1874), *Rise and Development of Organic Chemistry* (1875), and *Treatise on Chemistry* (1877). His treatise was one of the most important chemistry books in English until the 1920s.

Rudolf Fittig (1835–1910).   Alone or with his students, Fittig published about 400 papers on the pinacone reaction and the synthesis of diphenyl, alkaryls (Fittig reaction with sodium), mesitylene, isophthalic acid, phenanthrene, quinone, etc.

William Henry Perkin (1838–1907).   Perkin's syntesis of aniline blue or mauve was the beginning of the synthetic dye (from coal tar) industry.

Johann Friedrich Adolph von Baeyer (1835–1917).   One of the most successful and brilliant synthetic organic chemist of his period, von Baeyer worked on acetylene, indigo, and uric acid, and proposed the strain theory which explained the stability of five and six membered rings. Emil Fischer was one of von Baeyer's students at Munich.

Victor Meyer (1848–1897).   Meyer elucidated steric hindrance of the ortho position in aromatic carboxylic acids [*Ber.* **27**, 510, 1580 (1894)].

Albert Ladenburg (1842–1911).   Ladenburg published close to 300 papers alone or with his students (Breslau), and authored *History of Chemistry*, and *Lectures on the Development of Chemistry During the Last 100 Years* (1869), and the 13-volume *Handwörterbuch* (1882–1896).

James Mason Crafts (1839–1917).   Professor of chemistry at Cornell (1861–1869) and at the Massachusetts Institute of Technology (1870–1874), Crafts worked with Charles Friedel (1832–1899) in Paris (École des Mines) on the synthesis of organic compounds using aluminum chloride as catalyst, which became known as the Friedel–Crafts reaction.

Friedrich Konrad Beilstein (1838–1906).   Beilstein's monumental *Handbuch der Organischen Chemie*, which he started as notes to help himself keep up with the literature of organic chemistry, was first published in 1881 as two volumes.

Carl Graebe (1841–1927).   Graebe's work with Carl Liebermann (1842–1914) on anthraquinone, alizarin, and phenanthrene was important in the development of the synthetic dye industry. Graebe's

History of Organic Chemistry, published over the years 1920–1927, was a notable contribution.

Ira Remsen (1846–1927).   Translator of Wöhler's *Organic Chemistry* and author of *Principles of Theoretical Chemistry* for Americans, Remsen established the first doctoral program in the United States at Johns Hopkins in 1876, established the *American Chemical Journal* in 1879, and played an important role in chemistry education in the United States.

Emil Fischer (1852–1919).   Fischer established the fundamental configurations of monosaccharides by classical organic methods [*Ber. 24*, 1836, 2683 (1891)] and elucidated the structures of many organic compounds, such as the purines and polypeptides. He received the Nobel prize in chemistry in 1902.

Otto Wallach (1847–1931).   Wallach made many contributions in the field of terpene chemistry, authored many papers and several books, and received the Nobel prize in chemistry in 1919.

Ernst Beckmann (1853–1923).   Beckmann is famous for his work on ketoximes and their conversion to amides, known as the Beckmann rearrangement or transformation.

Ludwig Claisen (1851–1930).   Claisen is best known for the reaction (Claisen condensation) of esters, ketones, and aldehydes with ethyl acetate in the presence of sodium ethoxide or sodamide.

Paul Sabatier (1854–1941).   Sabatier received the Nobel prize in chemistry in 1912 for his extensive work on hydrogenation, most of which was reported in *Comptes rendus* with his students, such as Senderens, Mailke, and Murat, and in his book *La Catalyse.*

Theodor Curtius (1857–1928).   An editor of the *Journal fuer praktische Chemie* and a heavy contributor to it of papers, Curtius is best known for the Curtius reaction, a method for the preparation of amines from carboxylic acids through the intermediate formation of azide, hydrazide, isocyanate or urethane.

Arthur Hantzsch (1857–1935).   A classical organic chemist, Hantzsch, together with his many students, published over 500 papers.

John Ulric Nef (1862–1915).   Professor of chemistry at Purdue (1887–1889), Clark University (1889–1892), and University of Chicago (1892–1915), Nef is best known for his work on bivalent carbon.

Victor Grignard (1871–1935).   Grignard received the Nobel prize in chemistry in 1912 for his work on the reagent bearing his name and on its various reactions. This work has been of great significance in organic chemistry.

Richard Willstätter (1872–1942).   Willstätter received the Nobel prize in 1915 (shared with Sabatier) for his work on natural products, such as alkaloids, lecithins, pyrones, chlorophyll, hemoglobin, and enzymes.

Adolp Windaus (1876–1959).   Windaus received the Nobel prize in chemistry in 1925 for his work on vitamin D.

Heinrich Wieland (1877–1957).   Wieland received the Nobel prize in chemistry in 1927 for his work on organic nitrogen compounds, such as the alkaloids and bile acids. He revised Gattermann's *Die Praxie des organischen Chemikers*, an outstanding laboratory text, first printed in 1894 and followed by 24 editions in Germany plus various translations into English, Italian, and Russian.

Walter Norman Haworth (1883–1950).   Haworth received the Nobel prize in chemistry in 1937 for his work on sugars. His work on ascorbic acid (vitamin C) was of great significance.

Hans Fischer (1881–1945).   Fischer received the Nobel prize in chemistry in 1930 for his synthesis of hemin and for the role pyrroles play in the chemistry of blood and bile pigments.

Paul Karrer (1889–1971).   Karrer received the Nobel prize in chemistry in 1937 for his work on natural products (polysaccharides, glucosides, and vitamin A). His *Organic Chemistry* was an important textbook since published in 1928 (Germany) and in 1938 (translation of the fifth German edition into English).

DEVELOPMENTS IN INORGANIC AND ANALYTICAL CHEMISTRY SINCE 1850

Heinrich Rose (1795–1864).   His comprehensive *Analytical Chemistry*, first published in 1829 in German, with its sixth edition translated into French in 1861, was one of the most important texts in the nineteenth century.

Karl Remigius Fresenius (1818–1897).   In 1841 he founded the *Zeitschrift fuer analytische Chemie*, which became the outstanding journal devoted to analytical chemistry for many decades. His *Qualitative Analysis* in 1841 and *Quantitative Analysis* in 1846, which were translated into many languages, were regarded as among the best well into the twentieth century. The seventeenth German edition of the combination was printed in 1920.

Georg Lunge (1839–1923).   Of the more than 650 papers and 86 books that Lunge wrote, his best known work is *Chemisch-technische*

Untersuchungsmethoden, in four volumes. It was translated into English and French, and the sixth edition was issued in 1910.

Alexander Classen (1843–1934). Classen's works on electrolytic determinations made him well known, and his *Handbuch der analytische Chemie* and *Quantitative Analyse durch Electrolyse* were widely used for over 50 years.

Frank Austin Gooch (1852–1929). The perforated bottom crucible Gooch invented bears his name. Professor of chemistry at Yale from 1885 to 1929, he authored *Methods in Chemical Analysis* in 1912, in addition to many papers and other books.

William Francis Hillebrand (1853–1925). Chief chemist for the U.S. Bureau of Standards, Hillebrand wrote several books on the qualitative analysis of minerals and coauthored with Lundell the authoritative book on analytical chemistry (published after 1925).

Edgar Fahs Smith (1856–1928). Professor of chemistry at the University of Pennsylvania, Smith translated Richter's books on inorganic and organic chemistry, published over 200 papers, and wrote 20 books.

Frederick Pearson Treadwell (1857–1918). An American whose teaching career in analytical chemistry was at the Technische Hochschule in Zurich, Treadwell published his lectures as *Kurzes Lehrbuch* in two volumes, one in quantitative and one in qualitative analysis. His son, W. D. Treadwell, was also a well known analytical chemist and author of books.

Theodore William Richards (1868–1929). Professor of analytical and inorganic chemistry at Harvard beginning in 1889, Richards did outstanding work in determining the atomic weights of 28 elements, for which he was awarded the Nobel prize in 1914.

Francis William Aston (1877–1945). With the mass spectrograph he invented, Aston elucidated the isotopic ratios of various elements and won the Nobel prize in 1922.

Henri Moissan (1852–1907). Professor of inorganic and general chemistry at the Sorbonne, Moissan isolated fluorine by the electrolysis of potassium fluoride in hydrofluoric acid, for which he was awarded the Nobel prize in 1906. He is also well known for the development of the electric furnace, in which he produced artificial diamond and prepared new compounds: carbides, silicides, and borides. His books, *The Electric Furnace* (1897), *Fluorine and Its Compounds,* and the five volume *Treatise of Mineral Chemistry* (1904–1906) were valuable reference works for inorganic chemists.

Antoine Henri Becquerel (1852–1908). Becquerel discovered radioactive phenomena on the irradiation by x rays of uranium salts [*Compt. rend.* **122**, 420 (1896)]. Marie Curie (1867–1934), on extending Becquerel's work by fractionating pitch blends many times, isolated two new elements: polonium and radium. She gave the name radioactivity to the phenomena exhibited by uranium and the two new elements, which she described fully in her remarkable doctoral thesis of 1903, *Recherches sur les substances radioactives*. The work of Becquerel, Pierre Curie (1859–1906), and Marie Curie was recognized with the award of the Nobel prize in 1903. The Nobel prize was awarded again to Marie Curie in 1920.

DEVELOPMENTS IN PHYSICAL CHEMISTRY FROM 1850 TO THE EARLY 1900s

Marcellin Berthelot (1827–1907). Berthelot's two-volume book *Chimie organique fondée sur la synthèse* (1860), which used the same laws of chemistry for both organic and inorganic compounds and their reactions in arguing against the vital force doctrine, was a pioneer in thermochemistry [*Ann. chim. phys.* **5**, (5) 5–131 (1875)]. with the bomb calorimeter he designed, the heats of combustion of many compounds were determined. He introduced the terms *endothermic* and *exothermic*.

Francois Marie Raoult (1830–1901). Professor of chemistry at the University of Grenoble, Raoult elucidated the freezing point depression of solutions by the solute and the effect of the mol fraction of solute on the vapor pressure of solvents, now known as Raoult's Law [*Compt. rend.* **95**, 1030 (1882) and **104** 1430 (1887)].

Jacobus Henricus van't Hoff (1852–1911). The contributions of van't Hoff to stereochemistry have been mentioned already. He was one of the first to point out the analogy between solutions and gases. Dealing with osmotic pressure for solutions and elastic pressure for gases, he showed that solutes in dilute solutions obey the gas laws [*Archives neerlandaises des sciences extracts et naturelles* **20**, 239–302 (1885)].

Henry Louis Le Châtelier (1850–1936). Professor of chemistry at the College de France, Sorbonne, and École des mines, Le Châtelier's studies of chemical equilibrium and of solutions led him to state in 1884 that when a system in equilibrium is subjected to a stress (change in pressure, temperature, concentration, etc.), the system will tend to alter so as to undo the effect of the stress. This statement became known as the Le Châtelier law. He started the *Review de Metallurgie* in 1904, and remained as the editor until 1914.

Josiah Willard Gibbs (1839–1903). Professor of mathematical physics at Yale University, Gibbs has been considered by many the father of physical chemistry, yet none of his publications describe even a single experiment. He published his papers in the *Transactions of the Connecticut Academy*, a journal which was not widely read. His first paper, "Graphical Methods in the Thermodynamics of Fluids", in which he introduced the concepts of energy and entropy, was printed in the spring of 1873. In his second paper (October, 1873), "A Method of Geometrical Representation of the Thermodynamic Properties of Substances by Means of Surfaces," he extended his volume–entropy diagram to solid objects. Between 1875 and 1878, Gibbs published two papers, "On *the Equilibrium of Heterogeneous Substances*, in which he introduced the concept of chemical potential and deduced the phase rule (in a four-page paper, *Coexistent Phases of Matter*), which was a marriage of chemistry and physics. Despite the significance of Gibbs' publications, their strictly abstract mathematical nature, with no suggestion as to how the equations may be applied, kept them unread for over 10 years until Hendrik William Bakhuis Roozeboom (1854–1907), professor of chemistry at Leiden, showed the importance and value of the Gibbs' phase rule. W. Ostwald translated *On the Equilibrium of Heterogeneous Substances* into German in 1892, and Le Châtelier translated it into French in 1899. The collected papers of Gibbs were published in England in 1906, and in the United States not until 1928.

Svante Arrhenius (1859–1927). Professor of physics at the University of Stockholm, Arrhenius studied under or was acquainted with Ostwald, Kohlrausch, Nernst, and Boltzmann, wrote several books on physical chemistry, and received the Nobel Prize in 1903 for his work resulting in the elucidation of electrolytic dissociation.

Wilhelm Friedrich Ostwald (1853–1932). Ostwald's book *Lehrbuch der allegemeinen Chemie*, published in 1885, greatly contributed to the establishment of physical chemistry as a discipline of chemistry. With van't Hoff, he founded Zeitscrift fuer physikalische Chemie in 1887. Ostwald and van't Hoff strengthened the Arrhenius theory of electrolytic dissociation by their experiments on the ionic nature of molecules and the effect of this nature on the conductance and osmotic pressure of solutions.

Hermann Walther Nernst (1864–1941). Professor of physical chemistry at Gottingen (1890–1905) and at Berlin 1905–1922), he extended the work of van't Hoff, Ostwald, and Arrhenius to show that the electromotive force of galvanic cells is a consequence of the solution pressure of ions [*Z. physik. chem.* **4**, 129–181 (1889)]. He was editor of the *Jahrbuch der Electrochemie* and of the *Zeitscrift fuer Electrochemie.* In the twentieth century he discovered the third law of thermodynamics, for which he received the Nobel prize in 1920.

Richard Zsigmondy (1865–1929). Pioneer in the field of colloids, Zsigmondy published many papers and the classical book *Zur Erkenntniss der Kolloide.* He received the Nobel prize in 1925.

Fritz Haber (1868–1934). For applying the Le Châtelier and Gibbs principles to the industrial process for the catalytic synthesis of ammonia from hydrogen and nitrogen, Haber received the Nobel prize in 1918.

11

CONTRIBUTIONS OF AMERICAN CHEMISTS TO THE LITERATURE

Chemistry was first practiced in colonial America in 1632 by John Winthrop the Younger (1606–1676), who followed his father to Massachusetts Bay in 1631. Within a year of his arrival, he arranged to have apparatus, chemicals, and books shipped from England. He manufactured salt, erected iron furnaces, and produced saltpeter, potash, tar, alum, and medicinals. In 1662 Winthrop was admitted to the Royal Society (London), where he presented the paper *Of the Manner of Making Tar and Pitch in New England.*

Other early members of the Royal Society were John Clayton (late seventeenth century), William Byrd (1674–1744), Paul Dudley (1675–1751), John Winthrop the Third (1681–1747), and Benjamin Franklin (1706–1970).

In 1727 in Philadelphia, Franklin organized the Junto, the first scientific organization in the Colonies. Its name was changed in 1766 to The American Society for Promoting and Propagating Knowledge, Held in Philadephia, and in 1768 to the American Philosophical Society. The first wholly chemical society was formed in 1792 by James Woodhouse, professor of chemistry at the University of Pennsylvania. "The Chemical Society of Philadelphia," as it was called, ceased to exist with the death of its founder in 1809.

The New York Lyceum of Natural History was organized in 1817 and renamed the New York Academy of Sciences in 1876. Among its members were the following chemists: Samuel L. Mitchell (1764–1831), James Renwick (1792–1863), John Torrey (1796–1876), Lewis C. Beck (1798–1853), James J. Mapes (1806–1866), Charles F. Chandler (1836–1925), Henry Morton (1836–1902), Elwyn Waller (1846–1919), and Charles A. Doremus.

The American Association for the Advancement of Science (AAAS), formed by geologists in 1838 as the Association of American Geologists, assumed its present name in 1848. The AAAS Section of Chemistry and Mineralogy was organized in 1850, and the Section on Chemistry in 1973 (becoming Section C in 1882).

The American Chemical Society was founded on April 6, 1876, in New York City.

Following is a list (in chronological order by birth year) of American chemists (no longer living) who wrote books, edited journals, or taught:

Samuel Bard (1742–1821). Chemistry professor (1767–1773). at Medical School of King's College, which closed in 1776 and opened as Columbia University in 1784, Bard taught at Columbia from 1786 to 1787.

Edward Bancroft (1744–1821). A doctor from the University of Aberdeen, England, Bancroft authored *Experimental Researches Concerning the Philosophy of Permanent Colours and the Best Methods of Producing Them by Dyeing, Calico Printing, etc.* (1784), the first book on dyes in English. The second edition (1814) covered the state of chemistry as well as dyes and dyeing.

Benjamin Rush (1745–1813). The most outstanding of the early American chemists, Rush was educated as a doctor, but taught chemistry at the University of Pennsylvania (1769–1813). He wrote *Syllabus of a Course of Lectures on Chemistry* (1770), the first chemistry text published in the United States.

Thomas P. Jones (1773–1848). Jones wrote *Conversations on Natural Philosophy* and *New Conversations on Chemistry* (1831), which went through nine editions and were the most popular texts in the United States for many years.

Amos Eaton (1776–1842). A lawyer who studied chemistry with Benjamin Silliman and lectured on science, Eaton persuaded Stephen Van Rensselaer to establish Rensselaer Polytechnic Institute in 1824. He wrote *Chemical Instructor* (1822).

Benjamin Silliman (1779–1864). Educated in law, Silliman became the first professor of chemistry at Yale (1804–1853), after studying chemistry under James Woodhouse, and wrote *Elements of Chemistry* (1830). In 1818 he founded the *American Journal of Science*, the oldest scientific journal still being published in the United States.

Parker Cleaveland (1780–1858). Cleaveland became known as the father of American mineralogy from his work and his *Elementary Treatise on Mineralogy and Geology* (1816).

John Gorham (1783–1829). Author of the two-volume *Elements of*

Chemical Science (1819–1920), Gorham was one of the founders of *New England Journal of Medicine and Science*, and its editor for the 14 years of its existence (1812–1826).

James Cutbush (1788–1823).   Author of *The Philosophy of Experimental Chemistry* and *Synopsis of Chemistry* (1821), Cutbush was professor of chemistry and mineralogy at the U.S. Military Academy (1820–1823).

Jacob Green (1790–1841).   During his professorship of chemistry at Jefferson Medical College (1825–1841), Green wrote *A Textbook of Chemical Philosophy, Syllabus of a Course of Chemistry*, and *Chemical Diagrams*.

Thomas D. Mitchell (1791–1865).   Mitchell wrote *Medical Chemistry* (1819) and *Elements of Chemical Philosophy* (1832).

Daniel B. Smith (1792–1883).   Founder of Philadelphia College of Pharmacy and Science (1821), Smith helped establish *American Journal of Pharmacy* (1825), and wrote *The Principles of Chemistry* (1837).

Franklin Bache (1792–1864).   Author of *A System of Chemistry for the Use of Students* (1819) and (with G. B. Wood) *Dispensary of the United States* (1833), Bache published the American edition of Andrew Ure's *Dictionary of Chemistry* (1821). Bache taught at the Franklin Institute (1826–1832), Philadelphia College of Pharmacy and Science (1831–1841), and Jefferson Medical College (1841–1864).

Almira H. Lincoln Phelps (1793–1884).   Phelps wrote *Dictionary of Chemistry* (1830), *Chemistry for Beginners* (1834), and *Familiar Lectures on Chemistry*, based on his teaching at Troy Female Seminary (1823–1831).

Lewis Caleb Beck (1798–1853).   Beck wrote *Mineralogy of New York* (1842) and *Manual of Chemistry* (1831).

Williams H. Keating (1799–1840).   Keating wrote *Syllabus of a Course of Mineralogy and Chemistry* (1822).

Charles Goodyear (1800–1860).   Goodyear wrote *Gum-Elastic and the Discovery of Vulcanization* (2 vols., 1855) and *The Applications and Uses of Vulcanized Gum Elastic* (1853).

Lewis Reeve Gibbes (1810–1894).   Gibbes wrote *Synoptical Table of the Chemical Elements* (1870–1874).

James Curtiss Booth (1810–1888).   Booth, who edited and wrote most of the *Encyclopedia of Chemistry* (1850), served as president of ACS in 1883 and 1884.

John William Draper (1811–1882).   Author of *Textbook of Chemistry*

(1846), Draper served as professor of chemistry in New York University (1838–1882) and as first president of ACS.

Benjamin Silliman, Jr. (1816–1885).   Author of *First Principles of Chemistry* (1847) and *American Contributions to Chemistry* (1874), Silliman was editor of *American Journal of Science* (1838–1885) and professor of chemistry at Yale (1840–1870).

George W. Rains (1817–1898).   Author of *Rudimentary Course of Analytical and Applied Chemistry* (1872), *Chemical Qualitative Analysis* (1870), and *Interesting Chemical Exercises in Qualitative Analysis for Ordinary Schools* (1880), Rains served as professor of chemistry in the University of Georgia.

Thomas Artisell (1817–1893).   Author of *The Manufacture of Photogenic or Hydro-Carbon Oils* (1859), Artisell edited *New York Journal of Pharmacy* (1854).

John P. Norton (1822–1852).   Author of *Elements of Scientific Agriculture* (1847), Norton taught at Yale (1846–1852).

Henri Erni (1822–1885).   Author of *Coal Oil and Petroleum* (1865). Erni edited *Journal of Applied Chemistry* (1866–1868).

Charles M. Wetherill (1825–1871).   Wetherill wrote *The Manufacture of Vinegar* (1860).

Thomas S. Hunt (1826–1892).   Author of *Mineral Physiology and Physiography* (1886), Hunt also wrote *A New Basis for Chemistry: A Chemical Philosophy* (1887), and *Systematic Mineralogy* (1891).

Josiah P. Cooke (1827–1894).   Author of *The Elements of Chemical Physics* (1860) and *The New Chemistry* (1874), Cooke taught at Harvard (1849–1894).

Hyppolite Etienne Dussance (1829–1869).   Author of *Treatise on the Coloring Matters Derived from Coal Tar* (1863), Hunt also wrote *A Practical Guide for the Perfumer* (1868), *A General Treatise on the Manufacture of Vinegar* (1871), and *A General Treatise on the Manufacture of Soap* (1869).

Rachel L. Bodley (1831–1888).   First woman member of ACS, Bodley taught chemistry at Medical College of Pennsylvania.

Francis H. Storer (1832–1914).   Professor at MIT, Storer wrote *First Outlines of a Dictionary of the Solubilities of Chemical Substances* (1864), *A Manual of Inorganic Chemistry* (1867, with Charles W. Eliot), *Agriculture in Some of Its Relations with Chemistry* (2 vols., 1887), and *Elementary Manual of Chemistry* (1894, with W. B. Lindsay).

George Chapman Caldwell (1834–1907).   Author of *Agricultural*

Qualitative and Quantitative Chemical Analysis (1869) and *Elements of Qualitative and Quantitative Chemical Analysis* (1892), Caldwell taught at Penn State (1864–1868) and Cornell (1868–1907).

Charles William Eliot (1834–1926). President of Harvard for 40 years, Eliot wrote *A Manual of Inorganic Chemistry* (1865, with F. H. Storer), *Manual of Organic Chemistry* (1868), and *Compendious Manual of Qualitative Analysis* (1868).

Sidney A. Norton (1835–1918). Author of *Textbook of Inorganic Chemistry* (1878), Norton taught at Ohio State University.

George F. Barker (1835–1910). Professor of physics at the University of Pennsylvania (1873–1900), Barker wrote *Textbook of Elementary Chemistry.*

Charles Frederick Chandler (1836–1925). Editor of the American supplement of *British Chemical News,* Chandler founded the *American Chemist* (1870–1877) with his brother William Henry Chandler (1841–1906). An organizer of the ACS, C. F. Chandler served as its president in 1881 and 1889. He taught chemistry at Union (1857–1864) and Columbia (1864–1911).

Henry Draper (1837–1882). For his New York University students, Draper wrote *Textbook of Chemistry* (1866).

Henry Carrington Bolton (1843–1903). Bolton wrote three books on the history and bibliography of chemistry, subjects he taught at George Washington University (1892–1896).

John Howard Appleton (1844–1930). Author of *The Young Chemist* (8 editions), Appleton also wrote 13 textbooks and laboratory manuals (1878–1898) in general chemistry, qualitative and quantitative analysis, and organic and medicinal chemistry.

William Simon (1844–1916). Simon wrote *Manual of Chemistry* (1884, 13 editions by 1927).

Harvey W. Wiley (1844–1930). Author of *Principles and Practice of Agricultural Analysis* (3 vols., 1895–1897), Wiley was one of the founders of the Association of Official Agricultural Chemists and served as ACS president in 1893 and 1894.

Ira Remsen (1846–1927). Translator of Wöhler's *Outlines of Organic Chemistry* (1872) and author of *The Principles of Theoretical Chemistry* (1875), Remsen founded and edited *American Chemical Journal* (1879–1914), and served as ACS president in 1902.

Frank W. Clarke (1847–1931). Author of *The Data of Geochemistry* (1908), which contained the composition of the earth's outer crust he had calculated from 8600 analyses, Clarke served as ACS president in 1901.

Edgar H. S. Bailey (1848–1933).   Author of *A Laboratory Guide to the Study of Qualitative Analysis* (1901, with H. P. Cady), *Sanitary and Applied Chemistry* (1906), *The Sources, Chemistry and Uses of Food Products* (1944), *Laboratory Experiments on Food Products* (1915), and *Foods from Afar* (1922, with H. S. Bailey, his son), Bailey taught at Yale (1873), Lehigh (1874–1883), and University of Kansas (1883–1933).

John Uri Lloyd (1849–1936).   Lloyd wrote *Drugs and Medicines of North America* (1884–1887, 2 vols.) and *The Chemistry of Medicines* (1881).

Peter Townsend Austen (1852–1907).   Author of *Kurze Einleitung zu dem Nitro-Verbindungen* (1876), Austen taught at Dartmouth (1876), Rutgers (1877–1890), and Brooklyn Polytechnic Institute (1893–1898).

John Maxon Stillman (1852–1923).   Author of *The Story of Early Chemistry* (1923), Stillman taught at University of California (1876–1882) and at Stanford (1891–1917).

Thomas B. Stillman (1852–1915).   Author of *Engineering Chemistry* (1897), Stillman taught at Stevens (1886–1909).

John T. Stoddard (1852–1919).   Author of *Outline on Qualitative Analysis for Beginners* (1883), *Outline Lecture Notes on General Chemistry: Nonmetals* (1884) and *Metals* (1885), *Introduction to General Chemistry* (1910), and *Introduction to Organic Chemistry* (1914), Stoddard taught at Smith (1878–1919).

William P. Mason (1853–1937).   Author of *Water Supply* (1896) and *Examination of Water* (1899), both of which went through many editions, Mason taught at Rensselaer (1875–1925).

Edward Hart (1854–1931).   Author of *Volumetric Analysis* (1876), and *Chemical Engineering* (1920), Hart published and edited *Journal of Analytical Chemistry*, edited *Journal of American Chemical Society* (1893–1902), and taught at Lafayette (1878–1924).

Edgar Fahs Smith (1854–1928).   Author of *Chemistry in America* and six other books on the history of chemistry, Smith taught at University of Pennsylvania (1888–1928) and served as ACS president in 1895, 1921, and 1922.

Francis P. Venable (1856–1934).   Author of *The Development of the Periodic Law* (1896), *The Study of the Atom; or the Foundations of Chemistry* (1904), and *A Short History of Chemistry* (1894), Venable taught at University of North Carolina (1880–1930) and served as ACS president in 1905.

William A. Noyes (1857–1941).   Editor of *Journal of the American*

Chemical Society (1902–1917)., *Chemical Abstracts* (1907–1910), and *Chemical Reviews* (1924–1926), Noyes taught at University of Minnesota (1882), University of Tennessee (1883–1887), Rose Polytechnic Institute (1886–1902), and University of Illinois (1907–1926). In 1920 he served as ACS president.

John Jacob Abel (1857–1938).   Founder of the American Society for Pharmacology and Therapeutics (1908), the American Society of Biological Chemistry (1906), *Journal of Pharmacology and Experimental Therapeutics* (1908), and *Journal of Biological Chemistry* (1905), Abel served as professor of pharmacology at Johns Hopkins.

James Lewis Howe (1859–1955).   Howe wrote *Bibliography of the Metals of the Platinum Group* (over many years).

Arthur M. Comey (1861–1933).   Comey wrote *A Dictionary of Chemical Solubilities: Inorganic* (1896).

Edward C. Franklin (1862–1937).   Author of *The Nitrogen System of Compounds* (1935), Franklin taught at Stanford University.

Arthur D. Little (1863–1935).   Little wrote *The Chemistry of Paper Making* (1894, with Roger B. Griffin), the first American textbook on this subject.

William McPherson (1864–1951).   Author of *Elementary Study of Chemistry* (1905, with W. E. Henderson), McPherson taught at Ohio State University (1892–1937).

Samual P. Mulliken (1864–1934).   Author of *A Method for the Identification of Pure Organic Compounds by a Systematic Analytical Procedure Based on Physical Properties and Chemical Reactions* (1904–1922, 4 vols.), Mulliken taught at MIT (1895–1934).

Alexander Smith (1865–1922).   Author of *Introduction to General Inorganic Chemistry* (1906), one of the most important texts for about 25 years, Smith taught at University of Chicago (1894–1911) and Columbia University (1911–1919).

Oliver P. Watts (1865–1953).   Author of *Laboratory Course in Electrochemistry* (1914), Watts taught at University of Wisconsin (1905–1935).

Arthur A. Noyes (1866–1936).   Author of *Identification of Organic Substances* (1899, with S. Mulliken), *General Principles of Physical Science* (1902), and *A System of Qualitative Analysis for the Rare Elements* (1929, with W. Bray), Noyes taught at MIT (1890–1917) and California Institute of Technology (1918–1936).

Wilder D. Bancroft (1867–1953).   Author of *The Phase Rule* (1897) and *Applied Colloid Chemistry: General Theory* (1921), Bancroft founded and edited *Journal of Physical Chemistry* (1896–1932), and served as president of the Electrochemical Society in 1905 and 1919 and of ACS in 1910.

Forris J. Moore (1867–1926).   Author of *Outlines of Organic Chemistry* (1910), *Experiments in Organic Chemistry* (1911), and *A History of Chemistry* (1918), Moore taught at MIT (1902–1925).

Marsten Taylor Bogert (1868–1954).   ACS president in 1907 and 1908. Bogert taught at Columbia University (1894–1954).

Charles Baskerville (1870–1922).   Author of *Radium and Radioactive Substances* (1905), *General Chemistry* (1909), and *Qualitative Chemical Analysis* (with Louis J. Curtman), Baskerville taught at University of North Carolina (1894–1904) and The City College of New York (1904–1922).

Charles Albert Browne (1870–1947).   Author of *Source Book of Agricultural Chemistry* (1944) and *A History of the American Chemical Society* (1952, with M. E. Weeks), Browne served as assistant editor of *Chemical Abstracts* (1907–1910) and as editor of *Chymia*.

James F. Norris (1871–1940.   Author of *Principles of Organic Chemistry* (1915), Norris taught at MIT (1895–1940).

Louis A. Olney (1874–1949).   Olney edited *American Dyestuff Reporter*.

William T. Hall (1874–1957).   Translater of F. P. Treadwell's two-volume *Analytical Chemistry (1903, 1932, 1937)*, author of *Textbook of Quantitative Analysis* (1930), and reviser of F. J. Moore's *History of Chemistry*, Hall taught at MIT.

Gilbert N. Lewis (1875–1946).   Author of *Thermodynamics and the Free Energy of chemical Substances* (1923, with Merle Randall) and *Valence and the Structure of Atoms and Molecules* (1923), Lewis taught at University of California (1912–1946).

Austin M. Patterson (1876–1956).   Patterson wrote *A German–English Dictionary for Chemists* (1917), *A French–English Dictionary for Chemists* (1921), *The Ring Index* (1940, with L. T. Capell), and *A Guide to the Literature of Chemistry* (1927, with E. J. Crane).

Wilfred W. Scott (1876–1932).   Scott wrote *Standard Methods of Chemical Analysis* (1917), a multivolume work.

Eugene Cook Bingham (1878–1945).   First editor of *Journal of Rheology* (1929), Bingham taught at Layfayette College (1916–1945).

Atherton Seidell (1878–1961).   Seidell wrote *Solubilities of Organic Compounds* (1907 and periodic updates).

Harry N. Holmes (1897–1958). Author of the first laborabory manual for colloid chemistry (1921) and two series of general chemistry textbooks, which went through many editions, Holmes taught at Oberlin and served as ACS president in 1942.

Samual C. Lind (1879–1965). Editor of *Journal of Physical Chemistry* (1933–1950), Lind taught at University of Minnesota (1935–1947).

Henry D. Dakin (1880–1952). Dakin edited *Journal of Biological Chemistry*.

Arthur B. Lamb (1880–1952). Editor of the *Journal of American Chemical Society* (1917–1949), Lamb taught at Harvard (1912–1948).

Harrison E. Howe (1881–1942). Howe edited *Industrial Engineering Chemistry* (1925–1943).

Edward W. Washburn (1881–1934). Author of *An Introduction to the Principles of Physical Chemistry* (1915), Washburn edited *International Critical Tables* (1926–1930, 7 vols.).

Alfred L. Webre (1881–1863). Webre wrote *Evaporation* (1926 with C. S. Robinson).

Donald D. Van Slyke (1883–1971). Van Slyke wrote *Quantitative Clinical Chemistry* (1931, 2 vols.).

Peter J. W. Debye (1884–1966). Author of *Quantum Theory and Chemistry* (1928), *Polar Molecules* (1929), *The Dipole Moment and Chemical Structure* (1931), *The Structure of Molecules* (1932), *The Structure of Matter* (1934), and *Nuclear Physics* (1935), Debye edited *Physikalische Zeitscrift* (1915–1940). He received the Nobel prize in 1936.

Benjamin T. Brooks (1885–1962). Brooks wrote *The Chemistry of the Non-Benzenoid Hydrocarbons* (1922), *Science of Petroleum* (1937, 4 vols.), and *Chemistry of the Petroleum Hydrocarbons* (1954–1955, 3 vols.).

Harry Linn Fisher (1885–1961). Fisher wrote *The Chemistry of Natural and Synthetic Rubbers.*

Ross A. Gortner (1885–1942). Gortner wrote *Outlines of Biochemistry* (1929).

Howard J. Lucas (1885–1963). Author of *Organic Chemistry* (1935), Lucas taught at California Institute of Technology.

Walter Lucius Badger (1886–1958). Badger wrote *Heat Transfer and Evaporation* (1926) and *Elements of Chemical Engineering* (with W. L. McCabe).

Gustav Egloff (1886–1955). Egloff wrote *Reactions of Pure Hydro-*

carbons (1937), *Physical Constants of Hydrocarbons* (1939–1953, five vols.), *Isomerization of Pure Hydrocarbons* (1942), and *Alkylation of Alkanes* (1948).

Neil E. Gordon (1886–1949).   Gordon founded and edited *Journal of Chemical Education* (1923–1933).

Clarence J. West (1886–1953).   West prepared bibliographies on pulp and paper literature (1900–1953).

William Haynes (1886–1970).   Author of *This Chemical Age, The Chemical Front, Men, Money, and Molecules, The American Chemical Industry, 1609–1948,* Haynes published the first *Chemical Who's Who* in 1928, and founded *Drug and Chemical Markets, Chemical Week, Modern Plastics,* and *Drug and Cosmetics Industry.*

James B. Sumner (1887–1955).   Author of *Textbook of Biological Chemistry* (1927), *The Chemistry and Methods of Enzymes* (1943, with G. Fred Somers), and *The Enzymes, Chemistry and Mechanism of Action* (1951–1952, with K. Myrback), Sumner taught at Cornell (1914–1955).

Frank C. Whitmore (1887–1947).   Author of *Organic Chemistry* (1938), Whitmore taught at Penn State (1929–1947) and served as ACS president in 1938.

Carroll C. Davis (1888–1957).   Davis edited *Rubber Chemistry and Technology* (1928–1957).

Benjamin Harrow (1888–1970).   Harrow wrote *Eminent Chemists of Our Time* (1920), *Vitamins, Essential Food Factors* (1921), *Romance of the Atom* (1927), *The Making of Chemistry* (1930), *Romance of Chemistry* (1931), and *A Textbook of Biochemistry* (1935, with C. P. Sherwin).

Oliver Kamm (1888–1965).   Kamm wrote *Qualitative Organic Analysis* (1923).

Roger Adams (1889–1971).   Founder of *Organic Synthesis* and *Organic Reactions,* Adams taught at University of Illinois (1916–1957) and served as ACS president in 1935.

Farrington Daniels (1889–1972).   Coauthor of the fifth and subsequent editions of Getman's *Outlines of Theoretical Chemistry* (1931), Daniels wrote *Chemical Kinetics* (1938), *Solar Energy Research* (1955), *Photochemistry in the Solid and Liquid State* (1960), and *Direct Use of the Sun's Energy* (1964). ACS president in 1953, Daniels taught at University of Wisconsin (1920–1972).

Raymond E. Kirk (1890–1957).   Author of *Laboratory Manual in Inorganic Chemistry* (1927, with M. C. Snead), Kirk edited (with D.

Othmer) *Encyclopedia of Chemical Technology* (1947–1956). Kirk taught at Polytechnic Institute of Brooklyn (1931–1955).

Eduard Farber (1892–1969). Author of *Die Geschichliche Entwicklung der chemie* (1921), *Evolution of Chemistry, A History of Its Ideas, Methods and Materials* (1952), *Nobel Prize Winners in Chemistry* (1953, 1963), *Oxygen and Oxidation Theories and Techniques in the 19th Century and the Beginning of the 20th* (1967), Farber edited *Great Chemists* (1961) and *Milestones of Modern Chemistry* (1966).

Nathaniel Howell Furman (1892–1965). Author of *Potentiometric Titrations: A Practical and theoretical Treatise* (1926, with I. M. Kolthoff) and editor of *Scott's Standard Methods of Chemical Analysis*, Furman taught at Princeton (1919–1954) and served as ACS president in 1951.

Norbert A. Lange (1892–1970). Lange edited *Handbook of Chemistry and Physics* (1920–1932) and 11 editions of *Handbook of Chemistry* from 1934 on.

Homer Burton Adkins (1892–1949). Author of *Reaction of Hydrogen* (1938), *Elementary Organic Chemistry* (1928, with S. M. McElvain), and *Practice of Organic Chemistry* (1928, with S. M. McElvain), Adkins taught at University of Wisconsin (1919–1949).

Sidney D. Kirkpatrick (1894–1973). Kirkpatrick edited *Chemical Engineering* (1928–1950).

Nicholas D. Cheronis (1895–1962). Author of *Macro- and Semimicro Organic Chemistry* (1942), and founder and editor of *Microchemical Journal*, Cheronis taught at Chicago City College (1934–1950) and Brooklyn College (1950–1962).

Barnett F. Dodge (1895–1972). Author of *Chemical Engineering Thermodynamics* (1944), Dodge taught at Yale (1925–1964).

Morris S. Kharasch (1895–1957). Founder of *Journal of Organic Chemistry* and American editor of *Tetrahedron*, Kharasch taught at University of Chicago (1924–1957).

Victor K. LaMer (1895–1966). Editor of *Journal of Colloid Science* (1946–1966), LaMer taught at Columbia (1920–1961).

John H. Perry (1895–1953). Perry wrote *Chemical Engineers' Handbook* (1934) and *Chemical Business Handbook* (1953).

Ernst A. Hauser (1896–1956). Author of *Latex: Its Occurence, Collection, Properties, and Technical Applications* (1927), *Colloid Chemistry of the Rubber Industry* (1928), *Colloid Phenomena* (1939), *Experiments in Colloid Chemistry* (1940), and *Silicic Chemistry* (1955), Hauser taught at MIT.

Ernest H. Huntress (1898–1970).   Author of Organic Chlorine Compounds (1949), *Brief Guide to the Use of Beilstein* (1938) and *Problems in Organic Chemistry* (1938), Huntress taught at MIT (1922–1963).

NAME INDEX

SUBJECT INDEX